Paul McCartney

Behind the Myth

Paul McCartney

BEHIND THE MYTH

Ross Benson

LONDON
VICTOR GOLLANCZ LTD
1992

First published in Great Britain June 1992
by Victor Gollancz Ltd
14 Henrietta Street, London WC2E 8QJ
Second impression September 1992

A catalogue record for this book is
available from the British Library

ISBN 0 575 05200 7

Photoset in Great Britain by
Rowland Phototypesetting Ltd, Bury St Edmunds, Suffolk
and printed in Great Britain by
Butler & Tanner Ltd, Frome, Somerset

Prologue

THE boyish, agile figure of Paul McCartney can be seen most working mornings entering his office in Soho Square. He is shorter than you imagine, his hair longer than is fashionable. His clothes, rumpled and well worn, can most kindly be described as Oxfam chic. He often comes into London by train and bus from his unpretentious home in Sussex, just over an hour's journey away. He could afford a chauffeur and a limousine. He could afford to buy the train if he wanted. He doesn't. He is richer and more successful than any other pop star in history, but he is, he insists, just an 'ordinary bloke'.

Time seems hardly to have changed him. His face is youthful, his gait jaunty. Call his name and he smiles and gives the thumbs-up sign. He is still as determinedly cute as he was when he was Beatle Paul. It is an image that serves his purpose. It hides his complex and contradictory nature from a world that has been peering in at his life for almost thirty years.

For this 'ordinary bloke' is anything but.

Paul McCartney is an enigma wreathed in a smile, loved by millions who have never met him and disliked by many who have worked with him – most famously, of course, John Lennon. He is the 'cute one'. But cute, he says, is what he isn't, and John Lennon would have agreed with that.

'McCartney is a mess of contradictions,' observes Peter Brown,

7

who was working for Brian Epstein when 'Eppy' 'discovered' the Beatles playing in Liverpool's Cavern club, and who stayed with them through to the end.

He is a half-billionaire who prefers to travel by public transport; a vegetarian sheep farmer who refuses to eat anything that has a face; a law-abiding citizen and caring father with a string of drug busts to his discredit; the faithful husband who keeps his office in the old red-light district of London's West End.

He is a collaborator who finds it all but impossible to accept advice and always insists on being the boss; a composer who can produce songs as haunting as 'Yesterday' and as trite as 'Silly Love Songs'; an artist disciplined enough to write the *Liverpool Oratorio*, self-indulgent enough to produce disasters like *Magical Mystery Tour* and *Give My Regards to Broadstreet*.

Once the best-travelled and most international of the Beatles, he now rarely ventures abroad. The McCartneys ski occasionally and, until the death of Linda's father in 1991, they spent two weeks every summer at the Eastman vacation home on Long Island. But mostly he and Linda prefer the ordered routine of work and domesticity. Once a leading member of London's avant-garde set and the driving force behind the seminally influential *Sgt Pepper*, he now likes nothing better than to sit at home with his wife and children.

He can be, by turns, charming and arrogant, magnanimous and mean, sentimental and acerbic, obliging and ruthlessly ego-centric. It was McCartney who made his wife into a pop star and McCartney who insists she does her own washing and ironing; who holds his late father in the highest esteem, yet failed to attend his funeral.

And at the end of another day spent counting his royalties in his office in Soho Square, he will depart with a cheery wave and take the train home, perhaps stopping to pick up a bunch of flowers for his wife, to spend the evening in front of the television. If, that is, he isn't out on tour, and appearing before world-record audiences – sometimes as huge as 180,000.

8

It is a long way from the council estate in Liverpool where it all began and which McCartney, for all his wealth and fame, likes to pretend he never really left.

1

ON 18 June 1942, Britain's Prime Minister Winston Churchill arrived secretly in Washington to meet America's President Franklin D. Roosevelt and discuss the military strategy for crushing Germany's Führer, Adolf Hitler.

Of less immediate moment that same day, Mary Patricia, wife of cotton salesman and part-time fireman Jim McCartney, gave birth to her first child, a son, in the comfortable anonymity of the private ward of Walton Hospital, Liverpool. He was named James Paul McCartney. There was no guiding star over Liverpool to herald his arrival, only the occasional tracer bullet searching the wartime sky. Even his own father was unimpressed. 'He looked awful . . . like a horrible piece of red meat,' Jim McCartney said of his first-born.

When he got home to their set of furnished rooms near Liverpool football club's stadium in the district of Anfield, Jim McCartney broke down and cried. He felt better for it and the boy, in his turn, started looking 'better and better. He turned into a lovely baby in the end.'

He grew into a son the McCartneys had reason to be proud of long before he turned into Beatle Paul, songwriter, millionaire, cultural icon, fulfilling expectations beyond the most extravagant of parental ambitions. He was intelligent, good-looking in a cherubic sort of way, became a Boy Scout and was kind to little old ladies, caused trouble neither at home nor at school, and was good at his lessons. His mother Mary wanted him to be a teacher and if she had lived he might have become one. But she died and rock and roll claimed him. As it also did three other young men who were born in Liverpool at around the same time. Paul did not meet them until he was into his teens, and his parents did not like it when he had.

The McCartneys – hardworking, determined to make the best of their lives – wanted Paul and his brother Michael, born eighteen months later, to do well. The Starkeys and the Harrisons – much poorer, apparently condemned by birth and inclination to the economic under-class – seemed content to stay put where they started. As for John Lennon, well, as Lennon himself said, 'I seemed to disgust everybody.' Troubled, threatening even at an early age, he was not the kind of boy Paul's parents would have wanted their son to be mixed up with. The McCartneys were and remain a close-knit unit, with a strong sense of family pride and tradition. There is little room for outsiders in their self-contained world – 'My mum and dad didn't have friends,' Paul recalls – and certainly not for someone like the firmly middle-class Lennon who was intent on petulantly, wilfully throwing away everything the McCartneys were struggling to achieve. The interaction between city and character, family and friends, can produce dramatically disparate results and, as events would prove, it was by iconoclastically breaking the mould of his background and recasting himself as what he called the 'working-class macho guy' that John Lennon turned himself into a legend.

Conversely, it was by sticking to the values beaten into him from earliest childhood, values Lennon so publicly despised, that Paul McCartney made himself the richest rock star of them all, with an income estimated at something in excess of £20 million a year. Those values are as tough as Liverpool itself. Its inhabitants are noted for their wisecracking sense of humour but the laughter is a safety valve, an escape from the most brutal of economic realities. In 1914 the city handled a third of Britain's exports and at the peak of its prosperity boasted more millionaires than any other metropolis of its size in the world. Its wealth was founded on cargoes to and from the Americas, first of slaves, then of cotton, and it was cotton that had given Jim McCartney his first step up the ladder and the promise of a decent future.

He had started work at the age of 14 and a wage of six shillings (30p) a week showing cotton samples to prospective buyers. Fourteen years later his industry and honesty earned him promotion to cotton salesman and the grand salary of five pounds a week – an unusual elevation at the time, as his sons still proudly point out, for 'a working-class chappie'.

It was supposed to be a 'job for life.' It wasn't. The cotton trade never recovered after the Second World War, and the city crumbled away to become one of the poorest in Europe. The beleaguered inhabitants were faced with the stark choice of either knuckling down and, by thrift and labour, making the best out of the worst of times, or throwing in the economic towel and tagging themselves on to the end of the ever-lengthening dole queue.

Jim McCartney chose the first course. Society, as he was fond of observing, might be all arse over tit, but you had to make of it what you could. During the war he transferred to a job in an engine factory and then, when Hitler's Germany was finally crushed, he became an inspector with the Corporation Cleansing Department, checking to make sure the dustmen emptied the bins properly. Later he got a lathe-turner's job at the engineering factory, producing Sabre engines for the Air Force, which came with a council house on the Kowlsely estate in Wallasey. It wasn't much of a home – the inside walls were bare brick – but with a young baby it was better than furnished rooms.

Mary went back to work. A qualified nursing sister, she had once been in charge of the maternity wing at Walton Hospital, which was why she came to give birth to Paul in the private ward. To help out with the family's meagre finances, she became a health visitor and then went back to midwifery, looking after expectant mothers on first one, then another of Liverpool's large public housing estates. Because they were domiciliary posts, a council house was provided and the family then moved with her work. It was a slow but satisfying advance, each new house being slightly better than the one before, with better curtains and nicer furniture. The McCartneys were the first people in their street to get a television set.

'Most working-class people were, and still are, trying to achieve higher standards for their families, and our parents were no exception,' Michael McCartney would later write. 'In our family it was mainly Mum who wanted us to "better ourselves".' She was, said Paul, 'madly aspiring for her sons'. One of Paul's earliest memories is of his mother urging him to correct his accent. 'When she told me off, I imitated her accent and she was hurt, which made me feel uptight.'

In 1955 they finally came to domestic rest at 20 Forthlin Road in the 'respectable' – always an important consideration for the McCartneys – Liverpool suburb of Allerton. For the first time they had an inside lavatory.

The constant moving to what Mrs McCartney called 'better positions' was, says Michael, a 'pain' to her sons. No sooner had they settled into one school and made friends than they were uprooted and off again. It proved no disruption to Paul's education, however. His family provided him with the warm security he needed. He was bright and always worked hard enough to do well in his examinations; his eleven-plus results were good enough to earn a place at the Institute, Liverpool's finest grammar school which took the cream of the city's boys. His brother Michael followed him there, to their mother's uncontained delight – she wept tears of joy when Michael rushed home with the news that he too had passed his eleven-plus and would be joining Paul at the 'Inny'.

Surprisingly, Mary was less influential on the matter of her sons' religious upbringing. Irish by ethnic background, Mary Patricia Mohin was brought up a strict Roman Catholic. At the age of 31 she broke out of her faith to wed the Protestant Jim McCartney, eight years her senior. The marriage took place none the less at St Swithins' Roman Catholic Chapel in Liverpool's Gill Moss. And in keeping with her promise to the priest, her two sons were both formally baptised into the Roman Catholic faith ('and circumcised Jewishly,' Michael disclosed).

Jim McCartney adhered to an 'agnostic' view. He believed there was too much religion and not enough education in Catholic schools. His view won out and Paul and Michael were educated, not by priests and nuns, but in secular state schools. Not that Mary put up much resistance: she had not been impressed by the standards of education at the Catholic schools she saw in the course of her work as a health visitor.

More remarkably, when the boys did attend church it was not a Roman Catholic but a Church of England one. Paul sang in the choir at St Barnabas, near Penny Lane. On his father's prompting he auditioned to join the choir at Liverpool's Anglican Cathedral (he was turned down because he couldn't read music). Paul McCartney, christened a Roman Catholic, now describes himself as 'C of E'. His mother Mary had, as far as her own family were concerned, effectively rejected the religion of her childhood – as, by coincidence, did the future Mrs McCartney, Paul's wife Linda.

The absence of religious consistency was more than compensated for in the McCartney family's home by a strict code of conduct and responsibility. Mary was just and loving . . . the affection-giver; Jim was a man of his word, proud, hardworking, with a strong sense of duty. His wife earned more than him but, true to class and geography, he saw himself as the head of the household, the 'arbitrator', as Michael called him, who always had the last word and whose ruling was final. If Linda echoes Mary's religious fluidity, Paul is intent on recreating himself in his father's image.

Of his father, Paul said: 'He was just an average Jim, a cotton salesman, no great shakes. But he was very intelligent. He used to do crosswords to increase his word power. He taught us an appreciation of common sense which is what you found a lot of in

Liverpool. I've been around the world a few times, to all its little pockets, and, in truth, I'd swear to God I've never met anyone more soulful, more intelligent, more kind, more filled with common sense, than the people I came from in Liverpool.'

Peter Brown, who ran Apple, introduced Paul to Linda and, as a one-time executive director of Brian Epstein's NEMS Enterprises, was involved with the Beatles from their beginnings in the Cavern club through to the break-up, came to know Jim McCartney well. A Liverpudlian himself, he says: 'Paul was deeply influenced by the example of his father who was an unsuccessful man commercially but was tremendously nice and good and honest. Decent is the right word. If he hadn't been so decent he might have done better in life. Paul recognised the decency, this very admirable quality, in his father. He is trying to be as decent as his father was. It is a very northern-male thing: don't deny your past, be decent, keep the family together – as long as I'm the boss.'

In Jim McCartney's household this old-fashioned, chauvinistic approach to parenthood was moderated by a well-developed sense of humour and the love and attention he gave his sons. He encouraged their interest in the countryside and there were holidays on a farm in Wales where they were pictured proudly riding a pony. He saved up to buy Paul a three-speed Raleigh sports bicycle and took him on long country rides. A keen gardener, he introduced him to the smell of lavender freshly crushed between his fingers. Before he shaved he would rub his stubbly chin against his sons' cheeks and blow raspberries into their necks. He made 'marvellous' Yorkshire puddings, custard and rice puddings. He saved up his coupons – rationing was still in force in Britain – to give them bananas. He would apologise for not holding their tummies when they were being sick, explaining that it would make him sick too. He got them a dog, a half-breed sheep dog called Prince. To stop them fighting at night, he installed extension leads from the radio in the sitting room so that the boys could listen to 'Dick Barton, Special Agent' in bed on their primitive bakelite earphones and, when they were older, the crackling sounds of pop music on Radio Luxemburg.

Like the man himself, his views were decent and unpretentious. He expressed himself in proverbs such as 'Satan finds work for idle hands' and he was forever reminding them of what Paul called his ''ations'. The two most important things in life, he would say, are toleration and moderation. 'Toleration *is* very important,' Jim McCartney explained. 'They would laugh at people with infirmities, as kids do. I'd explain to them how *they* wouldn't like it. And moderation – a lot of trouble is caused without that.'

Trouble was something Paul intuitively avoided. If he did get into difficulties he kept his problem to himself – as he does to this day. Jim McCartney was not averse to smacking his sons if he felt their behaviour warranted it. Mary did not interfere. It was Michael rather than Paul who got the worst of their father's hand. While the younger McCartney boy was forever getting into scrapes, Paul, as his father said, 'did things much quieter. He had much more nous. Paul was able to get out of most things.' Which is perhaps just as well. For on the rare occasion he was beaten, he made it his business to take sneaky revenge. As he recounted: 'If I ever got bashed for being bad I used to go into their bedroom when they were out and rip the lace curtains at the bottom, just a little bit. Then I'd think, that's got them.'

On a gentler and more important note, Jim also introduced Paul to music at an early age. 'When I was very little I would lie on the floor in the living room while he'd be playing the piano,' Paul recalls. His father introduced him to the songs of artists such as Fats Waller and Fred Astaire, which he still enjoys and, in many cases, now owns the publishing rights to.

As a young man Jim, despite the eardrum he ruptured falling off a wall at the age of 10 and which kept him out of the Forces during the war, had had his own dance band. He had little time for classical music – 'Turn that bloody stuff off' he would shout when it came on the radio. It was jazz, and the big bands of the swing era in particular, that caught his musical interest. He formed a combo with a few like-minded acquaintances. After a false start as the Masked Melody Makers – in the heat the dye in their highwayman masks ran down their faces – they reformed as Jim Mac's Band and played the local dance halls. The band never enjoyed any great success, but it did help him find a wife.

Mary, Paul later discovered, had been courted by another man 'for a long time'. She got him to take her dancing. 'Then he suddenly twigged . . . it turned out that that was where my father was playing. She was following him round as a fan.' Paul McCartney's driving belief is that you make of your environment what you will, but he also inclines to the hereditary view. 'It made me think, God, that's where I get it all from.'

Jim McCartney played trumpet and piano. He gave up the trumpet shortly after he married when, as Paul described it, 'his teeth went' and he had to wear false ones. He kept up the piano, though, and singsongs were a regular entertainment at home. It was part of the family closeness Paul would come to place such store in. His parents, as he pointed out, had few friends ('They were rather snobbish,' one contemporary of Paul McCartney recalled) but they didn't need them. What they had and what they much preferred were relatives – aunts, uncles and cousins. And they had a lot of those. Jim was one of seven surviving children born to tobacco-cutter Joseph McCartney and his wife Florence, and they had gone forth and produced many more.

'As I was growing up I was always having babies thrust at me,' Paul remembered. 'It was like a big Italian family, someone always dandling a baby on the knee.' He loved the familial atmosphere and his favourite childhood reading were albums of the *Daily Express* cartoon character, Rupert the Bear, that anthropomorphic depiction of warm, homely, middle-class values. It is still a favourite of his. Of his family he now says: 'They're just very ordinary people but, by God, they've got something – common sense in the truest sense of the word. I've met lots of people. I've met Harold Wilson and Maggie Thatcher and most of the mayors in America. But I've never met anyone as interesting or as fascinating as my Liverpool family.'

The family idyll, when all its troubles seemed so far away, was shattered on 31 October 1956. Not for many years, not until McCartney started a family of his own three decades later and deliberately set about constructing it on the fragments of his bereaved memory, was the damage repaired. If it ever was.

Mary had been complaining of pains in her breast for months. As long before as the summer of 1955, on her way back from visiting her sons at a Boy Scout camp, the pains had been so intense that she had had to lie down. She put it down to the menopause, but the lump did not go away. Neither did the pain. One day Michael found her upstairs in her bedroom, clutching a crucifix and crying. Michael asked her what the matter was. 'Nothing, love,' she replied.

Eventually she consulted a specialist. He diagnosed breast cancer and operated but it was too late. Shortly before she was admitted to hospital she told Olive Johnson, a colleague of her husband: 'I don't want to leave the boys just yet.' Just before she died she said to her brother Bill's wife, Dill: 'I would have liked to have seen the boys growing up.' Paul was 14, Michael was 12.

When Paul was told that his mother was dead his first question was: 'What are we going to do without her money?' It was a remark as glib as it was hurtful (but, so his critics insist, McCartney is never less than glib and is more than capable of being hurtful). But he cried himself to sleep that night. He prayed for his mother to come back: 'Daft prayers, you know, if you bring her back I'll be very very good for always. I thought, it just shows how stupid religion is. See, the prayers didn't work when I really needed them.'

He sought more temporal solace. Jim McCartney had recently scrimped together fifteen pounds and bought him a guitar. It became his comfort and his escape. He took it everywhere with him, including into the lavatory. His brother Michael recalled: 'It was just after Mother's death that it started. It became an obsession. It took over his whole life. You lose a mother – and you find a guitar?'

What has been called the 'lifetime process of internalising his feelings' had begun. One evening, in the three-up, two-down loneliness of 20 Forthlin, the house a mother who was no more had been so proud of, Paul McCartney wrote his first song.

2

In the graveyard of St Peter's Church in Woolton there is a headstone that bears the name of Eleanor Rigby. On Saturday, 6 July 1957, Paul McCartney unnoticingly rode his bicycle past the grave on his way to the church fete from his home a mile or so away in Allerton. He was not there to buy any of the home-made cakes or secondhand books in the jumble sale. If he had an interest in the skiffle group who were playing that afternoon it was only a passing one. No, he was there because his schoolfriend Ivan Vaughan had told him there was a chance of meeting girls and he was dressed to kill. He was wearing a white sports coat 'with speckles in it and flaps over the pockets' and a pair of black drainpipe trousers. His hair was combed back in an Elvis-style pompadour, the brilliantined product of hours spent before the bathroom mirror. It was the peacock display of a young male in pubescent rut.

McCartney lost his virginity when he was 15, to a girl older and bigger than himself, at her house while 'she was supposed to be baby-sitting while her mum was out'. It was an experience he wished to repeat but he had tarnished his chances of doing so with that particular young woman when, to her intense embarrassment, he told everyone about it at school the next day. New 'talent' was therefore a necessity and Ivan, with all the endearing optimism of adolescence, had assured him that the Woolton parish church really was the place to pick up a willing girl who was bound to be just waiting to disappear into the bushes and get inside 15-year-old Paul McCartney's drainpipe trousers.

Ivan was wrong. There were girls there, of course, but Paul, for all his youthful braggadocio, had yet to acquire 'the flair for picking them up like that'. Young lust unsatiated, he ended up listening to the skiffle group. They were called the Quarry Men, after the nearby Quarry Bank grammar school they attended, and they were dreadful. There were five of them up there on the makeshift stage in the church grounds and, as Paul recalled, none of them had 'much idea' of how to play their instruments. The name of the singer and lead guitarist was John Lennon and he couldn't even remember the words of the song he was supposed to be singing and had to keep inventing them.

'John,' Paul remembers, 'was playing ukulele chords taught him by his mum and he was singing "Come Go with Me to the Penitentiary" by the Del Vikings, and he didn't know one of the words. Nobody had the record; we'd only heard it on the radio.' Lennon, dressed in a checked shirt and with his hair greased back in a quiff, was practising his stage craft. 'John was staring round as he played, watching everybody. He told me afterwards that it was the first time he tried sussing an audience, sizing them up, seeing whether it was best to twist a shoulder at them or best not to move at all.'

He hadn't mastered either technique. Most of the two hundred people there, all dressed in their Sunday best, found the tombola and the ball-in-the-bucket game more alluring than the sight of the young John Lennon dropping a shoulder or even the prospect of him dropping off the stage altogether, a distinct possibility considering the amount of beer he had consumed. Paul, though, was impressed. Music, rock and roll music, had taken its hold. 'The rock and roll bug,' he said, 'had bitten me,' as it had most of the Western world's teenagers, and if Paul wanted to do anything, it was to get out there and play it himself.

When the Quarry Men finished their set Paul went to meet them in the church hall. The 16-year-old Lennon reeked of alcohol. McCartney borrowed a guitar which he showed them how to tune.

He showed them how to play Eddie Cochran's 'Twenty Flight Rock', which he had laboriously learned on the evenings he was supposed to be doing his school homework. He sang them all the words and obligingly wrote them out for Lennon. Then he sang Gene Vincent's 'Be Bop A Lula', and taught them the words to that, for what they were worth.

Warming to his audience, he then gave a rendition of Little Richard songs, sung in the high-pitched Little Richard manner. McCartney knew the words to twenty-five rock songs, learned by listening to them not on the infrequent occasions they were broad-cast on the radio but on the 78-rpm records he had started collecting – 'Be Bop A Lula' was the first disc he bought – and which he played on the gramophone in the front sitting room in Forthlin Road.

Lennon was impressed – and wary. The Quarry Men was *his* band, he'd been kingpin up to then. Was he going to invite McCartney – and he only 15, an important consideration at that age – to join *his* band and possibly challenge him for the leadership? 'I thought, if I take him on, what will happen?' Lennon recounted. 'It went through my head that I'd have to keep him in line if I let him join.'

But McCartney was good, very good by the standards of the Woolton parish church garden fete. Lennon went away to think it over. He made his decision. It proved to be the right one – though how right, how spectacularly right, no one could have dreamed back in that summer of 1957.

Two weeks later Lennon's friend, Pete Shotton, whose mother had secured the Quarry Men their booking at St Peter's, chanced upon McCartney cycling in Woolton. On behalf of John Lennon he asked Paul McCartney if he would like to join the group. Paul said yes. The most momentous partnership in rock music was about to be forged.

The pair, as later events would painfully emphasise, had little in common. McCartney, Peter Brown observes, was 'conscientious and deferential to his elders'; essentially law-abiding with his father's

23

sense of responsibility and the determination, inherited from his mother, to 'better himself'. Lennon, the troubled product of a broken home, was rough, cruel and iconoclastic, too vain to wear the glasses he could hardly see without, a headstrong rebel without a cause intent on causing offence. McCartney had been taught by his father not to mock the afflicted; Lennon took a fiendish delight in making fun of cripples.

What they did have, though, was a consuming passion for rock and roll. And that, in the innocent, dreary days of the 1950s when youths like Lennon and McCartney had little else to interest or occupy them, was enough to bring them together. It was a meeting of opposites, prompted by emotional necessity and consummated by commercial ambition. It took them everywhere – around the world and into every home that had a radio, a television, a record-player, or a wall to pin a photograph on – and it would leave them both emotionally stranded. It was a marriage and it made them rich. And, for a long time after it was over, it left the abandoned McCartney emotionally 'shattered'.

It was, so one of their closest advisers believes, an inevitable union, given the time and their circumstances. Peter Brown says: 'You can choose your friends but not your family and they didn't choose each other, it just happened.'

On the night of October 18 Paul McCartney made his stage debut with the Quarry Men at a Conservative Club dance at the New Clubmoor Hall in Broadway, Liverpool. Later that night Lennon listened to McCartney play a couple of the tunes he had written. Not to be outdone, John, who until then had never progressed beyond the spurious achievement of setting his own lyrics to other people's tunes, responded by composing some melodies of his own.

Years later, long after their acrimonious parting, McCartney said: 'John and I were perfect for each other.' And the way they egged each other on, 'the competitive element' as Paul called it, was a vital part of the chemistry.

The song that McCartney played that night was entitled 'I Love My Little Girl', 'the first song I ever wrote. It was so naïve. What

24

really put me off was that I wrote, "Her hair didn't always curl", to rhyme with "girl".'

He misjudges. It was the tune, rather than the lyrics, that was weak and derivative. McCartney was no Liverpudlian incarnation of Mozart, who wrote his first symphony at the age of six; one of the greatest writers of popular melodies of this century had yet to find his musical feet. The my-girl-no-curl lyrics, on the other hand, compare not unfavourably to such later offerings as 'Michelle, my belle'. (A point that, not untypically, McCartney himself would make twenty-five years later when he remarked: 'It doesn't actually seem as bad these days – there must have been a lot of very bad lyrics meantime.') And at least it was a beginning. 'Once I got to know John it all changed. I went off in a completely new direction from then on.'

It was not a direction Jim McCartney, a widower at 53, had any reason to approve of. The death of his wife, Mary, had left him with the task of looking after two teenage sons on a paltry salary of eight pounds a week and he found it a struggle. 'I missed my wife – it knocked me for six when she died,' he said. He was determined to hold his family together until they were old enough to fend for themselves. Two of his sisters, Milly and Jinny, gave what help they could, coming in to clean and, their own commitments permitting, letting the boys in from school. But Jim McCartney was confused by the role the tragedy had cast him in.

'The biggest headache was what sort of parent I was going to be,' he said. Explained Michael: 'He had to decide to be a father *or* a mother to his two growing lads. Luckily he chose to be both, a very hard decision when you've got used to being the man around the house.'

'The winters were bad,' Jim would recall. There was no smell of hot scones in the oven, no maternal kiss to greet the boys, who 'had to light the fires themselves when they came home from school. I did all the cooking.'

Paul didn't help matters. Outwardly he remained, at least to himself, the same 'cocky sod' he had always been, but the consternation was there. He started playing truant. His school work suffered as a consequence and he had to stay back a class to catch up on the work he hadn't done to pass the required number of O levels. Without Mary's money, as Paul had worried when she died, the family was finding it hard to make ends meet. Yet against the specific orders of his father he brought friends home to raid the family larder and eat the food which Jim McCartney could barely afford to buy.

Without Mary's steadying influence, other signs of disquiet appeared. He started wearing clothes his conventional father thoroughly disapproved of, particularly the drainpipe trousers which were then height of backstreet fashion. He grew his hair long and swept back into a DA, a duck's arse, copied from Tony Curtis. The only people who dressed like that were members of the razor-carrying, bicycle-chain-wielding street gangs who slashed their way through performances of the Bill Haley film, *Rock Around the Clock*. Jim McCartney was concerned. He worried that Paul would turn into a Teddy Boy.

Paul got round his father's sartorial objections by first showing him a pair of trousers, getting his approval, and then promptly having them taken in during the school lunchtime at a nearby tailors. If his father noticed the change Paul would 'swear blind' that they were the same trousers he had given his blessing to. 'I was,' Paul admitted, 'pretty sneaky.'

Michael remembered: 'We were terrible and cruel. We gave Dad very little help plus a lot of cheek. He just bit his lip and carried on, day after day and night after lonely night.' He would have had 'every justification' if he had 'cracked up, got drunk, beat us up, brought women home'. He didn't. 'He just soldiered on.' And made, Michael insisted, 'an amazing job of it. Paul owes a lot to Dad.'

Not that Paul would have seen it that way, not then. It was an unhappy time for a man who would later make a jolly smile his international trademark. He rarely spoke. 'I had better conversations with brick walls around this period,' his brother recalled. It was only

26

through his music that Paul, tongue-tied by adolescence, silenced by a grief he kept bottled up, seemed able to express himself. In that he found a fellow in John Lennon.

An intelligent, sensitive child deserted by his mother, Julia, and his father, a seaman named Fred, shortly after he was born, Lennon had been brought up by his aunt Mimi in the pebble-dash respectability of Menlove Avenue, across a golf course and several social notches up from Forthlin Road. Like Paul, he had easily passed his eleven-plus. Unlike Paul, Lennon had no interest in learning. By the time Lennon hit his teens he was in revolt – against what, he couldn't say, but that only made it harder for his home-owning, determinedly middle-class aunt Mimi to deal with.

In the mid-1960s, when it was fashionable to proclaim working-class origins and boast of a lack of education, McCartney would disparagingly dismiss his grammar-school days as a waste of time. For Lennon they really were. While Paul could always stir himself enough to pass an exam, Lennon didn't even try. One typical end-of-term report from Quarry Bank described him as 'hopeless . . . certainly on the road to failure'. He failed all his O levels, including art, and it was only through the intervention of his aunt Mimi, who somehow persuaded his headmaster to write a lukewarm letter of recommendation, that he secured a place at Liverpool Art College. He is not, the headmaster wrote, 'beyond redemption and could possibly turn out to be a fairly responsible adult who might go far'.

The headmaster was eventually proved right, but not as far as Liverpool Art College was concerned. Lennon, as lazy and factious as ever, dragged along at the bottom of the class – when, that is, he bothered to turn up at all. His only interest – apart from those perennial interests of youth, as defined by McCartney, of 'women, money and clothes' – was rock and roll. In Paul he found a musical soulmate; someone who like himself was consumed by the skiffle of Lonnie Donegan, the strident shouts of Cochran and Vincent and Richard, the wailing of the Everly Brothers, and, above all others, by Elvis Presley.

They were not alone. In the drab 1950s, when the airwaves were controlled by the British Broadcasting Corporation and the seditious sound of rock and roll was severely rationed, the bedrooms of tens of thousands of British homes were filled with young men armed with broom sticks, air guitars, and, just occasionally, the real instrument, snarling into wardrobe mirrors, hair slicked back, bodies twitching, imagination in overdrive, pretending to be Southern Klansmen. The difference here was that the two youngsters playing out their fantasies in the front room of 20 Forthlin Road, Liverpool 18 – and had Elvis even heard of Liverpool until it was too late to make any difference? – had talent, a real talent greater than the hip-sneering, lip-curling original.

There was another bond between them. Shortly before they teamed up, Lennon's mother Julia had reappeared in his life. He was dazzled by her, by her light-hearted attitude to life and her sense of humour so similar to his own. A banjo-player herself, she taught her son the only chords he knew how to play on the £17-guitar Mimi had bought him in a moment of weakness. Says Peter Brown: 'It would not be inaccurate to say that John fell in love with Julia.' It was a tragically short-lived reconciliation. On the night of 15 July 1958, almost exactly a year after he had first met Paul McCartney, Julia was killed crossing the road outside Mimi's house.

'He lost his mum when he was seventeen; that was one of the things that brought John and me very close together,' said McCartney. 'It was a bond between us, quite a big one. We came together professionally afterwards. And as we became a writing team, I think it helped our intimacy and our trust in each other. Eventually, we were pretty good mates – until the Beatles started to split up and Yoko came into it.'

Mimi was not well disposed towards McCartney, the would-be Teddy Boy in the flecked jacket and skintight jeans. His as yet unpolished charm made no impression on her. When he arrived at her front door and asked, 'Hello, Mimi, can I come in?' she was wont to answer, 'No, you certainly cannot.' And if she did let him inside, she certainly did not allow the discordant guitar sounds of two would-be Presleys to pollute her neat, well-kept sitting room.

It was to the McCartney home, therefore, that they repaired to practise.

Jim McCartney did not approve of the friendship either. He disliked rock and roll and he disliked John Lennon. Michael recalled: 'Dad certainly didn't take too kindly to him.' He kept warning Paul: 'He'll get you into trouble, son.' Jim McCartney, however, practised what he preached. 'Dad actually *lived* his "toleration and moderation" adages,' said Michael. 'Johnny "Moondog" wasn't actually *banned* from 20 Forthlin Road.' He was in there more often than Jim McCartney knew or would have allowed, though.

Liverpool Art College was next door to the Liverpool Institute. Neither saw as much as they should have of their two pupils. Lennon turned up infrequently. McCartney, too, became a practised truant. 'We'd sag off class and nip over the fence into the cathedral cemetery a hundred yards away, where we boys would rather irreligiously sunbathe on the gravestones,' McCartney recalled. 'It was the best place for a doze and a tan.'

Lennon added variety to the truancy. Instead of the cemetery and a sleep, McCartney now headed back to Forthlin Road and a jam session with Lennon. They were sometimes joined by another youngster named John Lloyd, now a carpet salesman in Liverpool. He had met the novice musicians at the St Peter's garden fete on the same day they met each other. He recalls: 'Paul was pretty quiet, not very outgoing. He was also a bit on the pudgy side' ('fat' is how Michael McCartney describes his brother at that time; 'the college pudding', is how he described himself). 'He was very well mannered. I never heard him swear. If any grown-up spoke to him he was always very polite. He was not a rebel, not like John. John was completely different. There was a lot more to John than there was to Paul. John was very upfront, very outgoing. His mind was always ticking over. Paul was less obvious.'

At Forthlin Road they would listen to records on the gramophone – 'a nice piece of polished furniture' as Lloyd remembers it – and strum along on their guitars. McCartney would feed his young guests but they were not allowed upstairs. 'The McCartneys were very posh. You were lucky if you were allowed into the house,' Lloyd says.

Jim McCartney would have been angered enough had he known that while he was out at work there was anyone in the front sitting room at all, never mind the upstairs, when they were supposed to be at school. But the hours of practice had the sought-for result and the quality of their playing improved. McCartney conquered the problem of his left-handedness. 'When I first got a guitar I couldn't understand what was wrong with it because I really couldn't get it together,' he recalled. 'I just had no rhythm in my hands.' A picture of the left-handed country-and-western singer Slim Whitman – 'Now *there's* a name to conjure with,' he quipped – gave him the clue to what was wrong. 'He was the first lefty I'd ever seen and I said, "That's it! Turn the guitar upside down."'

It worked. And to keep up with his always more technically advanced partner, the right-handed Lennon would watch how Paul played his chords and then go and reverse the process again by practising in front of a mirror.

On Saturday evenings they watched 'Oh Boy!', the inspirational British television rock-and-roll programme recorded before a live audience which introduced a generation of fledgling rockers to the visual excitement of the music (Elton John wanted to be a performer from the moment he first watched the show). They didn't like Cliff Richard, a pink-jacketed, greasy-haired, carbon copy of Elvis and one of the show's resident singers, but they spent time enough practising how to play his songs and when McCartney worked out the guitar introduction to Richard's first hit, 'Move It', by watching it being played on 'Oh Boy!', 'I rushed out of the house straight away, got on my bike and raced over to John shouting, "I've got it!"'

They practised their harmonies. 'I had a little bit more knowledge of harmony through my dad – I actually knew what the word har- mony meant,' McCartney said. Lennon urged on McCartney's Little Richard-style vocals which became such a feature of the early

Beatles. 'I would often fall a little bit short, not have that little kick, that soul, and it would be John who would go, "Come on, you can sing better than that."'

Their songwriting, too, was developing. They filled exercise after exercise book with lyrics to over fifty songs including 'When I'm Sixty Four' and 'Love Me Do'. If the words remained the same, the tunes did not, however. Neither Lennon nor McCartney could read music – McCartney, after four attempts, still can't – and the melodies were often forgotten and had to be recomposed. When the Quarry Men, which became the Rainbows, then Johnny and the Moondogs, made one of their occasional appearances – at weddings and social clubs and arranged through friends – they would include some of their own compositions in their repertoire.

For all their efforts, however, no one was falling over themselves in the rush to sign them up. They were still only an amateur schoolboy outfit which often had trouble getting enough people together to make up a group and frequently found itself without a drummer (in the late 1950s not many boys wanted to be a drummer; everyone wanted to be Elvis). Membership worked on the revolving-door policy and they went through more personnel than name changes. Part of that was Paul's doing. Quiet he may have been, but as John Lloyd remembers, 'Paul had a mind of his own; he knew what he wanted.' And what he wanted was to play lead guitar. He got his way by so badgering the lad called Eric Griffiths who had the job that he eventually quit. Lennon, too, could also be tricky to work with, though, typically, he made his feelings known in a decidedly more straightforward manner. Pete Shotton took the hint when Lennon broke the skiffle-style washboard he had been playing over his head, and resigned.

One person who did stick in was a spotty-faced youth named George Harrison, the youngest of a Liverpool Corporation bus driver's four children. He was a year younger than McCartney and a chasmic two and a half years younger than Lennon. Like McCartney, he was a pupil at the Liverpool Institute and they first met, long before Paul was introduced to Lennon, on the bus on the way to school. They started talking when George's mother, Louise, had lent McCartney the money for his fare, and discovered that they shared a mutual interest in rock and roll and skiffle. George had his own guitar, bought secondhand for three pounds when he was 14, and one night Paul went round to the Harrisons' council house in Speke to peruse George's teach-yourself-how-to-play book.

Harrison remembered: 'We learned a couple of chords from it and managed to play "Don't You Rock Me Daddy O",' a hit in early 1957 for Lonnie Donegan, the king of skiffle, the artless, British-born, folk-based precursor to rock and roll played with washboards, guitars and basses made out of tea chests which had first aroused McCartney's interest in pop music. It was the beginning of a long but now ended friendship.

Louise Harrison, a keen dancer, encouraged her son's guitar playing, urging him on when he became despondent at his lack of progress – 'George never thought he was any good,' Mrs Harrison recalled – sitting up with him until two, three o'clock in the morning as he fretted over his chords, eventually investing thirty hard-earned pounds in an electric guitar, for which George had to take a job as a butcher's delivery boy to pay her back. His hard-earned proficiency did not impress John Lennon, however, not at first. It certainly didn't impress his aunt Mimi who was even more appalled by Harrison's Teddy Boy clothes than she had been by McCartney's. 'You always seem to like lower-class types, don't you, John?' she complained to her nephew.

Lennon, of course, had nothing against Harrison's pink shirts and greasy long hair. It was the way he would have liked to have dressed, if only Mimi had allowed it. It was Harrison's age that counted against him. They were introduced by McCartney at the Wilson Hall in Garston where the Quarry Men played on the night of 8 February 1958. Lennon didn't want to know his young friend's younger friend. 'George was just too young, a kid,' he said.

Harrison was not to be shaken off, however. He followed the Quarry Men around from gig to gig, hero-worshipping Lennon (a major plus point), putting up with his jibes, standing in if someone failed to turn up, until, without anyone really noticing, he became accepted as a permanent member of the group. And as the group became more proficient, so Jim McCartney's opposition started to ease. 'They were getting good, not just bashing about,' he said, and started sitting in with them, offering them the benefit of his musical experience, and, when that was rejected, warming up leftovers to sustain them.

It wasn't all rock and roll, though, not for Paul. Harrison would leave school without any qualifications at 16. Lennon, frequently drunk and even more troublesome since the death of his mother than he had been before, had no discernible ambition other than to marry a millionairess. But McCartney was still at school and his father was determined that he should remain there until he got the qualifications necessary 'to make an honest living by getting a steady job'.

That was not proving as easy as it should have, given the intelligence of a boy who had gained 90 percent for Latin in his first year at the Institute. The days missed playing truant, coupled with his reluctance to put his mind to his homework, had left gaps in his education which even his ability at turning it on at exam time was unable to paper over. His father was disappointed when he failed all his O levels except art and had to stay down a class to take them again.

Another boy in the form was Paul Fisher, now an executive with the Ford motor company. He used to share with Paul the occasional Woodbine cigarette, bought singly from a nearby tobacconist, behind the sheds in the upper playground during break. 'The Institute was a well-run, disciplined school and we had to wear a uniform, including a cap,' Fisher remembers. 'Smoking was against the rules but there was a tradition, an unwritten rule, that the prefects kept away from the smokers' corner. I used to meet McCartney there for a quick breaktime smoke.'

At school, out on public show, McCartney went out of his way to present himself as a 'likeable, humorous lad'. He was certainly not a trouble-maker and wore his school cap. He was, Fisher says, 'reasonably popular', with 'unusually good handwriting for a boy of his age' and a flair for drawing. He also had a talent for playing guitar, as Fisher recounts. At the end of term in the Remove form for O level failures the boys were allowed to put on a show. McCartney, ably assisted by Harrison on second guitar, a chap called Duff Lowe on piano and someone beating out the time on a tea-chest bass, entertained their fellow pupils in the Institute's music room.

'They really played well, George Harrison especially,' says Fisher. 'There were thirty or forty boys crammed into the room and when other people heard the music they tried to get in to listen. There was a rush of boys fighting to get in. We had to barricade the door to keep them out.' The first Beatle riot? There was another augury of things to come. In the summer of 1957, shortly after that fateful meeting with Lennon, Jim McCartney took his sons away to Butlin's holiday camp in Filey in Yorkshire where Paul entered the talent contest.

The compere's name was Mike Robbins and he just happened to be married to Jim McCartney's niece, Bett. With more accuracy than he imagined he announced: 'Ladies and gentlemen, every now and then you come across outstanding musical talent and today is no exception, so put your hands together for a young man from Liverpool . . . Paul McCartney.' With the reluctant assistance of his younger brother who was nursing an arm broken at Scout camp a few weeks earlier, McCartney sang the Everly Brothers' hit 'Bye Bye Love', then gave a youthful rendition of Little Richard's 'Long Tall Sally'. They were well received and McCartney won his first fan, a girl called Angela who came from Hull (though it turned out she really had her eye on the younger McCartney – much to the chagrin of Paul who hid the letters she wrote to Michael).

This time round, however, McCartney did not allow his music to interfere too much with his academic studies and on the second attempt he gained four more O level passes. 'Not that he cheated . . . but he was always good at applying situations and people, and still is,' his brother Michael would observe. He thought about

McCartney in Lennon's group, the Quarry Men, in 1958. Lennon had been doubtful about inviting him to join. *(Pictorial Press)*

On the verge of success with drummer Pete Best – who wasn't allowed to share it. *(Topham)*

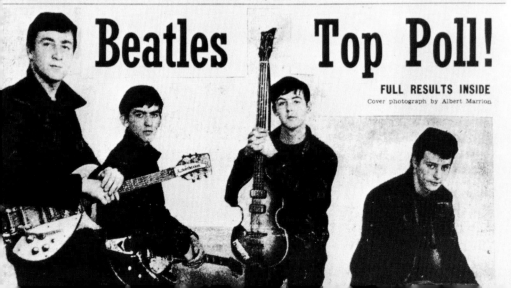

MERSEY BEAT

No. 13   JANUARY 4-18, 1962   Price THREEPENCE

Beatles Top Poll!

FULL RESULTS INSIDE

Cover photograph by Albert Marrion

The Beatles, 1963. Out of leather and into the suits Brian Epstein bought for them. Lennon hated the change; McCartney viewed it as a step on the way to stardom. *(Pictorial Press)*

Brian Epstein, the manager who made them stars and cost them millions. *(Topham)*

The embodiment of cheery youth: the Beatles in clean-cut pose with two friends, 1963. *(Pictorial Press)*

leaving and getting a job – 'school was still a complete drag' – but jobs, interesting jobs, were in short supply in Liverpool. Besides, his father wanted him to stay on. Following up his late wife's ambition for her first-born, he wanted Paul to become a teacher and, in respect for his father and the absence of any obvious alternative, McCartney stayed on at the Institute, moved up into the sixth form, and started studying for A levels in Art and English.

In truth, though, it was more out of duty than any real sense of purpose that McCartney struggled on through his academic work. Had he bothered to acquire the intellectual self-discipline necessary to complete his A levels successfully, the trite flaccidity of many of his later song lyrics might have been avoided, and disasters like *Magical Mystery Tour* and *Give My Regards to Broadstreet* might have been avoided. But there was no telling McCartney then, not when there were records to buy, songs to rehearse, more gigs to play, new friends to make, girls to be courted. It was the big world, not study or books that the young man, like most others of his age, found exciting.

John started going out with fellow art student Cynthia Powell, a prim and soft-spoken girl who came from Hoylake, socially a more desirable part of Liverpool than the areas John, Paul and certainly George came from. They started hanging out at the Jacaranda, one of the thousands of coffee bars that were springing up all over Britain at that time, and met its owner, Allan Williams, a stubby, talkative hustler who was just setting up as a booking agent for the city's proliferating 'beat' groups.

In the incongruous setting of a large Victorian house in the suburb of West Derby they met Pete Best, whose mother, Mona, in an extraordinary act of maternal indulgence, had converted her basement into a coffee bar-cum-dance hall called the Casbah for her son and his teenage friends. The Quarry Men started playing there on a regular if haphazard basis (they were still having problems with a drummer) and helped repaint it, Cynthia contributing a spider's web motif to the walls.

Now there was another member of the band. His name was Stu

Sutcliffe and, like John and Cynthia, he attended Liverpool Art College. His enigmatic, ethereal personality, lean, fragile frame, James Dean looks, and perennial dark glasses made him something of a role model for the other students, and, as it would turn out, for the other members of the embryonic group. Lennon, whose enthusiasm for people and ideas was consuming, often stayed over at Sutcliffe's studio, a shabby, soot-covered artist's garret near the college, to spend the night drinking and talking. Lennon ushered him into the Quarry Men – a step that would cost Sutcliffe his life.

An artist of genuine talent, Sutcliffe had entered some of his paintings in the John Moores Exhibition founded by the Littlewoods pools and mail-order family. He won a prize worth £60 – a large sum of money in those pre-inflationary days. Lennon cajoled him into investing the whole lot in a bass guitar. George would have been happier if he had opted for a drum kit. McCartney, on the other hand, would have preferred it if Sutcliffe hadn't joined at all. He resented Sutcliffe's friendship with Lennon and was exasperated by Sutcliffe's inability to learn how to play the instrument that had cost what it took Jim McCartney almost two months to earn. Underlying those objections was the more fundamental fact that the two men did not like each other.

McCartney had no right of veto, however; it was still Lennon's group and they needed a bass to provide the backing for John, Paul and George's alternating lead and rhythm guitars. And, for all McCartney's misgivings, Sutcliffe, despite his musical incompetence, had presence and style. As Pete Best put it: 'He was a powerhouse, simply because of his charisma.'

It was also Sutcliffe who came up with The Name. Playing around with variations of the name of Buddy Holly's group, the Crickets, he hit upon Beetles, then Beatals. Lennon, never one to resist a pun, turned that into Beatles, 'to make it look like beat music, just as a joke'.

One person who wasn't impressed was Casy Jones, who had his own group called Cas and the Casanovas. The vogue in rock and roll, he explained, was for longer names, like Marty Wilde and the

Wildcats, Cliff Richard and the Shadows, Tommy Steele and the Steelmen, and, the most famous band in Liverpool at the time, Rory Storm and the Hurricanes. The Beatles, he said, was too short, too simple, and suggested Long John and the Silver Beatles. Lennon refused to be called Long John but, for want of anything better, they eventually settled on the Silver Beatles and it was under that name that they turned up at the Blue Angel, a new club Allan Williams had just opened, for an audition organised by Larry Parnes.

A proselytising homosexual with an unpleasant reputation even by the unpleasant standards of pop management, Parnes was then the most powerful figure in British pop music. He recruited a string of handsome young men from building sites and harbour fronts and, in blatant sexual allusion, gave them names like Power and Fury. It was rumoured that some of his 'stable' had to do more than sing for their money. Now he was up from London, having fun and auditioning for a backing group for Billy Fury, another of the 'Oh Boy!' regulars and one of the biggest stars in the country at the time. The Silver Beatles were among the hopefuls crammed into the Blue Angel that May afternoon in 1960 when Parnes came making preparations for a forthcoming Fury tour.

Williams had secured them the services of a drummer named Tommy Moore, who, at 36, was old enough to be their father. But a drummer was a drummer and the Silver Beatles were not in any position to be choosy about their percussionist. True to what had now become a group tradition, however, he didn't turn up on time and they had to borrow Johnny Hutchinson from the Casanovas until Moore came panting in halfway through their ten-minute slot.

They didn't get the job. According to one version of what happened that afternoon, Parnes wanted to hire them, but only without Sutcliffe, who obviously couldn't play a note. Lennon is said to have loyally stood by his friend and refused the offer – to McCartney's considerable anger. Parnes's own memory, which is probably the more accurate one, was that he was put off, not by Sutcliffe (and with a stable of singers most of whom couldn't sing, what did a bass guitarist who couldn't play matter?), but by the ageing Moore. He was impressed enough, though, by what he had seen and heard to come back a week later to offer them £18 each for an eight-day tour of Scotland backing a 20-year-old former apprentice carpenter named John Askew who had been transmogrified by Parnes into a singer called Johnny Gentle.

The Silver Beatles were delighted. This – or so they thought – was the big-time and they set off in a rush of excitement. George took a holiday from work and renamed himself Carl in honour of Carl Perkins, the composer of 'Blue Suede Shoes'. Sutcliffe became Stuart de Stael, after the Russian artist Nicholas de Stael. Lennon stayed as John Lennon and got Cynthia to cheat for him in his lettering exams. McCartney, always the more showbiz-like, changed his name to Paul Ramon 'because it sounded really glamorous, sort of Valentino-ish'.

There was just one problem – McCartney was still at school, ostensibly studying for the exams he was due to sit in a few days' time. There was no chance his father would give permission. But Paul was a young man on the threshold of adulthood with a single-minded determination to have his own way, a trait that would become more pronounced with years. The former Boy Scout got round the problem by the simple expedient of lying. And his father, honest himself and decent and trusting enough to expect it in others, believed his son when he said the Institute had given him two weeks' holiday and told him to take it easy. The trip to Scotland, he said, would be a good rest and he would be back in time for the exams. Somehow Jim McCartney was persuaded to let him go.

He would have been better off staying at home. The tour was a horror – of 300-mile drives backwards and forwards across the Scottish Highlands from town hall to rundown ballroom, sleeping in cold-water accommodation, reduced to living on a bowl of soup a day, tempers fraying. Lennon fell out with Sutcliffe and spent the endless hours in the van verbally bullying him.

The manufactured Gentle was indeed no Fury and on one occasion they found themselves playing in a cramped upstairs room because a more popular 'old tyme' dance band was considered a better economic prospect for the main ballroom downstairs. They ran out of money and out of the Royal hotel in Forres without paying their bill. One night Gentle crashed the van and put Moore in hospital with two broken teeth. Lennon and the local promoter pulled him out of his sickbed and forced him on to the stage of the Dalrymple Hall in Fraserburgh.

To add further injury, the promoters were unhappy with the Silver Beatles' playing. Gentle denies that he joined the chorus of complaints, but when they got back to Liverpool Larry Parnes did not rehire them. Paul went back to school, sat his two A levels and, not surprisingly, managed to pass only one, English.

It was not what his father might have hoped for and it is certainly not what his mother would have wished. But there was one person who saw some lining in the cloud that appeared to be hanging over at least one of the Silver Beatles, and that was Allan Williams. The 'beat' boom was beating ever louder and Williams, a former door-to-door salesman, had quickly latched on to it and was flogging it for all he was worth. He had set himself up as a booking agent for a score of Liverpool groups, Gerry and the Pacemakers among them. The encounter with Parnes had whetted his appetite for the business, though at heart he was a small-time opportunist who dreamed big but never saw much further than the pound he took out of every ten his clients earned. London was the capital of British showbusiness, Liverpool a provincial outpost, and a man like Williams had to make do with the scraps that occasionally came his way and any local deals he could make for himself.

He opened a stripclub in the brothel area of Liverpool 8. When one of his artists, Janice, insisted that she would perform only to music provided by a live band, Williams booked the Silver Beatles. It was not an auspicious engagement. With grand ideas, somewhat above her artistic station, Janice wanted to undress to the sounds of Beethoven and Khachaturian. The Silver Beatles couldn't read a single note on the sheet music she handed them and, in a shabby compromise, Janice ended up stripping to the sounds of 'It's a Long Way to Tipperary' and the theme from *The Third Man*. It was, one

Beatle historian observed, 'quite simply the nadir of their career'.

There were other low points. Moore had predictably quit shortly after the Scottish fiasco. When they went round to his home to try to persuade him to change his mind his girlfriend leaned out of the window and yelled: 'You can go and piss off. He's not playing with you any more – he's got a job at the Garston bottle works on the night shift!' Taking work where they could find it, with whatever drummer they could pick up on the way, the Silver Beatles found themselves playing in some of the toughest dance halls in Liverpool. And they didn't come much tougher than they did in that mean city. Saturday night really was for fighting and the dance floors were battlefields for the rival gangs of rampaging Teddy Boys Jim McCartney was so concerned Paul would join.

He never did, of course. The gangs came from a poor, violent underclass a long way down the social scale from the aspirant respectability of the McCartney household. There was never the remotest possibility of Paul McCartney, the cap-and-blazered student at the Liverpool Institute, becoming a member of the Bath Hall Bloods or the Tanks, or any of the city's other hooligan bands. Paul was never more than a would-be Teddy Boy. The drainpipes and the pompadours were the adolescent attempt to mimic the working-class toughness and youthful rebellion so prized in the late 1950s and exemplified by Elvis's curled-lip snarl and the leatherclad bravura of Marlon Brando. The only bicycle chain at 20 Forthlin Road was still firmly attached to McCartney's three-speed Raleigh. It was the same with Lennon. As he said: 'I wasn't a Ted – I was only pretending to be one.'

There was someone who could not afford the pretence. One Richard Starkey, brought up in the rough Dingle district of Liverpool, had joined a gang in his early teens. 'You had to,' he said. 'This was deadly serious. In our area if you weren't in a gang you laid your life on end because you weren't protected. They had a terrible thing in Liverpool where you'd walk past someone and he'd say, "You looking at me?" If you said no, he'd say, "Why not?" If you said yes, then he'd get you anyway. There was no answer to that question, "Are you looking at me?"' His teenage years were a violent round of standing on street corners, 'beating someone up, getting beaten up, having a fight'.

As a change from the dull monotony of the streets, the Teds took their savagery with them into the dance halls. Rival gangs would converge, bottles would fly, knives and chains and steel-capped boots would be employed to lethal purposes, the bouncers would try to intervene, the police would arrive – and the Silver Beatles, in time-honoured tradition, would play on. Some of the incidents, McCartney said, were terrifying. During one show at the Grosvenor ballroom in Wallasey a battle broke out between a hundred local Teds and an invading horde of equal strength from nearby Seacombe. When McCartney went to rescue his amplifier, one Ted grabbed hold of him and said: 'Don't move, son, or you're fucking dead.' McCartney stood stone still. This was a threat he had reason to take seriously – one night when they were playing at a ballroom in Neston they had seen a 16-year-old boy kicked to death on the dance floor in front of them.

It was violence without reason and was almost impossible to avoid and one night, in the car park of Litherland Town Hall, it engulfed the Silver Beatles. Williams had booked them to play there and during the show either something was said or one of the gang's girls had taken a fancy to one of the band. Or it may just have been another manifestation of what Starkey called the 'terrible craziness' of gang ritual which did not consider a night complete until there had been a rumble.

Whichever, a gang of toughs was waiting for the group when they left. The Silver Beatles ran literally for their lives. Stu Sutcliffe didn't run fast enough. He was caught and punched to the ground. And as he lay there the boots went in and he was kicked repeatedly in the head. He would have been stomped to death then and there if Lennon, the one member of the band able to take care of himself physically, hadn't run back and, with fists and feet flailing, dragged him away to safety. But not quickly enough. Two years later, on 10 April 1962, Stu Sutcliffe, the artist who had never wanted to be a rock musician, died of a brain haemorrhage almost certainly brought on by the injuries he sustained that night. But at the time, once Sutcliffe appeared to have recovered, the group went back on to the ballroom and community-hall circuit around Liverpool. Williams, for his part, was looking towards more international horizons.

That summer the Royal Caribbeans, the Jacaranda's resident Jamaican steelband – Williams was nothing if not eclectic when it came to making money out of music – had flitted off to Hamburg, lured by a visiting German businessman's promises of fräuleins and Deutschmarks. The German was as good as his word and their letters back were filled with lurid tales of easy money and easier women.

Like Liverpool, Hamburg is a port with a long and prosperous past. They are both situated at the latitude 53 degrees north. There the comparison ends. Harrison would later say: 'When we grew up in Liverpool you could see a whole row of houses, then there was a bombsite. And those bombsites were there until I left at the age of seventeen. Whereas, when we went from there to Germany, the Germans had really built the country back.'

When Heinrich Heine, the German historian and poet, wrote, 'She can only describe the anguish in her heart through music . . . all the anguish at her own impotence, her longing for her past greatness, pathetic hopes, watching, waiting for help, all this is transposed into her melodies', he was referring to Renaissance Italy. He might as easily have been describing Liverpool in the late 1950s, a city spiralling into depression.

Hamburg, by contrast, was boldly facing up to the challenge of the changing economic circumstances. While Liverpool looked to heavy, state-funded industry for its future, Hamburg had set about encouraging small, specialised businesses, rarely employing more than half-a-dozen people, and to spectacular result: as Liverpool declined, so Hamburg thrived and was well on its way to becoming one of the richest cities in Europe. Its inhabitants, riding in the vanguard of the postwar boom, had money to spend and the city, true to its entrepreneurial tradition, was prepared to give them whatever they wanted, no matter how bizarre or kinky.

Intrigued by what he heard, Williams flew over there in a hired Dakota DC3 with his West Indian-born business associate, the self-ennobled Lord Woodbine, to see for himself and, while they were at it, enjoy a few days' revelling on the notorious Reeperbahn. He took with him a homemade tape-recording of some of the groups on his books, the Silver Beatles among them, but when he came to play it to club-owner Bruno Koschmider he found that it had been wiped clean of sound.

His Liverpudlian optimism, perversely honed bright by the city's incessant failure, must have made some impression on the German, however, for shortly afterwards Koschmider himself came to England intent on hiring bands for his club, the Kaiserkeller. He went, not to Liverpool but to London and the Two Is, the Soho coffee bar where Tommy Steele had been discovered and which still enjoyed a reputation as a well for untaped – and hence cheap – talent. By fortunate coincidence Williams happened to be there too, looking for work for Derry and the Seniors, another of his Liverpool groups. Koschmider immediately hired them and they were on stage at the Kaiserkeller within the week.

Like the Royal Caribbeans, Derry and the Seniors were impressed with what they found in Hamburg's rough, fun-loving red-light district and they too wrote home urging others to follow them out there. Koschmider, in turn, liked the band. There was a tough quality to Anglo-Saxon rock and roll which the Germans could never duplicate and the Seniors were popular with Koschmider's audiences. That meant more customers at the Kaiserkeller and he was soon on to Williams inviting him to send across another band.

Williams shuffled through his list. The top group was Rory Storm and the Hurricanes but they were booked at Butlin's. He offered the job to Gerry and the Pacemakers but they turned it down. In desperation, and despite the fact that they were again drummerless, he offered it to the Silver Beatles. The drummer problem was, for once, easily resolved. Paul telephoned Pete Best and asked him to audition for the band. The result was a foregone conclusion – there was not exactly a stampede of percussionists vying to play with the band – and Best was offered the post. The taciturn, painfully shy young man who had just left school to find himself without a job, readily accepted.

That left Jim McCartney. Paul was full of smiling enthusiasm but as Michael recalled: 'Dad wasn't easy to convince as he really wanted Paul to go to Teacher Training College and this is where, if Mum had been alive, the end of the start of the Beatles would have been nigh.' With Allan Williams's assistance, however, he was persuaded – after all, as Jim McCartney stoically observed, Paul was now 18 and there really wasn't much he could do to prevent him going. On 14 August 1960, the Beatles, yet to become the most profitable small, specialised business Liverpool ever produced, was on its way to being discovered in Germany.

3

'F AMILY' was a word much used by the Beatles and their entourage. It cropped up regularly, often unconsciously, in their conversation, and still does. And like the institution it describes, the Beatles' 'family' was both a protective shelter and an exclusion. People were either in it or they weren't.

Paul McCartney, whose youth was tragically disrupted by the death of his mother, is very attached to the concept of family. He constantly harks back to what he remembers as the dependable familial enclosure of his childhood and the recollections govern his life to this day. For that spectacular decade when he was between parents and parenthood, McCartney's family was the Beatles, and John Lennon in particular, and the bonds were forged in the threatening grime and wickedness of Hamburg.

The group arrived in the city via the Newhaven to Hook of Holland ferry in Allan Williams's battered green Austin van on 17 August 1960. They shed the Silver from their name on the way and it was as the Beatles that they made their debut that night on the rickety stage of Indra club in Grosse Freiheit. They were tired, hungry and apprehensive. They were still in their teens and this was the first time they had been properly away from home, the first time they had ever been abroad, and the five unworldly young men from Liverpool found the cultural change a disconcerting experience.

Their sleeping accommodation was vile and illegal – one room with two beds and a sofa and two filthy 8-foot by 6-foot cubby holes in the back of the Bambi-Filmkunsttheater porno cinema which Koschmider also owned. Their bathroom was the cinema's lavatory. Sometimes the Bambi's clientele preferred to deposit their excrement and worse where the Beatles were sleeping. The contract they signed bound them to a seven-day working week for an exploitative thirty Deutschmarks each.

The Indra club was a dingy, threadbare, depressing, recently converted stripclub, the patrons – a few drunks and off-duty prostitutes – apathetic. The Beatles did nothing to lighten their mood. Competent enough to play a few numbers to a crowd of teenagers in a provincial dance hall, they were completely untrained to face the world-weary denizens of Hamburg's red-light area. As Lennon recalled: 'In Liverpool we'd only done one-hour sessions and we just used to do our best numbers, the same ones, at every one. In Hamburg we had to play for eight hours, so we really had to find a new way of playing.'

It wasn't easy and it got worse when Koschmider, forced to close the Indra six weeks later due to the complaints of the neighbours who objected to living on top of a beat club, transferred them to the larger Kaiserkeller. Inexperienced and faced with an audience of drug-pushing, gun-carrying thugs, they froze. Their dispirited performances got what Lennon drily called 'a pretty cool reception' – cool enough, in fact, to put their continued engagement in jeopardy.

Derry and the Seniors, the other Liverpool band employed at the Kaiserkeller, were no encouragement. They looked down on the Beatles for being what a later generation would call a second-rate garage band. It was left to Williams, still in Hamburg looking after his ten percents, to sort out the mess that was appearing nightly on the Kaiserkeller's large, rotting stage. One evening in October he had had enough and started shouting at the Beatles to 'Make a show, boys!' That got picked up as 'mach shau' and the cry resounded throughout the club. It had a galvanising effect on the band and on

Lennon in particular. He started leaping around the stage like a demented dervish, sometimes pretending to be a spastic, sometimes imitating the crippled Gene Vincent whose leg had been irreparably damaged in a motorcycle accident. He would raise his right arm, shout 'Sieg Heil' – illegal in Germany at the time – goosestep across the stage and shout 'Nazis' at the audience.

The audience loved it. The Kaiserkeller was no afternoon tea dance. The people who gathered here were out for a good time and the rowdier and noisier the better. Fights were common and they were even more bloody than the gang fights the Beatles had played through in Liverpool. Hamburg, the gun-running centre of Europe at the time, was a very dangerous city, the Reeperbahn its most dangerous quarter, its waiters employed primarily for their skill with billy clubs and flick-knives. Lennon called them killers and half-dead bodies regularly littered the dance floor.

It was here that the Beatles honed their ability. McCartney says: 'My philosophy about a band is, if you can play your stuff in a pub, then you're a good band.' The Hamburg beer cellars were as tough a pub as you could wish to find and in several visits over the next two years the Beatles would emerge as a very good band indeed.

Said Lennon: 'To get the Germans going and keep it up for twelve hours at a time we'd really have to hammer. We would never have developed as much if we'd stayed at home.' Pete Best remembers: 'Eventually we were playing with no inhibitions whatsoever. It was freedom of music and we played as we wanted to play, the way we felt it should be played.'

They had little real contact with their audience off-stage, however, not at first. They spoke only a few words of German and had no real interest in either learning the language or making German friends. 'They were all half-witted,' Lennon remarked. It was to each other that they turned. Later Cynthia came out to visit them, as did Dorothy Rohne, another blonde art-college student who had been dating Paul and who, at one brief time, he might have married. The Seniors went home, to be replaced by the more affable Rory Storm and the Hurricanes whose drummer was one

47

Richard Starkey, now calling himself Ringo Starr, and they started hanging out with them. They became a family of Liverpudlian exiles – and, as is the way in all families, there were quarrels and rows.

McCartney was particularly prone to them. He often bickered with Harrison. He had rows with Lennon over the leadership of the group – a portent of worse rows to come. It was Sutcliffe, however, who suffered the brunt of McCartney's bouts of ill-humour. The move to Hamburg had not improved their relationship and Lennon recalled: 'Paul was always picking on him.'

On one occasion their antipathy degenerated into an on-stage fight. The artistic Sutcliffe, never as xenophobic as the others, soon acquired himself a girlfriend, the strange and enchanting photographic assistant, Astrid Kirchherr, who slept in a black bedroom ('My Jean Cocteau phase,' she explained to the uncomprehending Beatles – Cocteau was not exactly a household name in Forthlin Road). Astrid was not overly fond of McCartney. With calculated understatement she once remarked: 'Paul I found hard to get close to.' She was suspicious, she said, of his charm: 'It used to frighten me that someone could be so nice all the time.' She will not talk about him at all now.

McCartney's niceness was not always on obvious display. Whenever Astrid came into the club Sutcliffe would step up to the microphone and coo the Presley hit, 'Love Me Tender' to her – to the good-natured derision of the others. One night McCartney's remarks acquired an unpleasant edge to them. As Pete Best recalled: 'Paul said something that went a little bit over the top. Stu just turned round and clobbered Paul. He levelled him, knocked him back on the stage up against the piano. We split them up and we could tell that Stu was absolutely livid.' Order was restored, tempers calmed, and any residual antagonism buried under the surface of group unity. And whatever the lingering coolness between Astrid and McCartney, she stayed on in the 'family' to become one of the formative influences in the Beatles' development.

Sutcliffe had met her through her then boyfriend, a young

graphic designer named Klaus Voorman who had wandered into the Kaiserkeller after having a row with Astrid. He had been captivated by the 'loud, bang, bang' music of the Beatles and their strange, Teddy-Boy look. 'I couldn't take my eyes off them,' he recalled. He went back, and back again, this time with Astrid. Solidly middle-class, that black bedroom notwithstanding, she enjoyed the frisson that came from being surrounded by the lowlife that filled the Kaiserkeller. She was as entranced by the Beatles as Voorman had been. 'I'd always been fascinated by Teddy Boys. Suddenly there were five of them in front of me . . . I just sat there open-mouthed.' And she fell in love with Sutcliffe 'at first sight'.

The Beatles, overcoming their anti-German prejudices, were equally intrigued by the laidback, arty style of Voorman, Astrid and the friends they started bringing to the club. It was the era of the existentialist Beatnik and they were the leaders of the Hamburg chapter of the movement. They talked meaningfully about life, combed their hair forward, dressed in black and were like no one the Beatles had ever encountered. Lennon called them 'Exi's', as in existentialists. The intellectually inquisitive McCartney – the Exi's called him the Baby One – was inspired by their example and read Jack Kerouac's seminal Beatnik novel, *On the Road*. They all started drinking together between sets, conversing in that common human language of grunt, sign and gesture. Sutcliffe and Astrid, with the additional help of a German–English dictionary, soon became lovers.

The effect that Astrid and the Exi's had on the Beatles would have worldwide consequences. There was, in truth, little about them that was original – their philosophy was a Teutonic translation of the beat movement in the United States; the brushed-forward haircut came from the Left Bank of Paris; the collarless jackets were Pierre Cardin. But when it had been grafted on to a group of young lads with an accent that had not been heard outside of Liverpool, marketed, and combined with the songwriting genius of Lennon and McCartney, the result was a phenomenon.

In Arthur Koestler's words, 'Unexpected elements brought

49

together produce an act of creation', and in the case of Beatles they truly did. McCartney, always one for the quick social observation, has remarked: 'Think of Queen Elizabeth I and you always think of Raleigh. With Queen Elizabeth II you're going to think of the Beatles.' It was the music that did that.

Existentialism – the popular movement as opposed to Sartre's esoteric philosophy – had hitherto found its musical expression in modern jazz. The Beatles disliked jazz. 'We were anti-jazz; jazz never gets anywhere, never does anything,' Lennon said. They liked the Exi style, however, and adopted it as their own. And by setting it to a thumping rock-and-roll beat, by blending Kerouac with Little Richard, they took it out of the universities and off the campuses and turned it into a mass trend which reached its apotheosis in the flower-power hippy movement of the late 1960s. In those developmental Hamburg days neither Lennon nor McCartney had, of course, the faintest idea of what lay ahead of them. What they had to do then was get through twelve hours a night, every night, in front of audiences bellowing 'mach shau'.

McCartney always had ambition. He was always the one who was determined that the group was going to go somewhere, and preferably a long way from the rough-house audience of Hamburg. As difficult as he could sometimes be in private, his cheery, smily public persona was evolving and he was the most popular member of the group with the fans. 'He always did the talking and announcing and autograph bit,' said Astrid. 'Paul, even in those days, was more the impresario,' Best recalled. 'He was the PR man.' He was the one who was always looking ahead and asking, 'What are we going to do?'

In the existential world of the Reeperbahn, however, the future could be as short as the temper of the rampaging, knife-carrying, gun-wielding *Schlägers*, and they had to play for their lives. To sustain themselves in this Dantean inferno the Beatles resorted to the area's ubiquitous pick-me-ups – girls, pills and booze.

If the group was making good show, customers would send drinks up to them on stage. 'Sing "Hound Dog" for two crates of beer!'

someone would shout and they would. They drank a lot and sometimes too much – Best recalls Harrison adding to the already unspeakable filth of their sleeping quarters by vomiting over the side of his bunk bed after one drinking session.

As a chemical counter to the booze and on the pretext that they kept them going through their nightly sessions, the Beatles started popping pills. 'We learned from the Germans that you could stay awake by eating slimming pills, so we did,' said Lennon. Their first supplier was Rosa, the ankle-socked cloakroom attendant at the Indra who kept the pills in a large sweet jar and dispensed them readily. The first they took were the amphetamines Preludin, known as 'prellies', but they soon moved on to Purple Hearts and Black Bombers. 'It was the only way to keep going,' Lennon would insist.

The Beatles (with the exception of Pete Best, who never really fitted in with the others) were soon swallowing them by the handful. They insisted that they never became dependent on them but it was the beginning of what became a lifetime's association with drugs. And, taken in such quantities and combined with the amount of alcohol they were consuming, it often reduced them to stumbling, hyperactive incoherence, off stage as well as on.

Lennon, whose behaviour always veered towards the erratic, was made worse by these potentially lethal cocktails. Short of money and high on pills, he once tried to roll a drunken sailor. He appeared naked on stage with a toilet seat around his neck. He is said to have urinated out of a window on to some passing nuns, though McCartney denies that story. There are other tales of excess from those days.

Manager Spencer Mason remembers the pill-taking. He first met Ringo when he was working as a redcoat attendant and Ringo was drumming with Rory Storm's Hurricanes at a Butlin's holiday camp in North Wales. When the beat boom got underway Mason got to manage the Mojos, another Liverpool group that made it to Hamburg and at one time had in its line-up Lewis Collins, who became an actor and appeared in 'The Professionals'. Mason says: 'Everybody was on pills. It gave you a cheap high and it stopped you eating, which none of the groups could afford to do anyway. But it produced a certain madness. It made Lennon very boisterous. One day he bought a pig in the market. He used to walk around Hamburg with it on a lead.' The pig's association with the Beatles was brief. There was a hotel just off the Reeperbahn called the Phoenix where Allan Williams sometimes stayed. Lennon took the pig there – and threw it out of a top-floor window. Mason: 'He was out of his head, shouting, "Look, a flying pig."' The pig was killed by the fall.

'McCartney was much quieter,' Mason says. Off-stage, 'he was quite reserved, genteel almost'. But not so genteel as to refrain from availing himself of the women who were the Reeperbahn's *raison d'être*. A favourite drink, according to Mason, was 'schnapps, topped up with Fanta, topped off with "bluey" pills'. It was a mind-numbing combination but it did not seem to interfere unduly with the Beatles' sexual activities. They were young and certainly not the asexual, pre-pubescent Mop Tops Brian Epstein was later to portray them so adeptly as, and being in the Reeperbahn was like being let loose in a sweet shop. 'You got laid as much as you wanted,' says Mason. 'We had a lot of girls,' Best remembered.

Those casual encounters – with off-duty hookers, goodtime girls, dancers, the old, the young, backstage, in doorways, in the cess-pool of their lodgings – had their predictable medical consequences. The Beatles became a case study in venereal infections. Allan Williams, soon nicknamed the Little Pox Doctor, would be called upon to give instant diagnoses. They would meet him at the Gretel and Alfons bar which had become a hangout for the visiting English groups. He would take them into the lavatories where he would look for 'swellings in the groin, a discharge from the end'. He would ask if it hurt when they urinated. If the symptoms corresponded with 'all the things I'd read about', he would send them off to the free health clinics for a shot of penicillin. It was never long, though, before one or other of them had been infected again. As Peter Brown would observe: 'It was only when they returned from Hamburg for good that a venereologist managed to clean them up.'

Williams was more discerning in his choice of companions – but not discerning enough to avoid the sexual misadventure McCartney manoeuvred him into (or at least did nothing to prevent). One night Williams walked into the Beer House bar where McCartney, Mason, and a few others were drinking. He had with him what Mason describes as 'an absolutely amazing-looking tart' – high heels, tight dress, low cleavage.

McCartney knew the person and could guess where matters were leading. To chivvy things along, he pretended to make a pass at her, gracefully withdrew his attentions when Williams became irritated, and then, keeping a straight face, congratulated Williams on his good fortune. The moment Williams and his companion were out of the bar and on their way to a hotel, McCartney burst out laughing. He was still chortling when Williams stormed back into the Beer House an hour later screaming, 'It's a *man*.'

Yet, even in the midst of this dissipation, McCartney somehow found the time and, more remarkably, the energy to work on his songwriting. He would spend his free afternoons, between copulations and before the band was due on stage again, playing around with melodies on any available piano. 'I'll Follow the Sun' is one composition that can be traced back to Hamburg.

Best recalled: 'Trying to impress people, he'd say, "Look, I've written a song, what do you think?"' The answer was, not much, not yet. It was standard rock songs like Little Richard's 'Long Tall Sally', Chuck Berry's 'Roll Over Beethoven', Carl Perkins' 'Match Box', and Larry Williams's 'Dizzy Miss Lizzie' that the customers paid to hear and which formed the backbone of their repertoire. In all the trips the Beatles made to Hamburg in that two-year period they did not perform more than half-a-dozen Lennon–McCartney compositions and none of those was memorable.

Their stage craftsmanship and their ability to take hold of a song and give it a distinctive interpretation had improved dramatically, however, as they discovered for themselves when they made their first visit back to Liverpool four months later. It was an earlier trip than they had planned but they had no choice: it was a forced repatriation. At the end of October a rival club called the Top Ten had opened. Its owner, Peter Eckhorn, was determined to move in on Koschmider's territory, and started hiring away everyone he could from the Kaiserkeller. The head bouncer, a former boxer called Horst Fascher who was reputed to have killed a man in a fight, moved across. So did Rosa and her candy jar of prellies. Eckhorn then succeeded in luring Tony Sheridan, the Kaiserkeller's resident English singer whose star status was reinforced by the fact that he actually had a couple of record releases to his credit and had appeared on 'Oh Boy!'. The Beatles had become friendly with him and were soon to be found backing him in impromptu jam sessions over at the Top Ten.

It was an ill-considered move on their part. Koschmider, a one-time circus clown, may have been small but he was tough enough to look after himself and this assault on his business brought no smile to his face. Fights were soon raging between the minders of the rival establishments and the Beatles fell early victim to the feud. Koschmider had become quite impressed by the group and at one point there was talk of them transferring to West Berlin. When he discovered that they were on the point of defecting to the Top Ten he cancelled their one-sided contract, which specifically prohibited them from appearing anywhere within a 25-mile radius of the Kaiserkeller without his express permission.

Then the police were informed that George Harrison was only 17, too young even to be in the Reeperbahn after midnight. Harrison was ordered to leave West Germany and made his tearful exit 24 hours later. The others continued to work out their month's notice at the Kaiserkeller but, at Eckhorn's invitation, made plans to take up residency at the Top Ten. Koschmider warned them that if they did they would never play in Germany again. It was no idle threat. Club-owners in the red-light district of a city like Hamburg were not noted for the delicacy of their contract negotiations. Spencer Mason recalls seeing a man shot dead outside another nearby club, the Blue Peter: 'He lay there for ages. No one wanted to go near him.' This was Koschmider's parish and he played by the local rules. As Best said: 'He might have broken our legs.' He might have done worse and 'put us to sleep – that was for him to decide'.

Believing themselves safe under Eckhorn's protection, they moved out of the Bambi and into the attic room above the Top Ten. Lennon made the move without being seen. McCartney and Best were not so fortunate. When they went back to collect their clothes and Best's drum kit they found that the light in their den wasn't working.

'The only thing we could find to give us light was condoms,' said Best. 'Paul had some, so we stuck them into the wall and lit them. They sparkled and blubbered and gave off black smoke but they just about gave us enough light to throw our things together.' Within hours McCartney and Best had been arrested and thrown into jail facing charges, lodged by Koschmider, of attempting to set fire to the cinema. The following day they were put on the midnight plane and deported. Lennon and Sutcliffe followed soon afterwards.

It was a bedraggled, desperately undernourished McCartney who turned up at Forthlin Road. In the four months he had been away, constantly short of money, he had been living on a diet of cornflakes and the occasional cut-price dinner scrounged off the English manager at the Seaman's Mission. 'The emaciated skeleton that had once been my brother,' as Michael described the prodigal, had ankles 'as thin and white as Dad's pipe-cleaners'.

His father quickly repaired his body with home-cooked food and capsules of cod-liver oil 'swallowed daily after our main meal', as Michael recalled. It took a while longer for his spirit to revive. Hamburg had been a hard, exhausting experience which had ended with humiliating deportation and it was several weeks after their return before the Beatles bothered to make contact with each other.

Under pressure from his father, McCartney signed on at the labour exchange and went to work, first for a delivery firm, then winding electric coils for a company called Massey and Coggins which paid him £7 a week. His fellow workers called him Mantovani because of his long hair. The Beatles had got together again by then, 'but I didn't know if I wanted to go back full time . . . I quite enjoyed being a working man.' The company, impressed with his academic qualifications and his rarely less-than-obliging attitude, said that if he stuck to it he might end up an executive. He would probably have made a good one – he is honest and hardworking – but, as Jim McCartney observed, 'He wasn't really interested in either job. It was just to oblige me.' After two months he quit and went back to playing rock and roll.

By now, though, McCartney had some reason for optimism. Two days after Christmas, 1960, the Beatles played at a dance in Litherland Town Hall. The audience's reaction was frenzied. When Paul launched into 'Long Tall Sally', there was a spontaneous rush towards the stage. Four months of remorseless grind in Hamburg had turned a no-more-than-average local band into a rock-and-roll powerhouse. 'That was when we began to think for the first time that we were good,' said Lennon.

Rock music, once untamed and frenetic, was in the doldrums. Buddy Holly had died in an aeroplane crash, Eddie Cochran in a car crash. Chuck Berry was on his way to jail for taking an Apache prostitute across the state line in violation of America's Mann Act. Little Richard had become a priest. Jerry Lee Lewis had married a 13-year-old ('We're country boys – we knew she was only 12,' Johnny Cash wrily remarked) who also happened to be his cousin and the combination of age and their familial relationship had finished his career. Presley had been conscripted and came back a ballad-singing filmstar (the army, Lennon said, killed Elvis long before drugs finally did away with him). The army, the law and death had again ruthlessly pacified the South, as effectively as it had the Confederates a century before, and the pop charts were dominated by clean-cut All-American toothpaste advertisements almost invariably called Johnny or Bobby.

The British entertainment industry had followed the American example. 'Oh Boy!' had come off the air, to be replaced by the more prosaic 'Boy Meets Girl'; Cliff Richard now sang anaemic ballads like 'Living Doll' rather than snarling rockers like 'Mean

56

Streak'; a 14-year-old schoolgirl named Helen Shapiro who wore her hair in a bouffant had two of the year's ten best-selling records; Richard's backing group, the Shadows, had set the standard for well-groomed, carefully rehearsed, synchronised stagecraft.

These musical changes had made little impression on the 'mach shau' late-night world of the Reeperbahn, however, and the black leather-clad Beatles were still playing with a foot-stomping abandon which made Litherland Town Hall erupt.

'The kids went mad,' Best recalled. So did the dance's promoter, Brian Kelly, who, on the insistent prompting of Best's mother, signed the group up for thirty-five more dates. Mona Best, wife of a leading Liverpool boxing promoter, had started taking an increasingly proprietorial interest in the Beatles. She called them 'my son's group', and, with Williams fading into the background, had taken over much of the responsibility for organising their bookings. The Casbah club in the basement of her home became their headquarters. It was there that they met Pete's friend Neil Aspinall who soon afterwards gave up his career as a chartered accountant to join their 'family' as road manager and, eventually, director of Apple.

It was Mona who was instrumental in getting them their first engagement at the Cavern. In that she had the assistance of Bob Wooler, compere at the dance at Litherland Town Hall, who was soon employed at the dingy converted fruit-and-vegetable warehouse in the city centre that was to become the most famous beat club in the world.

Wooler had been as impressed with the group that night in Litherland as the audience had been. In an article for a music magazine published that summer he wrote: 'They hit the scene when it had been emasculated by figures like Cliff Richard. Gone was the drive that inflamed emotions. The Beatles exploded on a jaded scene. The Beatles were the stuff that screams were made of.' Mona pestered Wooler and he pestered the Cavern's owner, Ray McFall, until he agreed to book them.

The Beatles made their Cavern debut at a Tuesday lunchtime session in January 1961. They were paid £15. They were soon

57

appointed the club's resident group. They last played there in August 1963, when they were paid £300. In the intervening two years they appeared there 274 times, became the most popular group in Liverpool, and saw the formation of their first fan club.

'The Cavern was the place to be seen, the place to play if you wanted to make it,' Vic Hughes recalls. Hughes was the drummer in a group called the Blackwells which played the Cavern at the same time as the Beatles. He went on to back Shane Fenton who became Alvin Stardust before eventually quitting showbusiness and moving to Scotland where he now owns a carpet shop. The Cavern, says Hughes, 'was where the agents came. It was the shop window of Liverpool' – and a very dirty one. 'It was a real dump,' George Harrison's mother remarked. It stank of damp and perspiration and cigarette smoke and cheap Woolworth's scent and the Beatles loved it.

'You could see they were good,' Hughes says. 'They were laid back and they knew they were better than you.' Lennon, he remembers, was 'very approachable, one of the lads, even when he was on the way up. You could identify with the guy. McCartney kept himself to himself. He knew his talent and he knew what it was worth. He was a superstar before he was one.'

There weren't too many obvious fringe benefits of fame to be enjoyed at the Cavern. The Beatles, like all the bands that played there, had to pack up their own equipment and load it into the back of the old Austin Commer van that Aspinall, who was paid five shillings (25p) a gig for helping out, had bought for £80. 'And by the time you'd finished doing that any likely girl had almost inevitably gone off with some guy in the audience,' Hughes says. Sometimes McCartney would see out the night drinking warm Coca-Cola and chatting to mates in the small dressing room backstage and then catching the number 86 bus home to Forthlin Road in the early morning. His image as a rock-and-roll superstar was also dented by his father, who would often pop by during the lunchtime sessions to drop off the sausages he had bought for their evening meal.

Jim McCartney was still taking a close paternal interest in his son's health and welfare. He did not approve of the Cavern – 'You should have been paid danger money to go down there' – but he acknowledged that you had to be younger than he was to appreciate the noise, the discomfort, and what his younger son, Michael, remembered as the 'strong, heavy rock and roll which lifts the back of your neck off'. A father's reservations counted for very little in the turmoil of that dank cellar, on that wooden two-foot-high stage, before an audience of swaying, clapping youngsters whose cheering drowned out Jim McCartney's shouted instructions to his son to put the oven on when he got home. And besides, on a good week Paul was now earning more than Jim.

Paul McCartney's relationship with his father lies at the core of his personality and he has never perceived himself as anything less than a dutiful son. But he was in his youth, and, whatever his father might have counselled, playing rock and roll for a living was a more attractive proposition than winding electric coil. This was the period when McCartney was concerned with the business of creating himself. His stage patter was becoming more polished. As well as his throat-scorching Little Richard numbers, he was also developing his ballad singing. His brother Michael observed: 'Paul gets the girls (and some of the musical lads) going with "Till there was you",' from the 1957 Broadway show, *The Music Man*. 'It's a most unusual, Dad-orientated, melodic song in the middle of all the rock-and-roll screamers.' He also sang the old Judy Garland hit, 'Over the Rainbow' – to the apparent annoyance of Lennon who preferred his music with a harder edge.

Occasional exchanges notwithstanding, the rapport between Lennon and McCartney was all the while becoming more obvious, and there was an element of 'mach shau' to their on-stage rows which usually ended in laughter. When the trouble was real – as when the audience had been goaded into threatening retaliation by Lennon's shower of four-letter insults – it was McCartney who would step forward to calm the situation.

As Cynthia Lennon recalled: 'Paul, even in those early days, could have earned his living in public relations. He would work his backside off in potentially explosive situations in order to keep things on an even keel.' Except, of course, when he himself had provoked the situation, as he did with Sutcliffe. That happened less and less. McCartney, as his brother had remarked, had a 'lot of nous', and was always good at defusing situations and turning them to his advantage – no mean feat in the violent atmosphere of the Liverpool dance halls they continued to play alongside their Cavern gigs. And the more provocative Lennon was, the more skilled at diplomacy McCartney became.

McCartney maintains: 'I was very good at sarcasm myself. If I was in a bad enough mood, I was right up there with him. I *know* I wasn't always the "cute" one, and John wasn't always the acerbic one. But it's not convenient for some people to remember I wrote "Helter Skelter"; Charles Manson* is better known for that than I am. And John had a very sweet side.' He does concede, though, that it was 'the competitive element that was one of the best things about Lennon–McCartney'. And that arose, not out of their similarities but out of their differences: McCartney, smiling, pert, ever the matinee man, Lennon drawing off the vein of a dark appeal (Michael McCartney called him a 'caged animal'); Lennon a continuous improvisation, McCartney hanging on tight to conventional values; contradictory yet complementary.

If the development of this double act was the unwitting result of personality and circumstances, it was one they expediently learned to use to their mutual advantage. As dissimilar in character as they were, it was to each other that they increasingly turned – to the exclusion of the other members of the group.

That did not prevent them from making what use they could of the others – and Pete Best in particular. Neither Lennon nor McCartney was over-fond of him. Sutcliffe kept Lennon amused and provided a sounding-board for his ideas ('I depended on him to tell the truth,' Lennon said). Harrison played lead guitar and held

---

* Charles Manson and his 'Family', the infamous murderers of Sharon Tate, claimed to have found inspiration in the lyrics of 'Helter Skelter'.

the music together. Best's position was more invidious. The Beatles had needed to 'grow a drummer', Lennon said when they went to Hamburg, and Best was the only sprig in that hitherto barren garden. But whatever private reservations they may have harboured about him, they were more than happy to let him and his mother get on with organising their bookings and providing them with their Casbah base. And when they decided to return to Hamburg, it was Mona and Pete Best who wrote the endless letters to the German authorities, pleading with them to cancel the deportation orders and promising that, this time, they really would be on their best behaviour.

After Eckhorn had paid back the 158 Deutschmarks it had cost to deport McCartney and Best – which he deducted from their future wages – permission to return was finally granted and on 27 March 1961 the Beatles were back in sin city. It was the second of their five visits to the Baltic port and on each occasion they were booked into better clubs – this time at the Top Ten, eventually at the all-new Star Club. They were still not earning very much for their labours (Eckhorn paid them only 35 DM each a day) but that, as it transpired, was irrelevant.

They played, according to the best available count, a total of 998 hours on stage in Hamburg. It was invaluable experience. It was their rite of passage. It welded them into a unit and gave them the vital confidence to express themselves as entertainers, musically and as personalities. It also gave them what Liverpool couldn't – style.

Astrid was the inspiration, Sutcliffe the conduit. She dressed him in black leather, initially in just a jacket, then a long coat, then in matching trousers. John and George promptly followed suit. Paul took a little longer to be persuaded. He was and still is very careful with his money and eventually the others had to take him into the shop and instruct the salesman, 'This guy wants a coat like ours, size 38 to 40.'

The hair was next. Astrid washed and trimmed her lover's, and brushed it forward in the French manner. The others burst into peels of laughter when Sutcliffe turned up at the club sporting

61

the new style but soon afterwards George had followed Sutcliffe's example. Paul tried it too but for a while to come was constantly greasing it back into the old Teddy Boy quiff, because, the Beatles' official biographer Hunter Davies wrote, 'John hadn't yet made up his mind.'

The next innovation was the Cardin-inspired collarless jacket which Astrid made for Sutcliffe but the others drew the line at that, for a while at least. 'You're wearing your mother's suit, Stu,' they would jibe. Astrid also gave pictorial definition to the group, photographing them in deep shadow in stark black and white. Like most of what the Exi's did, there was little that was inventive here – the pictures were a copy of the *film noir* seen in Hollywood a decade before – but they were masterful interpretations which captured the early Beatles image. The Exi's may not have been raw originals, but they offered something fresher, more up to date than the tired, greasy kid-look the Beatles had brought with them from the dance halls of Liverpool.

There was an air of boredom about all this, however. Apart from fooling around with their hairstyles and their clothes and logging up several hundred more hours on stage, nothing much was really happening in their careers.

Stu left the group to enrol in the Hamburg art college and make his plans for marrying Astrid – to the considerable relief of McCartney who moved from rhythm guitar and piano to take over the bass fulltime. Relations between the two had never warmed. Paul put that down to Sutcliffe's musical inefficiency. 'Anyone who looked would realise he couldn't play it,' McCartney said. 'He just used to turn the amp down and sort of make a bass noise. He didn't know what key we were in half the time.'

Allan Williams's services were finally dispensed with in a letter written by Sutcliffe just before he left the group. That actually meant very little. Despite his later wails that he was 'the man who gave away the Beatles', Williams had never been more than a booking agent and for all practical purposes Mona Best had taken over that role.

Lennon and McCartney took a holiday in Paris on £40 John had inherited from an aunt in Edinburgh. There they were persuaded by one of the Exi's, Jurgen Vollmer, who also happened to be there, to adopt permanently what inaccurately, given its genesis in the Latin quarter, became known as the Beatles haircut. On the way back to Liverpool they stopped off at the bootmakers, Annello and Davide, in Covent Garden and bought some Cuban-heeled boots which were already fashionable in London but became known as Beatle boots.

On a more professional note, they also signed a recording contract. They were hired by Polydor, a subsidiary of the giant Deutsche Gramophon, to back Tony Sheridan on three tracks: rocking versions of the standards 'My Bonnie Lies Over the Ocean' and 'When the Saints Go Marching In', and a Sheridan ballad entitled 'Why (Can't You Love Me Again)'. Lennon was given the opportunity to wrap his vocal chords around an up-tempo version of the old Eddie Cantor song, 'Ain't She Sweet'. They also recorded a John Lennon–George Harrison instrumental called 'Cry for a Shadow', a reference to Cliff Richard's backing group which they claimed to despise but whose lead guitarist, Hank Marvin, could have outplayed Harrison with his eyes closed (Neil Young says that Marvin was one of the best rock guitarists of them all).

It proved a false dawn. They were paid a flat fee of 300 DM each but no royalties. The records were not even released under their name; Beatles sounded too much like 'peedles', local slang for 'penis', so instead they were listed as the Beat Boys on the label. The double-sided 'My Bonnie' and 'The Saints' was a hit in Germany but it wasn't doing the Beatles much good. They were a local success, both in Liverpool and in Hamburg. But so what? There were successful bands in Manchester and Newcastle and West Berlin and who had ever heard of them outside of their parochial enclaves? The rock industry is all about records and fame and both, in any meaningful sense, were still far beyond the Beatles' grasp.

Even McCartney, comfortable with his own talent and never short of self-belief, was suffering moments of doubt. Lennon wrote despondently to Sutcliffe, 'Something is going to happen, but where is it?' On 9 November 1961 it arrived, in the unlikely guise of a soft-spoken, public-school-educated young man in a well-cut suit. His name was Brian Epstein. The Beatles family was about to acquire its much-needed rich uncle.

4

PAUL McCartney was cute, personable and, by conventional definition, the best-looking member of the Beatles. But it wasn't Paul McCartney Brian Epstein was interested in. It was rough, raw John Lennon. 'He wanted John,' says Peter Brown.

The want was a physical one. When Epstein nervously ventured into the Cavern for that fateful lunchtime session he was transfixed by what he saw on the stage. There were four leather-clad rockers up there, joking and swearing and punching each other in the rough-house manner of male youth. Epstein was tantalised – particularly by the raucous rhythm guitarist showering insults at the two hundred or so teenagers munching sandwiches, drinking warm Coca-Cola, cheering and smoking in the musty catacombs of the Cavern.

He did not stand there salivating, McCartney insists, adding: 'I've heard of artistic licence, but that's ridiculous.' But as Peter Brown would record, that first glimpse of the leather-jacketed Lennon had an extraordinary effect on Epstein: 'It was in the most specific way a personification of his secret sexual desires.'

The scion of two prosperous Jewish families who had made their money in the furniture trade, Epstein was a troubled and lonely young man of 27 when he went down those eighteen steps into the old fruit-and-vegetable warehouse in Liverpool's Mathew Street. He had attended seven schools by the time he was 15 and had been asked to leave several. In those days, his mother Queenie loyally said, 'they just threw you out if they didn't like you'. And they didn't like little Brian Epstein, the petulant cliché of a mother's boy. 'I was one of those out-of-sorts boys who never quite fit,' he later wrote. 'I was ragged, nagged and bullied by masters and boys.'

He was a poor student. At 13 he failed his common entrance exam, private education's equivalent of the eleven-plus, and not even his parents' money could secure him a place at Rugby, Repton or Clifton. He eventually ended up at Wrekin College in Shropshire but, with no possibility of passing his exams, he left at 16 and went to work for his father as a £5-a-week furniture salesman. It was not what he wanted to do. He wanted to be a ladies' fashion designer, an ambition which had sent his father into a fury.

Compulsory national service claimed him two years later and he was drafted into the Royal Army Service Corps. He was never put forward for officer training – the only ex-public schoolboy in his intake not to be. He was, he admitted, 'the lousiest soldier ever', who turned left when he was ordered to turn right and fell over when he was told to halt. He appeared destined to serve his two years' conscription as a lowly, albeit always immaculately dressed, private. After ten months, however, Private Epstein was discharged on 'psychiatric grounds'. He was, so his references stated, a 'sober, reliable and utterly trustworthy soldier'. But the Army had discovered that he was also a practising homosexual.

In sexual disgrace, Epstein returned to Liverpool and a job running the Hoylake branch of his family's business. It gave him the opportunity to show off his promotional flair, his one real talent. He introduced the 'Scandinavian-style' furniture then in vogue, put it on interesting display and within a year was turning in profits that rivalled those of the main store. But if his parents were delighted by this unexpected upturn, he wasn't. Unstable, repressed and frustrated, he was off again a few months later to enrol in the Royal Academy of Dramatic Arts. This produced another little blaze of talent. Brian had done well to earn himself a place in the prestigious acting school with his readings from Shakespeare's *Macbeth* and

The Beatles about to take their first historic steps on American soil. McCartney leans back for the camera. *(Harry Benson)*

Miami, 1964, with the Beatles revelling in their fame, ordering the most expensive brandy, hanging out with the best-looking girls, driving in the biggest cars they could find. *(Pictorial Press)*

The 'singing champs of the world' meet the future 'boxing champ of the world', Cassius Clay. *(Harry Benson)*

George V Hotel, Paris, on the night in 1964 when the Beatles learnt that 'I Want to Hold Your Hand' had hit the top of the US charts. *(Harry Benson)*

TS Eliot's *Confidential Clerk*. He was a good actor, if rather inclined to become a trifle over-emotional (his performances were liable to end in him convulsed with sobs) and the director, John Fernald, who had been responsible for bringing on the talents of Albert Finney and Peter O'Toole, 'had great faith in me'.

The problem was that Epstein had little faith in himself. He was never able to stick to anything for very long before collapsing into depression. Unable to make friends easily, he was soon declaring that he loathed actors and their 'phony relationships' and their social life which he had never been invited to join. His mother had never approved of him leaving her maternal orbit and after just three terms he submitted to her pleadings and went home to Liverpool and yet another job in the family business, this time running the record department at their branch of NEMS, an old-established firm (Jim McCartney remembered playing on a NEMS piano during the First World War) which Brian's Polish immigrant grandfather had bought for its property value.

Back in commercial harness, Epstein's promotional abilities again came to the fore. He started with a staff of two. Two years later he was employing thirty people, including the young Peter Brown who had been hired away from the Lewis department-store chain. By diligent attention to his customers' requests, the introduction of a new stock-taking system which enabled him to reorder before he ran out, and the promise, usually fulfilled, that he could supply any record on release, he turned it into the most successful record shop in the north-west of England. He worked long hours, took pride in his achievements, and appeared to have found a job that could satisfy him.

Away from his desk it was a different matter. Those who knew him remember him as charming, personable and kind, but with a flip-side that swung into view all too often. He remained as insecure and lonely as he had always been. He often drank too much. He was overly sensitive about being Jewish and would blame his own failures on the anti-Semitism he perceived to be all around him. He was subject to irrational fits of temper punctuated by long periods when he retreated into icy silence. The slightest offence, real or imagined, could generate a torrent of odious abuse. Adding to this dark mental morass was his sexual predilection. Homosexuality was illegal in Britain at the time and Epstein, ashamed but driven, was condemned to taking his pleasure illicitly where he could find it.

When he was attending RADA he had been arrested for importuning in a public lavatory. Rex Makin, the Epsteins' family lawyer, rushed down to London and only his intervention prevented the case coming to court. Makin was soon called out again. Back in Liverpool Epstein took to frequenting a particular public lavatory in West Derby where like-minded men would meet for nameless, hurried encounters. One night Epstein picked the wrong man to approach. He was beaten up, his watch and wallet stolen. Shortly after the painfully battered Epstein had made it home to the comforting embrace of his mother, his attacker telephoned and attempted to extort more money. Makin insisted on calling in the police and, with Epstein help, the putative blackmailer was apprehended and imprisoned.

The incident only increased his sense of isolation and persecution. It did not curtail his activities, however; he continued to trawl the seedier parts of Liverpool, looking for all the 'rough trade' his flash maroon Hillman California and wallet could attract. This was the Brian Epstein who stood at the back of the Cavern during that lunchtime session in early November; the man who, by his own admission, couldn't keep his eyes off the Beatles.

According to Epstein's own account, he had first gone to see the group after a good-looking youth named Raymond Jones had walked into the NEMS store. Jones was dressed in tight jeans and a black leather jacket and Epstein had insisted on serving him himself. Jones had asked for a copy of 'My Bonnie'. 'Who is it by?' Epstein asked. 'The Beatles,' came the reply. Epstein professed to have never heard of them. When a couple of days later two girls came in and asked for the same record, Epstein, adhering to his policy 'that no customer should ever be turned away', started making enquiries. He discovered that the record was the one by Tony Sheridan, that it was being played at the Cavern club which was only two hundred yards away from his shop (Stu Sutcliffe had sent Wooler a copy), and that the Beatles themselves were now in residence there. Good businessman that he was, he decided to go and see what the fuss, albeit of an extremely limited kind, was all about.

In fact, Epstein must have known about the Beatles long before Raymond Jones excited his interest. The leather-swathed group were constantly in his store, whiling away their spare time listening to records which they could not afford to buy. NEMS was also one of the biggest outlets for the *Mersey Beat* newspaper, the second issue of which had carried a page-one picture of the group under a banner headline declaring 'Beatles Sign Recording Contract!', with an accompanying story which made considerably more of their German deal with Polydor than the facts warranted. Indeed, Epstein was contributing his own 'Brian Epstein of NEMS' review of new releases for the paper from the next issue onwards – and there wasn't an issue that did not heavily feature the Beatles. He only had to turn back a few pages to find Bob Wooler writing that the Beatles were the stuff that screams were made of, that 'here was the excitement, both physical and aural, that symbolised youthful rebellion', and it would have been surprising if, given his own interest in youth culture, he hadn't.

Wooler's prescient eulogy appeared in the *Mersey Beat*'s August 31 edition and five weeks later Epstein visited the Cavern by pre-arrangement with its owner. 'What brings Mr Epstein here?' Harrison enquired from the stage when he spotted the pinstripe-suited figure in the back shadows of the club.

Epstein's experience of pop music in its more strident form had hitherto been extremely limited. His favourite composer was Sibelius. The only live music he had listened to had been concerts by the Liverpool Philharmonic which his mother had taken him to. His column in the *Mersey Beat* had been restricted to such less than shattering revelations that the popularity of the Shadows 'seems to increase continually'.

Suddenly he was being engulfed by the Hamburg-honed, Little Richard/Elvis Presley rhythms of a type early critics were wont to condemn as the 'Devil's music'. Rock and roll was sex made audible and Epstein – rather late in life, it must be said – was swept away. He was too discreet, too reserved to acknowledge publicly what he felt. But of one thing he was certain, and that was his urgent desire to get to know them. And the way to do that, he decided, was to manage them.

Epstein went back to the Cavern time and again to see them. He went to see Williams, still angry at the way they had dispensed with his services, who told him not to touch them 'with a fucking barge pole', advice he ignored. 'He was hypnotised,' said Williams, adding that he sweated and blushed at the mere mention of their name. 'His main aim,' said Best, 'was to try and be accepted by the Beatles . . . to become one of the boys.' In imitation of their style, he was soon to be seen brushing his hair forward and dressing in black leather, but quickly discarded that affectation when everyone started laughing at him. He talked about them constantly to his staff. He would pick them up in his car and ferry them to their engagements. He followed their example and started popping amphetamines. What had begun as a chance encounter had become a fixation.

Rex Makin was discouraging. Epstein was a furniture-cum-record salesman. What, the family lawyer enquired of his client, did Epstein know about managing a pop group? The answer, of course, was absolutely nothing. That minor detail was not going to deter Epstein, however.

'I was fascinated by them,' he admitted. 'They were rather scruffily dressed – in the nicest possible way or, should I say, in the most attractive way – black leather jackets and jeans, long hair, of course . . . Whatever it is, they had it.' And whatever it was, John Lennon had more of it.

'He was infatuated by John,' says Peter Brown. 'That's why he was so dedicated to the group. That's not to say he didn't believe in their music, because he did. But he adored John. He wasn't in the least bit interested in the pretty boy Paul. Brian just wasn't interested in Paul in a physical way.'

The indifference was mutual, and would develop, on McCartney's part, into antipathy. Says Brown: 'Paul was certainly not above being charming to man, woman or beast to get his own way – he is a great charmer and very good at it – but not for sexual reasons. He was purely heterosexual.' So, of course, was Lennon, but he was always willing to experiment, to try something different, and believed it was vital to do so. He found Epstein's interest amusing and played it along for his own amusement.

McCartney, ever his father's boy, stuck to a more conventional path. Epstein had something else to offer McCartney, however. The round of Liverpool and Hamburg, initially so exciting, was becoming an aimless, provincial treadmill. McCartney was looking for something more and that is exactly what Epstein promised. 'I had money, a car, a record shop,' Epstein said. 'I think that helped.' He also had enthusiasm, contacts, and an apparently genuine interest in the aspirations of the Beatles, which, in the musical sense, meant Lennon *and* McCartney.

The Beatles had been managerless since the dismissal of Allan Williams and when Epstein offered to take them under his wing they agreed, though not with any alacrity. Harrison, Lennon, Best and, for reasons he was never quite sure about, Bob Wooler, arrived over an hour late for the meeting at NEMS Epstein had summoned them to. McCartney was even later; he was delayed in his bath. Epstein was angered by this affront. 'This is disgraceful; he's late,' he stormed.

'And very clean,' Harrison observed.

When the well-scrubbed McCartney arrived, Epstein's temper had cooled and an agreement of sorts was signed. There was no question but that it would be. The signing took place a month after Epstein had made his first visit to the Cavern and by then he was completely captivated by the group. He was like a lover obsessed. When Makin refused to have anything to do with what he regarded as the unhappy young man's latest irrational enterprise, Epstein wrote away for a standard contract. This was the formal agreement the four Beatles finally signed at Mona Best's Casbah club six weeks after McCartney's bath day.

Jim McCartney was suspicious of the whole deal. Epstein went to see him and his zeal won him round, as it did Lennon's aunt Mimi. 'John will never suffer,' he told her. 'The others don't matter, but I'll always take care of John.'

The contract, as it happened, was not a legal one. Both Harrison and McCartney were under-age and in his excitement Epstein forgot to affix his own signature. As far as Pete Best was concerned, the contract really wasn't worth the paper it was written on. For the other three, however, it proved the basis of a working relationship that saw them through the next six years, until Brian's death.

Epstein's terms were fairly standard for the time and better in many respects than they would have got elsewhere – if, that is, anyone else had been interested in signing them, which they weren't. Liverpool, 1961, was Hicksville UK. 'All we got in those days was, "Where are you from? Liverpool? You'll never do any-thing from there",' McCartney recalled. The agents and managers who came by the Cavern were local men offering local work.

Epstein, offering more than he knew how to deliver, promised to double their fees. Most important of all, he said he would get them a British recording deal. In return he demanded 25 percent of their income. They tried to cut him back to 20 percent but on that he stood firm. He needed the extra 5 percent, he explained, to cover promotional expenses.

It was a sell not so much hard as extravagant. Cynthia Lennon recalls John coming home to announce that they had got themselves a Jewish manager who swore that 'the Beatles were going to be *bigger* than Elvis!'

Epstein's father was predictably annoyed by this latest vagary on the part of his son. Brian assured him that it would only be part-time, that he would continue to devote himself to NEMS. His pledge proved to be as empty as all the others he had given his parents over the years – almost from the moment the group agreed to put their career in his charge, Epstein dedicated himself to the Beatles. He took over the bookings from Mrs Best. He persuaded them to clean up their act – to stop rough-housing and eating on stage, to work to a set programme of numbers presented in tight, pre-rehearsed sixty-minute sets.

The most significant change he effected was in the way they dressed. On 24 March 1962, just before they were due on stage at the Barnston Women's Institute in the Wirral, he presented them each with a £40, grey, brushed-tweed specially tailored lounge suit with narrow lapels and tie to match. Henceforth the Beatles were going to act and dress like professional entertainers.

Lennon disliked the change and would come to dislike it even more when groups like the Rolling Stones came on to the scene wearing what they liked and becoming almost as successful as the Beatles by behaving exactly as they wanted to. There was something pathetic and unmanly, effete almost, about four grown men dressing in the same way, right down to the Cuban heels of their Chelsea boots. They were, as Bill Wyman, the Stones' bass guitarist, sneer-ingly pointed out, 'Four stereotyped guys. They all looked exactly the same.' This was more Barbie doll than rock-and-roll outlaw and Lennon, who had adopted non-conformism as his personal creed, found the whole business insulting.

McCartney was altogether more amenable and obliging. When Epstein suggested the refashioning, McCartney gave his immediate approval and overruled the others' objections. The former schoolboy artist then sketched some rough designs for the suits Epstein was suggesting – with the pencil-thin lapels Epstein had had specially made up for them at Burton's. 'Paul just wanted to be successful and he thought that Brian was doing the right thing,' Peter Brown recalls. 'Brian was instrumental in deciding what the look should be. And being this tidy, organised, middle-class – or would-be middle-class – boy, Paul went along with it.' So, on McCartney's prompting, did Lennon.

Says Brown: 'Lennon resented the tidying up, right from the beginning, but he went along with it because he wanted to be a *star*. Another reason he went along with it was because he knew he could stop it any time he wanted to because of his control over Brian.'

It was, as it turned out, a master stroke, though the stardom Epstein assured them it would bring and which both Lennon and McCartney were so keen to achieve took rather longer in the coming than expected. Epstein's status as one of the largest record retailers in the north of England got his protégés an audition with the mighty Decca label but it did not go well and 'Eppy', as the group called him, discovered that, however influential he might consider himself to be in Liverpool, he was very small-time in London.

The audition was held on New Year's Day in 1962. Neil Aspinall drove them down. They got lost on the way and spent a desultory Hogmanay night wandering through London's West End where they were offered but turned down marijuana. They were kept waiting at Decca's West Hampstead recording studio. When they were eventually ushered in their battered amplifiers were not up to standard and they had to record on unfamiliar equipment. It was a repeat of those first dates at the Kaiserkeller eighteen months before. They were nervous and unsure.

The repertoire of fifteen songs that Epstein had selected for them did not help. It was an eclectic mish-mash of old standards like 'Red Sails in the Sunset' and 'Besame Mucho', with only three original Lennon–McCartney compositions in the whole collection. It was the last time Lennon and McCartney allowed him any say in their music.

'Paul couldn't sing one song,' Aspinall observed. 'He was too nervous and his voice started cracking up.'

Decca turned them down and signed Brian Poole and the Tremeloes instead. Epstein was furious and went to see Dick Rowe, head of the company's A & R department and so responsible for signing new talent. 'These boys are going to be bigger than Elvis!' he ranted. Rowe smiled condescendingly and dismissed him. As did Philips, HMV, Pye and Columbia. The Beatles became disenchanted with him and Epstein thought of quitting and going back to RADA.

According to Peter Brown, only his desire to be close to John Lennon kept him at it.

'He was dazzled by John, by his looks, by his wit, even by his cruelty,' Epstein's closest confidante recorded. 'Another passion might have burned itself out, but the eternal hope that one day Brian might consummate the relationship kept this one smouldering.' To ensure that it didn't extinguish itself before the hoped-for opportunity arose, Epstein had to keep working on the Beatles' behalf. But it was McCartney's talent, as much as Epstein's labour, that was responsible for the eventual breakthrough.

In April the Beatles had returned to Hamburg, this time with Epstein in tow. They were greeted on arrival with the news that Stu Sutcliffe had died. His mother gave his body to medical researchers who two years later finally established that the cause of death was a small tumour induced by a traumatic depression in the skull of the kind that would result from a kick in the head.

After offering what consolation he could for the loss of a friend he had never known, Epstein flew back to England and went back to his round of the record companies. Better to impress the disinterested executives, he transferred three Lennon–McCartney songs off the unwieldy tape he had been carrying around on to a black acetate disc at the HMV shop in London's Oxford Street. Two of them – 'Love of the Loved' and 'Like Dreamers Do' – were McCartney compositions and the engineer was impressed enough by them to send Epstein upstairs to the offices of Ardmore and Beechwood, a music-publishing subsidiary of EMI.

They, in turn, were impressed enough to send him along to see George Martin, head of A & R at Parlophone Records, another EMI subsidiary. It was a meeting immaculate in its timing. Epstein had just about run out of record companies – and Martin was head of an all but moribund label which EMI were considering closing.

Parlophone was at the back end of EMI's roster of interests. It was the company's 'joke label', partly because it released the Goons' comedy records, but also because its hits-to-releases ratio was so bad. Adam Faith, who was sporting a shorter version of the 'Beatles haircut' while they were still wearing theirs in pompadours, was signed to it, but after a couple of number-one hits his career had spun into terminal decline. Shane Fenton was another of its artists, but his career would not really take off for another decade. Head office were running out of patience and Martin desperately needed a hit if the label, and with it his £1,100-a-year job, was to survive. He had even been on a tour of the London coffee bars, looking for talent, but without success. Then along came Epstein whose opportuning, for once, was met with a welcome reception.

The two men met the following day, on May 9. Martin wasn't over-impressed by what he heard on the acetate disc that had been cut only twenty-four hours before. 'It was awful, dreadful,' he remembered. 'I can quite see why other people turned it down.' Given the pressures on his job, however, Martin was not in a position to be choosy. 'I was looking for something,' he conceded. 'I thought they were worth taking a gamble on.'

An agreement was struck and Epstein rushed off to the Post Office to dispatch two telegrams. One was to the *Mersey Beat*. It read: 'Have secured contract for Beatles to recorded [sic] for EMI on Parlaphone [sic] label. First recording date set for June 6th.' The other was to the Beatles in Hamburg. That one read: 'Congratulations boys. EMI request recording session. Please rehearse new material.'

According to official Beatle-lore, Epstein was jumping ahead of events, that June 6 date was not a recording session, only an audition. In fact Parlophone had agreed to take them on, unseen. On June 2 they returned from Hamburg. Two days later they went to London where they entered into contract with EMI. It was therefore as fully-fledged Parlophone recording artists that the Beatles made their first appearance in the Abbey Road studios in St John's Wood. Martin had indeed been desperate. But then, so had Epstein, and the contract he agreed for his 'boys' was quite the worst any manager could have agreed to.

All that Parlophone agreed to was to record four tracks in one year. The Beatles would receive a risible one-penny royalty per double-sided record – 'a grand sum to share between five of them!' as Martin said. Martin, who drew up the contract – 'it was a good indication of the EMI training/brainwashing to which I had been subjected' – included an increment of one farthing a year for five years. 'What that meant, if I chose to exercise these options, was that they were bound to EMI for five years,' Martin said, which took them to the grand rate of two pennies' royalty at the end of the five years. Epstein, who had never passed a mathematics exam and had wanted to grow up to be a dress designer, had been well and truly stitched up by the big city boys. It was a contract that would sour Epstein's relations with McCartney in the years ahead, and decisively influenced McCartney's attitude to future financial dealings.

In the summer of 1962, however, the Beatles were too inexperienced to bother with the fine print. After all those years of hard work and unfulfilled dreams, just to have a recording contract was reward enough. And in Martin they had found someone who quickly came to share their belief in their own talent and had the ability to do something with it.

'They were cheeky, they had a great sense of humour,' Martin said. 'I had been making a lot of comedy records and I liked them. I knew they had great charisma.' The humour was summed up by Harrison's answer to Martin's question, 'Is there anything you don't like?' 'Well,' Harrison replied, 'I don't like your tie for a kick-off.'

This jolly sense of irreverence became a Beatles' trademark, though McCartney never regarded it as anything special. 'As kids on the streets we just called it wisecracks,' he says. 'It was a wise-cracking kind of time, the fifties. And it also had a lot to do with Liverpool, where wit is a prized thing.'

It wasn't particularly prized that day. When Harrison made his remark the others, he recalled, 'were like, "Oh no, we're trying to do a record deal here."' But Martin, he observed, 'also had a sense of humour', and the incident was brushed off.

The music proved rather more problematic. Martin initially thought of reshaping them as a singer with a backing group, in the manner of Cliff Richard and the Shadows, and with Paul, the best-looking one, as the front man. 'Luckily for me and the world I decided against it,' McCartney said, adding, accurately, 'Not that John would have stood for it.'

When it came to the matter of how to record, however, the Beatles had to listen to what Martin was telling them. He was the expert, they were the acolytes. 'At first they needed me enormously,' he said. 'They knew nothing and they relied on me to produce their sound.' But even then they insisted on certain conditions. The first session had gone well – they had recorded McCartney's 'PS I Love You' and 'Love Me Do', Lennon's 'Ask Me Why', and the ubiquitous 'Besame Mucho' – but not well enough for a record release. When Martin got them back into Abbey Road in September he wanted them to record 'How Do You Do It', a catchy number written by an established pop composer named Mitch Murray. They refused (it later went to another Liverpool group, Gerry and the Pacemakers, who had a number-one hit with it) and that angered Martin. This was the song, he said, 'that's going to make the Beatles a household name – like Harpic. When you can write material as good as this, I'll record it.'

Lennon and McCartney were adamant, however. They wanted to record their own material and their version of 'How Do You Do It' died on their indifference. 'We hated it,' Paul said. 'We didn't want to do it. We felt we were getting a style that was the Beatles' style and were known for it in Hamburg and Liverpool. When we came down to London we didn't want to blow it all by suddenly changing our style and becoming a run of the mill group. We knew that "How Do You Do It" was a number one and George insisted it was, but we wanted our own song. We said we've got to live or die with "Love Me Do"; we know it's not as catchy but that's the way we've got to go. We were trying to keep the integrity.'

Paul was the most insistent on them recording their own songs. He had been writing since the age of 14 and he was convinced that his own compositions sounded as good as anything then in the charts. It also happened that 'Love Me Do', and 'PS I Love You', the two 'Lennon–McCartney' songs they wanted to record, were McCartney compositions.

The 'Lennon–McCartney' designation was formed out of mutual convenience. They were never a team, as Martin pointed out, in the Rodgers and Hart mould, 'but songwriters who helped each other with little bits and pieces'. McCartney was initially the more productive of the two. He could turn out songs almost to order. 'I'm just very lucky,' he says. 'I've got a gift. If you said, do a tune now, I could go off and in five minutes I could guarantee I'd come back with a tune.'

'He can turn out excellent potboilers,' Martin would observe, adding, 'I don't think he's particularly proud of this.' But John Lennon was around then to add the break, the edge, and often the words that would strip a McCartney song of its banality and give it point and direction. It was a symbiotic process and without thinking about it they often came close to a genuine collaboration. One would work out a series of chords, the other would add to them, and so it would go, backwards and forwards until a finished song would be arrived at. Given this system, they decided it was only fair if both of them shared the writing credit.

McCartney, predictably, wanted his name first but was eventually persuaded that Lennon–McCartney sounded better. That was symptomatic of the competition between the two. But it was healthy and productive and the result was the greatest songbook in popular music. And all the time, Martin said, McCartney was 'trying to do better, especially trying to equal John's talent for words'. McCartney also took careful count of whose songs were being recorded (as did Lennon) and was not averse to pushing his own compositions to the front of the queue. And in those simpler days, before he became attuned to their different talents and styles, it was McCartney's simpler melodies that first caught Martin's attention.

Not that Martin really liked 'Love Me Do' or 'PS I Love You'. Classically trained, he found the tune trite, McCartney's 'love me do, you know I love you' lyrics insipid. Those first songs, he said, 'were pretty awful'. He chose 'Love Me Do' for the A side of their first single, he said, because it was the best there was. Before it got to that point, however, there was one more pressing problem that had to be resolved. It involved the drummer, as it always had.

Pete Best had been with the group for two years. 'I had been with them through the hard times,' he bitterly pointed out. Now, as their fortunes were about to change, the door was slammed shut on him. But why? There are several theories and the truth is probably a combination of them all.

He had never really been part of the Beatles' 'family'. He had been hired out of necessity on the eve of their first visit to Hamburg but he had never fitted in. He continued to wear his hair greased back. He didn't pop pills like the others did. 'He was on his own really,' Astrid observed. Then there was the matter of his drumming. George Martin did not think he was very good and neither did Paul McCartney, an all-round musician who could play them better himself. Martin told Epstein: 'This drumming isn't regular enough. It doesn't give the right kind of sound,' which only confirmed what McCartney had always believed.

Jim McCartney once admonished Best for drawing all the attention to himself, that it was 'very selfish of you to do so', but Paul denies that Best was fired because he was good-looking and rivalled him in popularity. Mona Best was not convinced. Her son, she insists, was the most popular member of the band, with the largest following in the Cavern. The others resented that. 'Pete's beat had made them. They were jealous and they wanted him out.'

John Lennon told photographer Harry Benson, who went to the United States with the Beatles for the *Daily Express* and stayed to become one of America's top photographers, that they were 'fed up with Mona Best', that she was trying to take over the group and run their careers for them, and that to get rid of her they had to get rid of her son.

Neil Aspinall blamed Harrison. The junior of the Beatles' three founder members, George was an ardent admirer of Ringo, had become friendly with him and wanted his mate in the band. The Beatles, after all, were all about mateship and that meant there was no place for Best. Ringo concurs. George, he says, was the 'main instigator for getting me in because he liked me playing'.

Spencer Mason says it was Brian Epstein's doing. 'Eppy tried to get up Best,' he says. Epstein had made a pass at Pete Best. He had taken him for a ride in his new Ford Zodiac and asked him to a hotel for the night. Best had insisted on being driven home. 'Eppy never liked Best after that,' Mason says. 'Best's drumming was a bit frilly, Ringo's a lot straighter. But that didn't matter. It was because Best was straight, as a man, that Eppy had him out.'

Epstein insisted that he always liked Best, that he was 'incredibly good-looking with a big following', that he was 'very upset when the three of them came to me one night and said they didn't want him'.

Best was called into Epstein's office on Thursday morning, August 16. 'He was very apprehensive,' Best recalled. 'He talked around the subject for a while, but then he had to come out with it. He said, "Pete, I've got some bad news. The boys want you out and Ringo in."' He gave George Martin's criticism of his drumming as the excuse. 'If I wasn't that great, why was I kept on for two and a half years? When we first returned to Liverpool, why didn't they get another drummer then? Why wasn't Ringo asked then, instead of two years later, on the eve of success?' The answer to that plaintive question lay with the problem the Beatles had always had with their drummers. Finding them had proved hard enough, keeping them even more so, and because Best was prepared to stick it out they let him – until the record contract gave them the clout to go out and hire someone else.

Not that Ringo was that much better. 'There were a dozen as good as him in Liverpool at the time,' says Mason, and Epstein's original choice as Best's replacement had been Johnny Hutchinson. But he didn't like the Beatles, and turned the job down. It was only then that Epstein made the telephone call to Ringo to lure him away from Rory Storm's Hurricanes for a probationary £25 a week and the promise that if he fitted in, he would soon become a fully fledged member of the group.

Best's sacking caused a furore among the Cavern crowd. Epstein's car was vandalised, Ringo was booed and Harrison was punched, arriving at the Abbey Road recording session with a black eye. As it transpired, Ringo, the puny waif from the back streets who had spent much of his childhood in hospital, was essential to the Beatles' conquest of America. Without knowing it – but how could they have known it then – they had got the drummer they needed, someone vital to their early success.

It was as a drummer rather than a focus for every love-struck pubescent girl's maternal instincts that Martin judged him, however, and his verdict was dour. Having suffered Best, the producer was in no mood to take another chance. Ringo, as Martin pointed out, 'was not a "technical" drummer. He couldn't do a roll to save his life. Men like Buddy Rich and Gene Krupa would run rings round him.' So could Andy White, the session drummer Martin brought in for the 'Love Me Do' recording. Ringo, much to his distress, was reduced to banging a tambourine. 'I was shattered,' Ringo recalled. 'I thought, that's the end, they're doing a Pete Best on me. How phony the record business is, I thought.'

McCartney, on the other hand, was immediately captivated by the studio and the possibilities it offered. Martin encouraged his interest by getting him involved right from the start in the techniques of recording. By adding Lennon's harmonica (shoplifted by him in Holland on the way to Hamburg), Martin gave 'Love Me Do' a different feel. By upping the tempo and giving it a new arrangement, he completely altered the sound of 'Please Please Me'.

Norman Stone was the engineer on those early sessions and he recalled: 'It was nearly always Paul who was the MD, the musical director, as early as this. Obviously John would have quite a lot to say, but overall it was always Paul who was the guv'nor. Which is fair, because he was the natural musician and, even at this stage, the natural producer.'

While the others were still trying to work out what the red light over the studio door meant, McCartney was up in the control box, listening to the playbacks, asking questions, trying to work out which switch did what. In Epstein's eyes Lennon was the force, the leader of the group. Martin, however, was in no doubt as to who had the real musical talent. It was Paul McCartney and it was a McCartney song that introduced the Beatles to the record-buying public.

On 2 October 1962 – six months after the death of Stu Sutcliffe, just under seven weeks since the sacking of Pete Best, just over five weeks since Lennon had 'done the decent thing' and married his pregnant girlfriend, Cynthia, two days after the Beatles had finally signed a formal management contract with Epstein, and ten days before Little Richard tried to seduce McCartney – 'Love Me Do' was released. With Epstein's assistance – he ordered thousands of copies to help buy it into the charts – it went to number 17.

Said McCartney: 'In Hamburg we clicked, at the Cavern we clicked, but if you want to know when we *knew* we'd arrived, it was getting into the charts with "Love Me Do". That was the one. It gave us somewhere to go.' On 11 January 1963, 'Please Please Me' was released. It went to number one. The Beatles were really going somewhere.

5

PAUL McCartney's declared ambition, according to the first official Beatle handout, issued in October 1962, was to make a lot of money. After he'd done that, he said, he wanted to retire. Three decades and several hundred million pounds later, retirement is still in the future. 'People say to me, "Why are you still in music, you've made your money; why don't you sod off and go on holiday?" Because I'm still fascinated,' he says, by the business that made him rich, by the continuous excitement of doing something new.

Making the money – and no one in pop music has made more – did not prove as easy as his talent suggests it should have been, though. Epstein saw to that. 'From Me to You' followed 'Please Please Me' to the number-one spot. The next single was 'She Loves You', written in a Newcastle hotel room and based on the simple idea of Paul's of substituting 'you' for 'me'. It notched up sales of 1,300,000 and became the biggest-selling disc in British recording history.

In November they released 'I Want to Hold Your Hand', which Lennon and McCartney wrote 'eyeball to eyeball' in the cellar of Jane Asher's parents' house in London. That, too, went to number one with sales that rivalled 'She Loves You'. Their EP, *Twist and Shout*, sold over a quarter of a million copies. Their first album, *Please Please Me*, stayed at the top of the album charts for twenty-nine weeks, only to be replaced by their follow-up LP, *With the*

Beatles, whose advance orders of 270,000 were a world record, beating the 200,000 set by Presley's *Blue Hawaii*. By the end of 1963 £6,250,000-worth of Beatles records had been sold and EMI's profits had soared by 80 percent. By the following year Beatles-generated business had topped $40 million.

Yet when it came to actual cash the Beatles found themselves relying on handouts from the brown paper bags stuffed with pound notes that Epstein collected at every concert they played. Even at the usurious royalty rates Epstein had negotiated, Lennon and McCartney were soon up in the 83-percent tax-bracket set by the new Labour government for its highest-earning citizens. To make up the shortfall and to keep his boys in pocket Epstein went into the black economy, demanding – and getting – up to a £1000 a night in cash from theatre managers who were only too happy to pay it to secure the appearance of the most successful entertainment act Britain had ever witnessed. He would then scrupulously divide the illicit takings between the four members of the band, having first taken his 25 per-cent off the top. 'For the first time in our lives we could actually do something and earn money,' McCartney recalled.

It was hardly the most sensible way to run the most profitable small specialised business in Britain. And all the while other sources of income which should have been coming the Beatles' way were being ignored or dissipated or sold out for ludicrously small fees. Manufacturers, quick to leap on to the Beatle bandwagon, started producing Beatle wigs, collarless Beatle jackets, Beatle boots, and anything else that the name could be attached to, and usually without authority.

'Brian was weak at making deals,' observed Brown, with dry understatement.

In the effort to bring some sort of order to what was turning into a financial cautionary tale, Epstein employed Bryce-Hamner, a staid, traditional accounting firm with little experience of showbus-iness. Dr Walter Strach, the senior partner in charge of the Beatles' account, knew nothing of the brown paper bags and would have been horrified if he had. His advice was to invest it while they were still making it and prepare for the hefty tax bills that would soon be arriving. For no one, least of all the four Beatles, believed that they had a lifetime's ticket to ride this gravy train.

Ringo thought he might just make enough to buy a chain of hairdressing salons. Harrison said he was going to buy a bus for his bus-driver father. Even McCartney, more intelligent, more 'bourgeois', as Brown called him, seemed a little unsure what to do. McCartney recalled: 'I always thought you could put it in the bank, lovely, marvellous, pay my taxes, leave it there. They said, no you can't, you've got to invest it.' And the obvious thing to invest it in was their own talent.

Epstein had been disappointed by the failure of Ardmore and Beechwood, who had sent him to see Martin and had been given the publishing rights to 'Love Me Do' in return, to do more to promote the record. Epstein complained that he had had to do it all himself (shortly after the song was released McCartney remarked that he hadn't eaten all day 'because somebody had to pay for those ten thousand records Brian bought'). He was determined to find someone else.

Martin sent him to see Dick James. A former big-band singer, James had recorded the theme song to the Robin Hood television series under Martin's direction, his and, until the advent of the Beatles, Martin's only memorable hit. James, Martin told Epstein, 'is hungry. He needs work, he needs money, he badly needs a hit.'

However hungry James may have been, he was still experienced enough in the ways and wiles of showbusiness to see a sucker deal when it was presented to him on a plate. He listened to a tape of 'Please Please Me' and immediately recognised the potential. He offered to form a company in which he owned 50 percent of the shares, the Beatles and Epstein the other half. On top of that the company would be managed by Dick James Music who would charge a 10 percent handling fee off the top.

Epstein was delighted – just as he had been delighted by the terms of the Parlophone contract. McCartney wasn't, for very good reason. Under James's terms Lennon and McCartney, whose talent, after all, was what the deal was all about, only received 15 percent each, Harrison and Ringo 1.6 percent each. James, meanwhile, had 50 percent – after his company had skimmed 10 percent off the top. Epstein had given away 50 percent of what quickly proved to be the most prolific songwriting partnership in musical history – for nothing. Within eighteen months James was a millionaire with an income greater than either of the songwriters whose musical efforts were earning it for him.

Says McCartney: 'When John and I were writing, all our business people came to us and said, "Do you want to own your own company?", and we said, "Not half." As we were setting it up we suddenly realised it wasn't actually going to be *our* own company, it was within somebody else's company but they were calling it our own company. That was a big mistake we made. We should have sat down and said, "No, you said it was going to be our company, couldn't we please have it all in our company and we'll give you a bit." We were too naïve. We didn't understand all this majority shareholding.' He drolly adds: 'I think we were ripped off.'

The company was called Northern Songs 'because we came from Liverpool and there was already a company called Southern Songs'. It would become the cause of endless legal battles over the next three decades. By bitter irony, the company that was set up ostensibly to safeguard the product of their collaboration became one of the wedges that forced McCartney and Lennon apart.

It was only later, though, that the full import of what had happened sank in. When the deal was struck they were still young and, as McCartney pointed out, naïve. They were riding the crest of a phenomenon and they were revelling in it. Their records were at the top of the hit parade, riots started breaking out wherever they appeared, and by the end of 1963 they were on the front of every national newspaper in the country. Eppy, or so they assumed, was looking after the money.

'Somebody said to me, "But the Beatles were anti-materialistic",' McCartney recalled. 'That's a huge myth. John and I literally used to sit down and say, "Now let's write a swimming pool." We said it out of innocence, out of normal working-class glee that we were able to write a swimming pool.'

According to William Mann, the music critic of the august *Times*, it wasn't just swimming pools they were capable of writing. On 27 December 1963, he reviewed their second album, *With the Beatles*. He gave the Lennon composition, 'Not a Second Time', particular attention. 'One gets the impression,' Mann wrote, 'that they think simultaneously of harmony and melody, so firmly are the major tonic sevenths and ninths built into their tunes, and the flat-submediant keyswitches, so natural is the Aeolian cadence at the end of "Not a Second Time" (the chord progression which ends Mahler's "Song of the Earth").' The critique sounds faintly ridiculous now. But everything that happened then seems ridiculous in the coolness of hindsight.

The explanations advanced for what took place are as multifarious as the experts called upon to give them. It was all to do with sublimated sex. It was an eruption of immense social significance that signalled the dawn of a new age. It was a reaction to the tawdry Profumo call-girl and spy scandal which was indirectly responsible for bringing the Labour Party to power. It was a cynical exercise in hype perpetrated by a media short of an amusing story. It was the musical protest of a generation brought up under the shadow of the atomic bomb.

It might just have been something as simple as the effect of good old-fashioned rock and roll, of the kind that had always provoked hysteria, set to better melodies and presented in an original way by four humorous, engaging, unthreatening, seemingly identical, apparently clean-cut young men with funny haircuts and provincial accents who enchanted everyone with their style and wit.

The Beatles themselves certainly had no idea why it was happening or even what people were talking about sometimes. Aeolian cadences? 'To this day I don't have *any* idea what they are,' Lennon would remark seventeen years later. 'It was just chords, like any other chords.' They were too busy getting on with it to worry about the intellectual rationalisations for their success. They were not above playing it for all they were worth, though, and working on ways to encourage it. Kenny Lynch toured with them early on in 1963: 'I remember John and Paul saying they were thinking of running up to the microphone together and shaking their heads and singing, "whoooo". I said, "You can't do that. They'll think you're a bunch of poofs."' Despite the warning, they were soon doing just that, and, observed Lynch, it 'became a very important, terrifically popular part of their act'. It was the Beatles' answer to Presley's thrusting pelvis and it came with their signature 'yeh, yeh, yeh', which Jim McCartney had pleaded with Paul to make a more dignified 'yes, yes, yes'.

What they actually said and sang on stage soon became irrelevant in the cacophony of screams that greeted their every appearance. The band that prided itself on its musical ability was being drowned out by its own success. They ordered new Vox AC60 amplifiers to replace the AC30s they had been using before but it didn't make the slightest difference. They still couldn't hear a note of what they were playing. They couldn't even count in to the beginning of a song at the same time, such was the bedlam, and as often as not they ended up playing out of sync. The fans, caught in the throes of mass hysteria, there to scream themselves into blithering, incoherent ecstasy, didn't care. As several critics pointed out, for all the difference it made the Beatles could have been singing 'Mary Had a Little Lamb' – a song which McCartney would record a variation of on his first Wings album.

None of this had seemed remotely possible when 'Love Me Do' was first released. When they appeared with the yodelling Frank Ifield in Peterborough – their first major theatre booking – they were greeted with stony, uncomprehending silence. The reaction was not noticeably better when they went out on tour early in 1963 as the last of five supporting acts for Helen Shapiro. The only notable incident was when they were thrown out of the Carlisle Golf Club dance at the Crown and Mitre hotel in Carlisle for wearing leather jackets.

They were still, as far as the entertainment industry at large was concerned, a bunch of Liverpool scruffs and the efforts to convince the top promoters to employ them had proved almost as difficult as getting anyone to offer them a recording contract. It was for that reason that Epstein had started putting on his own shows. With his brother, Clive, he had formed a limited company grandly called NEMS Enterprises, which had its office in a room over the family shop, to handle the Beatles. It did not get off to a resounding start – the first booking NEMS Enterprises made for the group was at a seaside café in Cheshire. After expenses Epstein was left with a profit of just over one pound. By October 1962, however, he was operating with greater success.

'The only way to get the Beatles proper gigs was to do our own promotion, because you always needed a headliner to get the crowds in,' says Peter Brown. On October 12 NEMS staged a concert at the Tower Ballroom in New Brighton. There were eleven acts on stage that night – including, to Epstein's and the Beatles' considerable embarrassment, Lee Curtis and the All Stars who had just acquired a drummer by the name of Pete Best.

Little Richard, one of McCartney's boyhood heroes and the singer whose vocal style he had spent years copying, was top of the bill. He was now out of priestly retirement and right back to his old ways. McCartney was overawed. 'I never thought I'd ever meet Little Richard. We never thought we'd be playing on the same bill as a big star like that. So when Brian told us he'd set up a gig at the Tower at New Brighton, with Richard and about ten other groups, we were knocked out. We were going to meet Little Richard!'

The screamer from Macon, Georgia, was just as excited about meeting Paul McCartney. 'He thought that Paul was just the cutest thing he had ever seen, which he was when he was twenty years old,' Brown recalls. 'Little Richard chased him round and round the dressing room, Paul just managing to keep one step ahead.'

Little Richard – fingernails varnished, hair curled – got on much better with Epstein, much to the irritation of Don Arden, who was looking after the singer on his British tour and had nothing but trouble with his temperamental star. Harsh words were exchanged between Epstein and Arden, which ended with Arden making the obvious innuendo and Epstein shouting back, 'I shall call your office on Monday, Mr Arden. I don't think you'll be working there very long after that!'

Asked about Epstein's homosexuality, McCartney answered: 'We were more confused by it than turned off. We really didn't know what it meant to be gay at the time.' There is a ring of McCartney-style public relations to that reply. His smile might have been innocent, but McCartney had seen enough to know where Little Richard – and Brian Epstein – were coming from.

Says Brown: 'Paul had lived in Hamburg in the most sleazy conditions, and had been propositioned in various ways. He and the others had seen all kinds of life when they were seventeen, eighteen years old. It wasn't something to horrify or upset or anger him. It didn't bother him. Paul wasn't going to turn round and bash Little Richard. He was just going to make sure he kept one step ahead of him in that race around the dressing room.'

Lennon was no innocent, either. He was well aware of Epstein's interest in him. When it was suggested, back when Epstein was still trying to hustle a record deal, that he should take up Brian's offer of a holiday in Copenhagen, just the two of them, Lennon had replied, 'Shut up. Can't you see he's after me?' The chase continued and in April of the following year he was finally persuaded to accompany Epstein on a holiday to Barcelona. Epstein had first visited Spain in 1959, shortly after that painful encounter in the lavatory in West Derby. He had been back several times since and had developed a deep, if predictable, interest in bull-fighting and, more especially, in certain young matadors.

Cynthia objected to the trip. She had only just given birth to their son, who would eventually be christened Julian in his father's absence. She wanted her husband to be with her, a husband who, in the manner of all pop stars at the time, refused to acknowledge that he was married and compounded the public rejection by treating her with cruel indifference in private. Lennon said he was tired from touring, that he deserved a holiday and that Epstein had no one else to go with. Over his wife's protests, he went.

Peter Brown has no doubts about what took place between Epstein and Lennon in the hotel room they shared. McCartney dismissively says, 'That's been rumoured for years,' and refuses to add to the speculation that was soon the subject of common gossip in the Beatle 'family' and beyond. 'We all knew what had happened,' said Spencer Mason.

It was Bob Wooler's ill-judgement to mention to Lennon what everyone was saying behind his back. In June McCartney held his 21st birthday party at the Birkenhead home of his aunt Jinny who had helped out after his mother had died. The Fourmost, another group recently signed to NEMS Enterprises, played. So did the Scaffold, a band whose members included Paul's brother Michael who had changed his name to McGear to avoid any suggestion that he was cashing in on Paul's escalating fame. A lot of alcohol was consumed. When Wooler, the disc jockey who had been instrumental in getting the Beatles their Cavern bookings, suggested, most probably in jest, that Lennon and Epstein were closer than Liverpool convention expected, the drunken Lennon went berserk.

'I smashed him up,' Lennon remembered. 'I broke his bloody ribs for him.' Three of them, in fact. 'He called me a bloody queer.'

Wooler sued and Lennon settled out of court for £200. It was a sad dénouement to a relationship that had been very profitable for the Beatles. 'Bob Wooler was one of the ones who got the least for all the early work and devotion he put into the Beatles,' Mike McGear said. 'Anyone who wrote, "The Beatles are truly a phenomenon. I don't think anything like them will happen again" in *Mersey Beat* back in 1961, two years *before* Beatlemania, can't be all that bad.'

The Beatles' caravan was about to pack up and move on, however, and Wooler, like Liverpool itself, was about to be left behind. They had had enough of the city. They had outgrown it. 'We didn't

93

like to say it, but we really didn't like going back to Liverpool,' Lennon admitted. 'Touring was a relief, just to get out of Liverpool and break new ground. We were beginning to feel stale and cramped.'

Epstein was the first to make the break. He said goodbye to the family business for the last time, and in one week in October had moved all of NEMS Enterprises down to London. He hired a black manservant, ordered a red Rolls Royce and set himself up in a flat in Knightsbridge which he decorated with white carpet and black leather furniture. The boys followed shortly afterwards, though not into anything particularly grand; Dr Strach was keeping a tight rein on their finances.

Lennon and Cynthia and baby Julian rented a rather dingy flat in Kensington in the bedsitter region near to Earl's Court. Harrison and Ringo shared a flat in the same block Epstein had just moved into. Only McCartney made the transition to the capital with any style. In May, shortly after he had nearly drowned on a holiday in the Canary Islands with Ringo and George, he joined the other Beatles at a pop concert at the Royal Albert Hall. There he met Jane, the actress daughter of Dr Richard Asher, a top London psychiatrist. Her mother, Margaret, was a distinguished professor of music who, by coincidence, had taught George Martin how to play the oboe when he was a student at the London School of Music.

Jane Asher was a celebrity in her own right. She had appeared in the film *Mandy* at the age of five, playing a deaf mute. She had starred in Walt Disney's production of *The Prince and the Pauper*. She was also a regular on *Juke Box Jury* and Paul and his brother, as Michael said, 'both fancied her'. She also reeked of class and that was immensely important to the socially ambitious McCartney. Jane, only 17 but already full of poise and cool detachment, was just what this lad from Liverpool was looking for. She had, said Michael, 'a well-cultured, Dad-admired accent', which Paul's late mother, who was always keen for her son to imitate the tones she heard on the BBC, would certainly have approved of. She was also, so everyone insisted, a virgin, a not unimportant consideration in England's chauvinistic North-West at the time.

After the show she joined the Beatles for refreshments at the Royal Court hotel in Chelsea's Sloane Square. They started seeing each other whenever possible. Soon afterwards Mrs Asher invited McCartney to move in with them in their grand family home in Wimpole Street. It was an important move for the young McCartney. He was 21 and, after his experiences in Hamburg, very streetwise. He still showed all the rough edges of his provincial, lower-middle-class upbringing, however. He was determined to lose them and the Ashers – urbane, intelligent, cultivated – were delighted to do the rubbing. They introduced him to classical music, encouraged his interest in literature, spent hours talking at the dinner table – a new experience for a young man used to eating his food as quickly as possible and then rushing out. He started quoting poetry – not very accurately, as it happens – and attending the theatre and the ballet. It was a development, a refinement of his tastes that would come to its intellectual fruition three years later in *Sgt Pepper*.

It also introduced the public to the great guessing game of Will they, won't they marry? that lasted until Jane found him in bed with another woman and ran out of his life in tears, pausing only to send her mother round to collect the pots and pans. But then women's sobs, off-stage as well as on, were already a mark of McCartney's young life.

His relationship with Dorothy Rohne, Cynthia Lennon recalled, had ended when McCartney had rushed in one evening, told her it was all over, and rushed out again, leaving her in tears. Soon after that he had picked up with Rory Storm's sister, Iris. That affair had expired on the deathbed of his infidelities and she later married Alvin Stardust. Now it was Jane's turn to provide the stability to counterbalance his promiscuity. He was one of the world's most desirable bachelors and he made good use of that fact.

Jane refused to give up a career she had enjoyed since childhood. She was often away touring. In the later years of their relationship

95

she spent a lot of time in America with the Old Vic. Says Brown: 'He got lonely.' Jane either didn't know what was going on or pretended she didn't. The final betrayal had been a long time in the preparation, however, and there could be no way back after she was confronted with a woman in her own bed with Paul.

Until that happened Jane Asher remained on call to provide the love and security McCartney needed. He would come to resent her independence but in that first bloom of romance he was proud to be seen with her, proud enough to take her home to Liverpool which was something he hadn't been noted for doing before. His brother Michael remembers the excitement when Paul telephoned from London and said he was bringing her to Forthlin Road. 'It was all too much for a young teenager and a working-class Liverpool cotton salesman to take in at once.' So overcome were they that they retired to bed to await the grand arrival of the Beatle prince and his well-bred consort.

Jane Asher was much more than the prize for a gauche Liverpudlian's social aspirations, of course. The good manners that were second nature to her included putting people at their ease. She took the trouble to get on well with Jim McCartney and her boyfriend's extended family of cousins, aunts and uncles, and was always a welcome guest on her visits north, infrequent as they were in that wild, reckless year when Britain succumbed to the Fab Four.

The Beatles relegated everything – family, friends, ordinary social life, girlfriends, children – to the back seat. For it really looked for a while as though the world had gone stark staring Beatle-mad. A year which started quietly ended in screaming chaos. That was just the beginning. And there was no escape – Epstein, determined at all costs to keep them in work, had them solidly booked for months ahead.

After the Helen Shapiro tours they went out as the supporting act for Tommy Roe, a wannabee Buddy Holly who had had a hit with a record called 'Sheila', and another American one-hit wonder called Chris Montez who had made the charts with 'Let's Dance'.

By the first night the screams for the Beatles had inverted the running order – as they did when the Beatles went out on tour with Roy Orbison, who, unlike Montez and Roe, was a genuine star.

Orbison remembered the Beatles pleading to be allowed to close the show. 'In Europe it means a lot to top the bill,' he said. 'They said, "You're making all the money, please let us close the show."' In the face of popular demand, he had to. 'I always thought they would be as big in America as they were in Europe,' he observed. From then onwards they were the headliners. There was no need for Epstein to hire the likes of Little Richard to fill an auditorium – the Beatles were more than capable of doing that themselves now.

Only the mighty Grade family resisted. The three brothers – Lew, Leslie, and the third, who worked under the name of Bernard Delfont – held a virtual stranglehold on British showbusiness. Delfont controlled a number of West End theatres. Leslie was the most powerful booking agent in the country. Lew owned ATV, the independent television company which presented 'Sunday Night at the London Palladium', the most important variety show on television.

Leslie Grade had approached Epstein with a view to taking a hand in staging the Beatles' live shows. Epstein turned him down and in the process succeeded in rubbing him up the wrong way, thereby closing doors that might otherwise have been open to him.

But even the Grades had to surrender eventually to the tide of hysteria. They were shrewd enough to recognise a business phenomenon when they encountered one and it was all smiles and handshakes when it was announced that the Beatles would be appearing on 'Sunday Night at the London Palladium' on October 13. Fifteen million people tuned in to watch them that night, almost a third of the population. It wasn't the people at home watching who made that such an important night; it was the girls rioting outside the theatre who appeared in every British newspaper the following day.

Even if the number of girls had been greatly exaggerated to make the story, the Beatles were now front-page news.

Three days later Delfont announced that the Beatles would top the bill at the Royal Command Variety Performance to be televised from the Palladium on November 4 because, he explained, his 10-year-old daughter liked them. This was the ultimate accolade in British entertainment. The Beatles had truly arrived.

And not just in England. On October 23 they embarked on a seven-day, nine-concert tour of Sweden which earned them a mere £2,000. It was their first proper tour abroad and pandemonium greeted them everywhere. They arrived back to more screams. Several hundred fans had gathered at the airport in what was to become the ritual of the Beatles' airport receptions. The British Prime Minister, Sir Alec Douglas Home, was ignored in the mayhem. Everything the Beatles touched was turning to gold, in the figurative if not the literal sense.

The press and public were now firmly behind them. Stories of their stand-up 'wenching' sessions in the dressing rooms, of Lennon's cruelty, of the way cripples who were brought to meet them were forcibly ejected by their newly employed bodyguard, the former Cavern club bouncer Mal Evans, never appeared in print. They were the Fabulous Beatles. A veil was drawn over their indiscretions, their normality. They were becoming what Lennon had feared they would – four smiling pop-up Barbie dolls. They were the salve to a troubled age. Now they were going to work their magic on the royal family at the Royal Command Variety Performance. They *had* to succeed. And they did.

When he stepped up to the microphone to sing 'Twist and Shout' Lennon said: 'For this number we'd like to ask your help. Will the people in the cheaper seats clap your hands? All the rest of you, if you'll just rattle your jewellery.' What Lennon had said when they were backstage practising their 'ad libs', however, was: 'I'll tell them to rattle their fucking jewellery.'

That was not going to happen. This wasn't Hamburg. The Beatles were locked into their clean-cut image. It had assumed a force of

The London Airport scene became a
Beatles tradition. With thousands of
fans in screaming attendance, George,
Paul, Ringo and his wife Maureen,
and John, with his wife Cynthia in a
rare public appearance, fly out to Austria
to work on *Help!* *(Hulton Deutsch)*

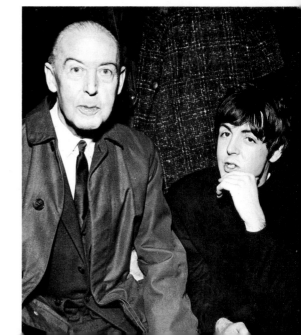

Jim McCartney, the decent, honest
father. *(Pictorial Press)*

The Mop Tops recording their 1965 Christmas special at the height of
Beatlemania. (*Hulton Deutsch*)

Mal Evans, the Beatles' road manager,
pictured in 1966 returning from
Manila. (*Topham*)

Bohemian aristocrat Tara Browne, heir
to a Guinness fortune. A close friend
of Paul's, he was killed in a car crash in
December 1966 aged twenty-one.
(*Syndication International*)

its own. It was Epstein who had suggested they recast themselves as lovable entertainers. McCartney had embraced the vision. When Lennon objected, McCartney had talked him round. McCartney had seen the future and it worked – with a vengeance. Over 26 million people tuned in to watch them on the Royal Command Variety show. They were captivated. The *Daily Mirror* summed it all up in a one-word headline. BEATLEMANIA.

6

O N 7 February 1964, the Beatles flew into New York aboard Pan Am flight 101. Paul McCartney was nervous. He kept his seatbelt strapped all the time they were in the air. America, he said, had everything. He kept asking, 'Why do they need us?'

America did. Like a computer virus, Beatlemania had spread through the telecommunication networks of Marshall McLuhan's global village, and was about to infect, to epidemic proportions, the world's richest, most media-orientated nation. For one chill moment, though, it looked as though this rare moment of McCartney's self-doubt was to be worryingly realised. The plane landed at 1.35 in the afternoon. The Beatles were first down the steps. They were greeted – by silence.

Photographer Harry Benson was the fifth person off the plane. He recalls: 'There was a crowd there waiting to meet them but nothing to the crowds they had come to expect. There were photographers, airline officials, a few policemen. But that, as far as they could see, was the sum of it. They had hoped there would be thousands of screaming fans. They weren't there.' On Benson's call the Beatles turned round as they walked down the aeroplane's steps and on to American soil. There is a plaintive appeal in the four faces who smiled into the camera lens.

No British act had ever succeeded in the United States and success was very important to McCartney. 'It is important to succeed everywhere,' he said. For that disconcerting instant, however, it looked as if the Beatles were about to go the way of Cliff Richard, whose own tilt at the American market had died in ignominy four years earlier at the bottom of the bill on a Frankie Avalon tour.

Even Epstein, whose faith in the group was almost religious in its fervour, was worried. Capitol, EMI's American arm, had consistently refused to release their records and had only recently been persuaded to change tack. To get them over to the United States he had discounted their appearance money to the point where the Beatles themselves were paying for the privilege of strapping on their guitars and shaking their hair in that scream-provoking rite Lennon and McCartney had so assiduously practised. Epstein, as would quickly be proved, had yet again seriously underestimated the commercial value of his boys. On this occasion, though, no one could blame him for that – for no one huddled at the newly renamed John F Kennedy airport that winter's morning could have foreseen the hysteria about to consume a nation still in mourning for the president shot dead in Dallas only three months before.

The signs that something was afoot were there, however, and there were men smart enough to spot it. Walter Cronkite, the doyen of American news anchors, had carried a report about Beatlemania in Britain on the CBS evening news. Ed Sullivan, host of the most influential entertainment programme on American television, also had an inkling of what might be happening and how he could turn that to his advantage. Sullivan was famed for spotting new talent. Elvis Presley had appeared on his show and become a star. 'Ed was such a superb showman,' Cronkite recalls, 'that he called me almost before I was off the air. He said, "Who were those four guys?" So I told him the name and he said, "I'm going to have to try and get them over here".' And that, says Cronkite, 'was the beginning of their coming to the States. I think they would have come here eventually, but that was the historic record of how they came here.'

Sid Bernstein got in even earlier. A tubby former ballroom manager with ambitions to become a fulltime concert promoter, he was taking a course in English government in 1963 at the New School for Social Research in New York. As part of his studies he was required to read the British newspapers. He recalled: 'I began to read about a group making noise out of Liverpool. I, as a promoter, thought, It's time to strike! I just had a feeling that the timing might be right. It was just a hunch.'

Without hearing a Beatles record, he contacted Epstein and, over the manager's reluctance – 'Nobody knows us in America, we don't mean anything,' Epstein protested – signed them for two shows at the Carnegie Hall in a year's time, on 12 February 1964. When Sullivan learnt that Bernstein had them booked for that date he co-ordinated their appearance on his show and booked them for February 9. Sullivan contacted Bernstein 'and asked me if I'd heard them. I said, "No, Ed, I haven't, but I've been following them in the newspapers and they're a phenomenon, so I took a chance." He said, "So am I."'

Sullivan had originally wanted to sign them as a novelty item. Epstein was horrified when that suggestion was put to him by the show's producer, Sullivan's son-in-law, Bob Precht. If the Beatles were going to appear at all, he grandly declared, they were going to be the headliners. They wanted to appear on the Sullivan Show because it was the best programme of its kind on television. But the Beatles, he insisted, were also the best. In the end Precht agreed that the Beatles would top the bill. And not just once, but on two consecutive Sundays. Sullivan was indeed taking a chance but not as much of a one as he intimated to Bernstein. With the form in Britain as his guideline, he shrewdly calculated that the odds were shortening in his favour. If the Beatles succeeded he would take the credit. If they didn't he could dismiss them as a freak novelty.

Epstein, too, was pleased with the arrangement. He called a meeting with Capitol and, armed with the Sullivan contract, persuaded the company to release 'I Want to Hold Your Hand', a song written, he said, with the 'American sound' in mind. Capitol put it out on a 'limited basis' on 13 January 1964. Two weeks later, to the bewilderment of the Capitol executives, it hit number one on the Cashbox chart. The Beatles were playing in Paris and staying at the ritzy George V hotel when the news came through. They shouted and cheered and started punching each other with delight. A pillow-fight broke out that night in Harrison's room.

Albert Goldman, a biographer of Lennon, claimed the rumpus was staged, that Lennon – cool, calculating, streetsmart – would never have demeaned himself by indulging in anything so adolescent as a pillow-fight except as a publicity gimmick. Harry Benson, who took the famous photograph, dismisses Goldman's hypothesis. 'There was no way,' he says, 'that the picture could have been set up.' Benson says he was simply photographing them the way they were: four young men isolated by their fame. The only people allowed into their rooms, apart from their entourage and girlfriends, were good-time girls. They were there to serve a singular purpose. Once it had been fulfilled they left, leaving the group on their own again.

'Things like pillow-fights were a release,' says Benson. 'They were always indulging in violent fun like that. Paul got that one going. He didn't want to go to bed.' And when the fight broke out, he was 'smart enough to know that the photograph would be good for the image of the group, good for him'.

They were noticeably less exuberant when their plane touched down at Kennedy three weeks later. The record-buying public had judged 'I Want to Hold Your Hand' a hit. Now they were about to judge the Beatles themselves. 'We all felt a bit sick,' Ringo admitted. Says McCartney: 'There's no such thing as a perfectly confident person,' and for those first few silent moments in America even his self-belief was under siege. The doubt didn't last.

The New York police, mindful of security, had marshalled the fans inside the airport building. When the Beatles walked into the terminal they were engulfed by the noise they hadn't heard when they stepped off the plane, generated by as many as ten thousand people in the throes of mass hysteria, screaming, *We love you, Beatles, oh yes we do,* and hurling themselves against the police cordon. An estimated 70 percent of the fans were male; if the Beatles were sexual objects to the girls, they were role models to the boys, though the girls were equally frenzied when they joined in the charges against the police lines. One young female fan was hanging from the third storey, held up by two boyfriends, and screaming, 'Here I am! We love you!' It was the most tumultuous reception even the Beatles had experienced.

There was a hint of cynical manipulation in the scene. Capitol, coming late to the case, had at last caught up with the idea that the Beatles might turn into a money-spinner after all and, following the unexpected success of 'I Want to Hold Your Hand', had distributed five million free 'The Beatles Are Coming' posters and car stickers as part of an unprecedented $50,000 'crash publicity program'. Their record pushers had been strong-arming the pop radio stations and New York's influential WMCA had gone on to 'Beatle time', giving minute-by-minute updates on the Beatles' arrival with breath-less, 'the temperature is thirty-two Beatle degrees' hyperbole.

Nicky Byrne, who was in charge of Beatles merchandising, went so far as to claim to have 'fixed' the airport crowd, and reports of students at a high school in the Bronx being bribed to go out to the airport and scream did appear in several newspapers the following day. There was more than hype to what was happening, however. The New York police estimate that a quarter of a million people lined the route from the airport to the Plaza hotel where they were staying and no pop hustler could ever have 'fixed' that. Epstein and the Beatles had chosen their moment well.

American pop music, emasculated and blow-dried into respect-ability following the payola scandal of four years before which had ended the career of Alan Freed, the disc jockey credited with inventing the term 'rock and roll', was languishing in a trough. Since the close of rock's first Sun Record-inspired era, the US charts had been dominated by the teen idols like Bobby Vee and Bobby Rydell, Johnny Tilletson and Frankie Avalon. Only the Beach Boys, with their uniquely Californian vision of surf and long-limbed girls, offered any resistance to the fresh sound of the Beatles which was sweeping all before it.

Allen Ginsberg, the Beat poet and friend of Jack Kerouac, was so excited when he first heard 'I Want to Hold Your Hand' in a New York nightclub that he got up and danced, which was the first time Ginsberg had been seen to dance in public. Jerry Lee Lewis, in disgrace since his ill-considered marriage, took particular, and particularly fiendish, pleasure in the demise of 'all those Bobbys and Johnnys', as he called them, with their crooned laments to puppy love, who had been groomed to take his place. They were cut down, the Killer snarled, 'like corn before the reaper' of the Beatles.

It wasn't just the music that swung America behind the group. Two hundred hard-bitten journalists turned up to meet them at the airport. They came to bury the four Mop Tops with their long hair and their funny clothes. They stayed to praise them. The New York *Herald Tribune* dismissed them as 'seventy-five percent publicity, twenty percent haircut and five percent lilting lament'. WNEW, the established radio station, also held out. Their top disc jockey, William B Williams, played a few bars of 'I Want to Hold Your Hand' and then earned himself a footnote in history by telling his audience: 'They want to hold your hand – a lot of people would like to hold their noses.' These dissenting voices were about to be silenced by the avalanche. Almost everyone else at that press conference was enchanted by their humour and irreverent wit.

'What do you think of the campaign in Detroit to stamp out the Beatles?' they were asked.

'We've got a campaign of our own to stamp out Detroit,' McCartney replied with a cute smile.

Everyone laughed. Even when they were being caustic, the Beatles had a way of delivering their lines which amused rather than offended. Pop stars had never behaved like this before. And, by an extraordinary metamorphosis, it was Ringo – the ill-educated drummer who considered himself lucky just to be in the group – who most encapsulated this spirit of wit and homely sophistication.

McCartney was astonished at the way America lionised Ringo. He held him in lesser regard and made his feelings plain enough for people to notice. Harry Benson thought it was to do with class

– that the socially aspiring McCartney looked down on Ringo and his rougher, backstreet attitudes and manners. Peter Brown says that McCartney's dismissiveness had more to do with Ringo's education. Yet it was Ringo, Brown insists, who deserved the greater share of the credit for the Beatles' American success. It is a view which, at first glance at the senior trinity of the group, makes little sense.

Lennon and McCartney wrote the songs. Lennon, when the Americans finally managed to sort out which Beatle was which, was seen to represent the rebellious element. Harrison was deemed to have a certain brooding appeal. McCartney, the best looking, the most obviously talented, the most amenable, was quickly labelled (to his quiet satisfaction) the 'star'.

Ringo appeared to be the least important factor in this equation. He was the new boy at the back often hidden behind one of the others, and in Britain he had never commanded any great following. The Americans, however, were enamoured by what they saw as his undernourished, waif-like pathos and for a now-all-but-forgotten while he was the most popular member of the group.

Far more important, from the viewpoint of the group's long-term success, was the way Ringo acted as the catalyst that brought the other elements together. Brown's view of Ringo's contribution is given illustration by the press conference where the Beatles were accused by an aggressive reporter of being four imitation Elvis Presleys. Harrison, ever 'the quiet one', stayed silent. Lennon visibly bristled. McCartney, the closest to the microphone, was confused by the insult. Before he could recover his aplomb, Ringo leapt forward.

Yes, he said, that's exactly what they were – and promptly convulsed into hip-waggling contortions, with the others dutifully following suit. It was amusing, and irresistible. A situation which had non-plussed the immaculate McCartney and disconcerted the scathing Lennon had been neatly diffused. The hard lessons learned on the streets of Dingle, where humour was the last line of defence, were paying extravagant dividends.

But if Ringo was the lovable clown, McCartney was still the

ringmaster of what was turning into an international circus. 'McCartney was the real Beatle,' Harry Benson says. 'He knew the image he wanted to project. He was the one who would always do things for publicity.' That willingness to tailor his behaviour to fit the public's expectations would lead to accusations of hypocrisy. 'But that,' Benson insists, 'was better than not doing anything at all,' which is what Lennon very soon decided he wanted to do.

It was always McCartney who was willing to pose for photographs, who was available to give an extra quote, ever keen to ingratiate himself with the 'men in suits' on whose goodwill they were still dependent. Away from the arc lights he could be truculent, arrogant even. But when he was on public show he was obligingly keen, almost 'subservient'. At the rehearsals for the Sullivan programme McCartney went out of his way to be polite. 'It was "Mr Sullivan, sir" all the way,' Benson recalls. The old showman Sullivan, like just about everyone else, was charmed by the Beatles. By now, of course, he knew he was on to a thing of epoch-making proportions.

The Plaza hotel, where the Beatles were staying (much to the chagrin of the management who thought they would be entertaining four British businessmen), was besieged by screaming fans. Other stations caught on to the wave of the trend started by WMCA, and Beatles records were being played every few minutes on almost every radio station in the city. Murray 'the K' Kaufman, the WINS disc jockey who called himself the Fifth Beatle, had inveigled himself into the Plaza and was broadcasting live from the Beatles' suite – and had gone to the top of the ratings as a consequence.

Sullivan himself was caught in the maelstrom. He had received over 50,000 requests for tickets for the show which was broadcast from a theatre that held only 700. With masterly aplomb, Sullivan passed all responsibility for what was happening over to his networked audience. He read out a welcoming telegram purporting to come from Elvis Presley (in fact the 'King' had nothing to do with it, it was sent as a publicity stunt by his manager 'Colonel' Parker). He then said: 'America, judge for yourself!'

America did. An estimated 73 million people, the largest television audience in history, tuned in to CBS that night to watch the Beatles sing 'All My Loving', 'Till There Was You', 'She Loves You', 'I Saw Her Standing There', and 'I Want to Hold Your Hand'.

It was the Beatles themselves who worked out what to play. 'Brian never interfered in their music,' says Peter Brown. 'Brian would talk with them and say what he thought would work from the point of view of popularity – and what the record companies wanted. But they always made the final decision about what they were going to play. They were all very savvy. They had been playing together for a long time. They knew what would work best in this particular circumstance.'

The reaction was one of overwhelming approval. 'I thought the Beatles would die in New York,' Frank Sinatra said. 'I was very surprised by the reception they got. I guess I was wrong.' And how. The second show, broadcast from Miami seven days later, broke the record they had just made by pulling in 75 million viewers. Sullivan's gamble in giving the 'unknown' group from England a chance had paid off beyond even that old trouper's wildest expectations – as had Epstein's presumptuous demand that the Beatles would appear only as headliners.

The financial aspects of the trip were less encouraging. Epstein got his way with the billing, but Sullivan allowed him no say in the production of the show. When Epstein said, 'I would like to know the exact wording of your introduction', Sullivan replied: 'I would like you to get lost.' And when it came to the money, Epstein got taken to the cleaners. Sullivan agreed to fly them to the States but that cost him nothing – their tickets had been provided as a 'promotional consideration' by Pan Am. The fee itself was a paltry $3,500 for each of the two appearances, plus $3,000 for taping. 'Even for an unknown act,' Precht said, 'that was about the least we could pay.'

The Bernstein-promoted concerts added another $7,000 to the balance sheet but with the actual cost of the trip adding up to around $50,000, the Beatles stood to lose as much as $30,000 – a staggering sum for a band that only a few months before had considered itself lucky if it earned £30 a night. But then money was never Epstein's strong point. His promotional flair combined with Lennon and McCartney's songwriting abilities and McCartney's instinct for showbusiness theatricality had created the Beatles phenomenon. And in that early dawn of Beatlemania there appeared to be no limit to what he could achieve. While 'Colonel' Tom Parker had confined himself to managing Presley, Epstein, in the manner of Larry Parnes, had gone out and built himself a stable.

Gerry and the Pacemakers had been signed to NEMS and they had had a number-one hit with 'How Do You Do It', the song the Beatles had turned down. A host of others had followed. They included Billy J Kramer and Priscilla White, the former cloakroom girl at the Cavern who had been persuaded up on to the club's stage to sing a song with the Beatles and had been immediately signed by Epstein who renamed her Cilla Black (Vic Hughes, the drummer with the Blackwells, thinks it was McCartney who persuaded Epstein to sign her 'because he fancied her', though in fairness to McCartney, no one appears to share that recollection). Also on his roster was Jane Asher's Cambridge-educated brother, Peter, who sang in a duo named Peter and Gordon. With a supply of Lennon and McCartney songs to draw on, all Epstein's acts were enjoying chart success. Whereas Parnes had only succeeded in Britain, Epstein's success was worldwide.

When it came to financial management, however, Epstein had neither the resources, the expertise, nor the 'nous'. NEMS was a whited sepulchre – glorious to behold in all its chart success but dangerously incompetent in its operation. If the Sullivan deal could be justified on the grounds of the exposure it would afford the Beatles, there was no excuse other than gross ineptitude for the way Epstein signed away millions of pounds. All the Beatles should have been millionaires for life within a few weeks of their American debut. They weren't and it would take years and a confetti of lawsuits to give them the financial security that should have been theirs, by right of talent, almost from the beginning.

Four months before they arrived in the United States Epstein had committed the Beatles to a three-picture deal with United Artists. Walter Shenson, the producer hired to make them, went to see Epstein with Bud Orenstein, head of UA's British operation. They offered the Beatles a salary of £25,000 for the first movie plus a percentage. 'He agreed to that,' Shenson recalled. 'Then we asked, "Mr Epstein, what would you consider a fair percentage of the picture?" Brian thought for a minute, then he said, "I couldn't accept anything less than seven and a half percent."' The UA men couldn't sign quickly enough. They had been prepared to offer 25 percent. For the price UA also got the rights to the movies' sound tracks (EMI had inexplicably forgotten to add in films in their gouging contract). To compound the mistake, all rights to the movies reverted to Shenson after fifteen years.

Even more spectacular in its incompetence was the way Epstein handled the merchandising contracts. Unaware of just how much money was at stake and without bothering to find out, Epstein gave his new London lawyer, David Jacobs, power of attorney to handle all negotiations. Jacobs, like Epstein a homosexual, was London's most powerful society solicitor with a well-deserved reputation for getting the transgressions of his clients swept under the legal carpet with a minimum of publicity. He was not, however, a contract lawyer and he, in turn, chose to pass on the responsibility for dealing with the licensing arrangements. He gave it to a young man named Nicky Byrne, a bright young member of what was then called the Chelsea Set whose most obvious qualification for the job was that he had once amused Jacobs at a party.

Byrne was at first strangely reluctant to accept this proffered licence to print money. The market was flooded with shoddily made Beatles merchandising ranging from wigs to lunch boxes with no one quite sure who was legally allowed to manufacture what. As Byrne complained, 'Brian Epstein had a very bad name in the business world at the time.' It was only on Jacobs's prompting that Byrne eventually agreed to accept the job. He formed a company called Stramsact to handle the British side of the business and a subsidiary named Seltaeb (Beatles spelt backwards) to look after the

American end. When Jacobs, who drew up the contract on NEMS' behalf, asked Byrne to write in his percentage, 'I put down the first figure that came into my head – ninety percent. To my amazement, David Jacobs didn't even question it. He didn't think of it as ninety percent to us, but ten percent to the Beatles. He said, "Well, ten percent is better than nothing."'

The full enormity of this financial catastrophe was impressed on Epstein shortly after the Beatles appeared on the Ed Sullivan show. Beatle wigs were selling at the rate of 35,000 a day. There were Beatle games, ice-creams, masks, counterpanes, biscuits, T-shirts. Woolworth and JC Penny started negotiating to open Beatle counters in their nationwide stores.

When Byrne, fresh from 'fixing' the Beatles' airport reception, met up with Epstein in New York, he handed him a cheque for $9,700.

'How much of this do I owe you?' Epstein asked.

'Nothing,' Byrne replied. 'That's your ten percent.' Ten percent of the first $97,000 Byrne had already banked of a business which the *Wall Street Journal* estimated would gross $50 million by the year's end.

Epstein professed himself pleased. Byrne recalled Epstein saying: 'You must work for *me*, Nicky. I'll make you a president, I'll give you a thousand a year.' Byrne thought he was joking. 'Then all of a sudden I realised he was crazy.'

In Epstein's defence Peter Brown argues: 'If you're in almost any kind of business these days, there is somewhere you know where to start. You look at what was done before. But in the case of the Beatles, truly almost everything we did was the first time it had ever been done. It was very difficult to know what to do. They were a rock-and-roll band. No one had any conception of their long-term wealth or value or that they would be a major part of the history of the second part of the twentieth century.'

Epstein wasn't so crazy that he did not know, however, that if the Beatles, and especially McCartney who had always harboured reservations about Epstein's abilities, discovered just how much money he had signed away, his future association with the group was likely to be a short one. The Beatles, McCartney said, were in rock and roll for the fun, and to avoid having to 'get a proper job'. But, as he also pointed out, they were in it for the money too. And Epstein had just lost them a fortune of several million pounds.

He did the only thing he could think of: he didn't tell them. Then he set about trying to salvage something from the financial wreckage. He started signing merchandising contracts himself. But because he was doing so without reference to Byrne, two or more manufacturers often ended up with the same licence. Lawsuits followed. In turn Byrne and NEMS became involved in a $22 million lawsuit, which ended with an out-of-court settlement to Byrne of £10,000. More dangerously, some $80 million dollars' worth of contracts ended up being cancelled. In the ensuing chaos threats of retribution were made against Epstein.

These fiascos were the seed capital for McCartney's later hostility towards Epstein. 'Rip off' is the phrase he uses to describe what happened. He is too intelligent, too streetwise to ever let it happen to him again and the financial debacle shaped the rest of his life.

McCartney was always careful about money – as Pete Best had observed, he was always the last to offer his cigarettes or buy his round of drinks. After this he became more parsimonious, more determined to keep control of what he believed was his – and sometimes much more than others considered his rightful due. It would lead him into bitter legal conflict with the three other young men from whom he had appeared inseparable in those halcyon days when the world went Beatle-mad and the Four Mops from Liverpool seemed to personify everything that was fresh and honest and exciting.

It would also expose the irreconcilable contradiction in his personality – the dichotomy of wanting his own way but wanting to be liked at the same time. That can lead him to justify the most ruthless act of self-interest with transparently inconsistent pledges of praise and support. He would happily call Ringo Starr 'the greatest drummer in the world' – then dub over the drum tracks himself after

Ringo had left the studio. During the making of the *White Album* Ringo quit the group because of the criticism he was receiving and, according to Peter Brown, it was McCartney 'who played drums on at least "Back in the USSR"'. He would praise Harrison's songwriting abilities – but refuse to collaborate with him. He would maintain that the Beatles were a partnership – and then insist on taking charge. They are actions that give fuel to those charges of 'hypocrisy' that dog him into his middle age. McCartney himself sees it in a different light, arguing that whatever he did was done, not for himself, but for the good of his 'family': his group and, later, his wife, his children, the finer principles of musical integrity, and, more recently, for the rights of animals.

In this amalgam of contradictions the constant has been his determination to keep control of his finances. It still rankles that he did not take a closer interest in them earlier. In those early days of Beatlemania, however, McCartney, like everyone else, was being swept along by an irresistible tide beyond his comprehension – and, as he would later discover to his chagrin, that of his manager. Only Harrison took the time to ask how much they were earning, where the money was going, and he didn't understand what the answers he was given really meant. McCartney was still only 21, still overwhelmed by what was happening to the Beatles, to him, still, though with increasing reservations, prepared to leave the money side to Epstein.

Says Jill Haworth: 'He was very shy. He was amazed by the reception they were receiving. He was flabbergasted. They all were. They couldn't believe it.' Jill Haworth is the Bognor-born actress who five years before, at the age of 14, had been selected by director Otto Preminger to play the part of the young concentration-camp victim in the film, *Exodus*. She was later unofficially engaged to the actor Sal Mineo. In February 1964 she was to be found in the company of Paul McCartney.

They met at a press conference at the Plaza hotel where she had been taken by a friend who wrote for one of the fan magazines. McCartney took an immediate shine to her. Shortly afterwards he visited her apartment. 'He came round for tea, believe it or not,' she says. 'He wanted a good cup of tea and he couldn't get it in the Plaza and he came to my apartment.'

It was a foolhardy thing to do. The Plaza was surrounded by fans and the Beatles, as Jill recalls, 'couldn't even put their heads out of the window without causing chaos'. To leave the hotel without an escort was to risk serious injury. But he made it. 'He came by a cab,' Jill says. 'He just walked out with a scarf over his head. I guess everyone was expecting all the limousines and all the craziness.'

Even the best-laid plans of a Beatle could go astray, however. Jill wasn't there. She was on her way to the Plaza to see him. McCartney ended doing exactly what he said he wanted to do – drinking tea, but with Nancy, Jill's mother. It was not until Miami where she joined him for the second Sullivan Show that they got to know each other properly.

'He called up and said, "Do you want to come down?"' Jill remembers. 'I said, all right. He paid, somebody did. I know I didn't.' The Beatles were staying at the Beauville on Miami Beach. In the interests of discretion she was put in another hotel. 'A car would be sent for me to take me over there,' she says. Finding the opportunity to be alone 'wasn't easy. For one thing, they doubled up in rooms', with Paul usually sharing with Harrison. For another, McCartney 'had a girlfriend back in England; he had Jane Asher', and he was anxious to keep this friendship out of camera range of the besieging press. Despite such tactical difficulties, the two became close friends. 'He was charming, very charming, not a bit cocky,' she says. 'I suppose he was witty but it was really Lennon who was the witty one who made everyone laugh. Paul was quieter. He was sweet.'

Even McCartney's fabled cuteness started to fray a little, though, as the 'craziness' kept building and building towards a crescendo that never quite arrived. They played three shows on the first American trip, the first at the 8092-seat Coliseum in Washington, and two at New York's famed Carnegie Hall. They couldn't hear themselves play above the screams. They would never again be able to hear themselves when they were playing live.

The outings from their hotels became less and less frequent. In New York McCartney had managed to take Jill to a nightclub. They went to the famed Peppermint Lounge, birthplace of the Twist, where the resident band, the Epics, had donned Beatle wigs and given an impersonation of their famous guests. On another evening McCartney had visited the Playboy Club and left with a willing Bunny girl. Murray the K had also managed to talk Ronnie and Mary of the singing trio, the Ronettes, past the security guards at the Plaza for an introduction to Lennon and Harrison.

But as their fame grew – they couldn't turn on a television or open a newspaper without seeing themselves – the Beatles found themselves imprisoned by their own celebrity. Even a cup of tea with Nancy Haworth became out of the question. The limousine lifestyle had been replaced by armoured cars. When they went for a roast-beef dinner at the home of Buddy Dresner, the Miami police sergeant assigned to guard them, they had to leave their hotel in the back of a requisitioned butcher's truck.

Forced to live on top of each other they became irritable. To pass the time they amused themselves by getting Ringo to telephone down to room service and order up the most expensive things they could think of, like a bottle of the finest Remy Martin cognac. When it arrived they would take a few sips and then order something else. At the Beauville hotel they would phone down and ask the management to clear the pool so they could go for a swim. 'They thought that was great fun,' says Benson.

A silly competitiveness started up between them. If one of them got a plastic sword or a woolly doll, they all wanted one. There was also a furious row over the girls that were being allowed into their rooms. Epstein, terrified that one of them would be caught with an underage fan which would have 'ruined them before they got started', tried to restrict them to prostitutes. Before they were allowed up to see the Beatles, the girls had first to be vetted by Mal Evans and others and they, as is the way of roadies, kept the best-looking ones for themselves. The Beatles eventually found out. Lennon, for whom the presence of his wife Cynthia, who was having a terrible time of it, had proved no great impediment to his extramarital engagements, was particularly incensed. He blamed Epstein for lumbering them 'with the grotty ones'. It was left to McCartney to sooth tempers. The attractive qualities of their nocturnal visitors improved noticeably after that.

There were other, more personal strains. McCartney, as ever obsessed with his own vision of perfection, started rowing with Harrison, complaining about his guitar playing, talking to him without looking at him. The others complained, jokingly at first, but soon with an edge of irritation to their voices, at the way Paul always pushed his way to the front during the photo calls. McCartney, in turn, was upset by the way the American press kept calling Lennon the Beatles' leader. He had acknowledged as much himself in the first radio interview the Beatles ever gave, to Cleaver and Clatterbridge hospital radio in the Wirral on 27 October 1962, when he said, 'John Lennon is the leader of the group.' But that was eighteen months and several McCartney-written records ago. To hear the Americans say it rankled. 'He used to get his feelings hurt,' says Benson. 'John would always deny it and say that the Beatles didn't have a leader, but he certainly believed it himself. McCartney would look sullen whenever it was mentioned. He would raise the glass he was holding and look through it.'

In Miami McCartney went into a sulk for another reason. In a few days' time Cassius Clay was fighting Sonny Liston for the heavyweight championship. Attempts were made for the Beatles to meet Liston. That growling bear of a man refused to have anything to do with what he called 'a bunch of faggots', so instead of the champion and odds-on favourite they were driven out to the training camp and introduced to the future Mohammad Ali.

Harry Benson took the photographs that day. He recalls: 'Clay mesmerised them. He completely controlled them. He shouted, "Get down, you little worms!" and they all lay down on the canvas.'

Clay said: 'You're the singing champs of the world, right? It's proper that you should want to meet me because I'm the greatest champion the boxing world is ever going to know.' The Beatles didn't want to know and hadn't wanted to meet him. 'They were furious,' Benson remembers.

McCartney was asked who he thought was going to win the fight. 'Clay, I suppose, because he's the funniest,' he replied. He was being tactful. McCartney, aware as always of his 'image', was actually convinced that Liston was going to win and angrily blamed Benson for involving them 'with a loser'. As events would have it Clay won his fight with Liston in dramatic style; by luck not judgement the singing champs of the world had met the right man after all.

The outcome in Washington where they played their first American concert, organised at the last minute by Epstein and his newly appointed US lawyer, Nat Weiss, in an attempt to make good some of the trip's losses, was not so felicitous. They were supposed to fly there but a heavy snowstorm and a collective rock-and-roll memory of Buddy Holly's death in similar weather conditions had necessitated a change of travel arrangements and, on Harrison's insistence, they made the journey by train. One of McCartney's amorous transgressions caught up with him on the way.

Back in Hamburg a young woman was claiming that he was the father of her daughter. The story had reached Britain. The *Daily Express* ordered its New York correspondent, David English, to put the matter to McCartney. English travelled to Washington with the Beatles in their private rail carriage. The Cute One was in grand mood, smoking, drinking, moving among his courtiers. What he wasn't doing was answering questions. Whenever English quietly tried to broach the subject with him, McCartney would reply, 'Later, later,' and move off again.

English, now the knighted editor of the *Daily Mail*, was a tenacious reporter. He chose his moment with finesse. There were scores of journalists waiting at the station for the Beatles. As McCartney, back in smiling PR mode, stepped on to the platform at Union Station English shouted out, 'Paul, there's a woman who says she's had your child . . .'

McCartney rounded on English. 'Oh fuck, why did you have to say that *now*?' English looked blank.

It was the Beatles' second brush with scandal. In New York Epstein had entertained a party of rent boys in his suite at the Plaza and one of the gutter tabloids had lowered a photographer down the side of the hotel in a bosun's chair to take pictures through the window of the un-American activities taking place. The photographs were shown to Byrne who promptly bought them out of the marketplace.

The story of the illegitimate child went the same way. Like so many other incidents that might have cast a shadow over the image of the Fab Four, it was consigned to the archives. The American public wanted the Beatles squeaky clean. So did the British, chauvinistically proud of this most visible export. The press, reflecting the wishes of their readers, chose to ignore their peccadillos and excesses. The Beatles were enjoying an immunity from criticism only afforded to the royal family. What they didn't enjoy, at least not yet, was the respect afforded to those whose regal status was inherited.

Brian Somerville, their public relations officer, had arranged for them to be invited to the British embassy. After a private champagne reception they went on to an embassy-organised ball. The upperclass embassy staff treated the lower-middle-class Liverpudlians with unconcealed contempt.

'They can actually write!' a middle-aged woman in a pink dress shouted as they started signing autographs. When Lennon said that they wouldn't be able to sign autographs for everyone, they were surrounded by a group of young men with cut-glass BBC accents and old school ties who arrogantly informed the Beatles: 'Yes you can – and you will.' In the final dénouement an 18-year-old gatecrasher named Beverly Markowitz took a pair of scissors out of her handbag and snipped off a lock of hair from behind Ringo's left ear. Ringo complained: 'This lot are terrifying.'

Harry Benson was at the party. He recalls: 'They were treated like yobs.' For once the Beatles' cheerful self-possession deserted them. They had never been to anything quite that grand and they were out of their social depth. They had the strained look of people without an escape. Says Benson: 'They were sad. They looked as if they wanted to cry, Lennon in particular. And they were stuck, they couldn't get out. They weren't pugnacious – they were humiliated.'

Sir David Ormsby-Gore, who succeeded to the title of Lord Harlech on the death of his father two days later, was the British ambassador. An intelligent, urbane man who came to epitomise the modern, 'with it' aristocrat and whose daughters, Jane and Alice, became notable figures in the Beatles-inspired counter-culture, he was disturbed by the treatment meted out to the Beatles. So was his wife, Sylvia (after her death in 1967 Harlech squired President Kennedy's widow, Jackie). As the Beatles left she went over and apologised to them. 'It couldn't have been much fun for you,' she said. 'I really am terribly sorry about the scene in the ballroom.'

Epstein neatly defused what threatened to become a diplomatic incident by writing a polite thank-you note to Lady Ormsby-Gore. When the Conservative MP Joan Quennell asked the Foreign Secretary if it was true that the group had been manhandled by embassy staff, Rab Butler was able to reply that, on the contrary, he had a note from the Beatles' manager saying how much they had enjoyed the evening. Privately, however, Epstein vowed that his 'boys' would never again be put on display for the amusement of government officials, no matter how important – a policy that would backfire dangerously on them in the Philippines two years later.

Yet whatever the slights and despite the seeds of long-term problems that had been planted, that first visit to the United States had been a glorious, unique success. America, which only a few weeks before had never even heard of the Beatles, had been ravished by the music and the cheeky charm of four young men from Liverpool.

No entertainment act had ever enjoyed such a complete and total triumph. Epstein's prediction that the Beatles would be bigger than Elvis had been proved right.

7

FOR two sublime years the Beatles enjoyed a celebrity that spanned the globe. Their photographs hung like icons on the walls of suburban American bedrooms and African mud huts. Their records were worldwide number ones. Their first film, A *Hard Day's Night*, was a huge critical and box-office success and they were hailed as the new Marx Brothers. Their hairstyle and clothes redressed a generation. They were courted by presidents and prime ministers and the Queen of England hummed their tunes and made them MBEs. Their concert tours were sell-outs and in Adelaide, Australia, over 300,000 people turned out into the streets to see them – the largest crowd of its kind in history. On 4 April 1964, they had the top five singles in the Billboard chart and seven others in the Top 100, an unprecedented and unrepeatable feat.

McCartney revelled in it. 'Hey man, the performance, there's no substitute,' he said. 'If I was some 24-year-old bachelor I sure as hell would want to be on tour, just for the women.'

In those two years when they toured the world they presented a unified picture – four men moulded into one image, their individual personalities submerged in the whole. 'We spent more time together in the early days than John and Yoko,' Yoko's John later observed. 'The four of us sleeping in the same room, practically in the same bed, in the same truck, living together night and day, eating, shitting and pissing together. Doing *everything* together.'

Epstein, still consumed by the fantasy he had helped create, wanted to enshrine that togetherness in bricks and mortar, in a suburban compound of mock-Tudor mansions with a house for himself on the Beatles' estate. For a while it looked as if he might get his way. Lennon and his wife, Cynthia, were installed in a £30,000 home in Weybridge, Ringo and his new wife, Maureen, in a similar house nearby. George, who would soon marry Patti Boyd, the elfin model he had met on the set of A *Hard Day's Night* – the title came from a saying of Ringo's – bought a bungalow in Esher.

McCartney broke the dream. He wanted nothing to do with Epstein's ludicrous reworking of JM Barrie's story of Peter Pan and the Lost Boys that would lock them together forever in sunny adolescence. Leafy suburbia held no allure for him. If McCartney was going to live a fantasy it was the one of Swinging London.

Socially adept, inherently intelligent, fascinated by the intellectual milieu the Ashers had introduced him to, he preferred the stimulus of the city *Time* magazine had declared to be the most avant-garde, the most exciting, the most innovative in the world. He attended the theatre, went to concerts, developed an interest in modern art, drank the fashionable Scotch and Coke in fashionable nightclubs like the Ad Lib and the Scotch of St James's, cultivated the rich, like Guinness heir Tara Browne, and the famous, like opera singer Joan Sutherland. He drove an Aston Martin and, as was only right for any paid-up member of the 'in crowd', a customised Mini Cooper. And when he eventually bought a house it wasn't in the stockbroker belt but right in the heart of London, in the upper-class area of St John's Wood.

'*I* was there when all these things started to happen in London,' he reminds us. Let the others rot away beside their golf courses in 'bloody' suburbia; *he* was imbued with the feeling special to the age that things, as he sang, were getting better. The council estates and the meagre wages and the social restrictions seemed of the past. Now anything seemed possible and for McCartney it was. He was the prince of a new golden era that blended aristocrats with the new meritocracy, spoke with a regional, working-class accent (real or, in the case of Mick Jagger, affected), made heroes out of photographers and models and hairdressers, came swathed in colourful raiments – and shrouded in its own exotic incense.

The Beatles and Epstein had been introduced to marijuana by Bob Dylan at the Delmonico hotel in New York on 28 August 1964. What do you want to drink, they had politely asked the pop poet when he was introduced to them in their suite. 'Cheap wine,' Dylan replied. The Beatles, still ordering according to price, only had expensive wine to offer. Dylan suggested a joint. 'We've never smoked marijuana,' Epstein replied. Dylan was astonished. 'What about your song?' he asked. He was referring to 'I Want to Hold Your Hand', and started singing '. . . and when I touch you I get high, I get high . . .' The words, Lennon sheepishly corrected him, were '. . . I can't hide.'

It was about time then, Dylan replied, for less concealment and more elevation. The curtains were drawn, wet towels placed at the foot of the bolted door. After half an hour of preparation, Dylan was at last allowed to light up. He passed the joint to Lennon who fearfully passed it on to Ringo whom he dubbed 'my royal taster'. Ringo took a hit and soon afterwards started laughing. The others, in their turn, followed suit.

McCartney was overwhelmed. 'I was thinking, I'm *really* thinking for the first time,' he declared. It was the beginning of a lifetime's psychological addiction that would lead him to prison. It would also have a noticeable effect on his music. As it did on Lennon's. Their simple, 'I love, she loves' lyrics gave way to more textured compositions like 'Eleanor Rigby', a poignant study of loneliness inspired by the subconscious recollection of the name on the gravestone in the churchyard where he first met Lennon. The competition between the two songwriters is illustrated in the song. Lennon would later claim: 'I wrote a good lot of the lyrics, about seventy percent.' To which McCartney replied: 'He says he helped on "Eleanor Rigby". Yeh – about half a line.'

McCartney, overdosing on stimuli, maintains that he 'got the name Rigby from a shop in Bristol' when he was walking about waiting for Jane Asher who was rehearsing a play at the repertory theatre. 'And I think Eleanor was from Eleanor Bron, the actress we worked with in the film, *Help!*' The subconscious memory of that name in the cemetery cannot be discounted, however. But whatever its origins, 'Eleanor Rigby', who, as McCartney said, 'didn't make it, never made it with anyone, didn't even look as if she was going to', was a significant improvement on 'I want to hold your hand'. And when the psychedelic ingredient of LSD was added and combined with the inspiration of Dylan's poetic explorations, the Beatles' music acquired an impetus which gave artistic and cultural direction to a generation.

'We'd heard of Ellington and Basie and jazz guys smoking a bit of pot, and now it arrived on our music scene,' McCartney said. 'It coloured our perceptions. I think we started to realise there weren't as many frontiers as we'd thought there were. And we realised we could break down barriers.'

What didn't change was McCartney's ability to turn out melodies of stunning quality. 'I've developed a system of how to write "McCartney" kind of stuff,' he says. 'I just sit down and I'm in the mood and I grab a guitar and I get lucky. I'll hit some chord that interests me and in that there is the opening chords. Simplicity is the best thing.'

'Yesterday' is McCartney's genius at its simple best. The song, he says, 'fell out of bed' in the Ashers' Wimpole Street home. 'I had a piano by my bedside and I must have dreamed it because I tumbled out of bed and put my hands on the piano keys and I had a tune in my head. It was just all there, a complete thing.' Even McCartney himself, whose tunes glide down a conveyor belt, was astounded. 'It came too easy . . . I couldn't believe it,' and for a while he didn't. 'I didn't believe I'd written it. I thought maybe I'd heard it before, it was some other tune, and I went around for weeks playing the chords of the song for people, asking them, "Is this *like* something? I *think* I've written it." And people would say, "No, it's not like anything else, but it's good."'

The working title was 'Scrambled Eggs' and when he played it to Alma Cogan, the statuesque 1950s singing star whose friendship he was courting, in her apartment, he cutely sang, 'Scrambled eggs, Oh, how I love your legs.' There was a 'harder edge' to the finished version. '"Yesterday" isn't cute,' he says. '"I'm not half the man I used to be" – that's pretty strong. And remember, I wrote it when I was 24.' (In fact, he wrote it when he was 22 – it was recorded at the Abbey Road studios on 14 June 1965, four days before his 23rd birthday.) It is, he says, 'the most complete thing I've ever written. It's very catchy without being sickly.'

Typically, he needed other people to tell him how good the song was before he realised it himself. McCartney has never been a sound judge of his own material. He seems incapable of exercising quality control. The melodies are produced on demand – because he wakes up with it in his head, because he needs another track for an album, because he likes showing off – in a matter of minutes. Says Peter Brown: 'Because he is so prolific he is not really aware of the quality. It's stream of consciousness. He puts it down, and that's it, he's on to the next project.'

If they all carry the distinctive McCartney hallmark, many would benefit from a little honing, which was where Lennon was so important. McCartney was always wary of Lennon and that markedly improved the quality of his songwriting; fearful of being subjected to his partner's scorn, McCartney worked hard to avoid it. Peter Brown recalls: 'It was not a dominant–supplicant relationship but if Lennon didn't like something he would tell McCartney.' They did not row, not at this stage; it was more a case of casual hints, perhaps a caustic look, a suggestion here and there. Lennon would add a verse, or a middle break; he would take a 'story that Paul would start' and then figure out where to go with it.

It was a contribution that could immeasurably improve a song. The example of that is 'I Saw Her Standing There'. Paul had written it in the living room of Forthlin Road one afternoon when he was playing truant from grammar school. The original lyrics were: 'she was just seventeen, she was a beauty queen'. It was Lennon who changed the second line to, 'You know what I mean' – and didn't that make the difference.

Lennon's help was not required on 'Yesterday' but it needed George Martin to take charge and point the song in its rightful direction. This was not a 'Beatle song', he ruled, to be played to a backing of guitars and drums. Instead a string quartet was hired. 'It was on "Yesterday" that we first used instruments or musicians other than the Beatles and myself,' he said. 'It was the turning point', the moment when the Beatles 'started breaking out of the phase of using just four instruments and went into something more experimental'.

With telling insight into his own musical judgement, McCartney says: 'The hits are the ones that you thought wouldn't be hits, like "Yesterday" or "Mull of Kintyre". I didn't want to put them out.'

'Mull of Kintyre' would become the top-selling record of all time in Britain. 'Yesterday' was issued as a single in the United States on 13 September 1965. It went to number one and held the top spot for four weeks. It has since been recorded by over 2,500 artists, including Frank Sinatra, Lou Rawls, Ray Charles and, rather less impressively, the Californian surfin' duet of Jan and Dean, making it the most covered song in the history of popular music. It has been played on the radio over five million times, two million more than any other song. Even Lennon was impressed. 'Wow, that was a good one,' he said. 'Well done, beautiful.'

It wasn't all McCartney. The Beatles hadn't yet turned into a one-man band. Ringo had been the undoubted star of A Hard Day's Night, his engaging naturalness diverting attention from McCartney's decidedly more wooden performance.

Lennon enjoyed considerable success with In His Own Write, the McCartney-suggested title for his book of Lewis Carrollesque jottings. The Times Literary Supplement declared it worthy of study by 'anyone who fears for the impoverishment of the English language'. It was praise more extravagant than McCartney thought it worthy of and he was right. 'People said it was Joycean, like James Joyce,' McCartney observed. 'And John said, "Who's he?" I mean, we didn't have that kind of schooling.' What he meant was that

Lennon, Ringo and Harrison hadn't – McCartney, on the other hand, was the A-level English student and he helped Lennon with the book. He denied, however, that he was in any way jealous of Lennon's literary triumph.

'It wasn't a question of envying each other – each of us was as good as the other,' he insisted.

They were now. As they grew older the age gap narrowed and McCartney no longer held his partner in quite the awe he had when they first met. Separated from his Beatles 'family' when they weren't touring, the cocky self-assurance of the elder child reasserted itself. If the group was still the centre, it was no longer the only focus of his life.

He had as a girlfriend Jane Asher, who came from a background very different from his own. She gave, Cynthia Lennon drily observed, 'an enormous boost to Paul's ambitious ego'. He started acquiring the accoutrements befitting his new status. He opened an account at Coutts, bankers to the Queen. He would order Jane's birthday cake from Maxim's in Paris. He paid £40,000 for the house in elegant Cavendish Avenue, St John's Wood, hired a married couple as housekeeper and butler, and got a dog, an Old English sheepdog named Martha. There was deep-pile grey and brown carpet on the floors. The master bathroom was decorated with imported tiles and had a tub large enough for two. The glass came from Tiffany. The Porthault bed linen was changed daily. Home life for Paul and Jane who, for decorum's sake, never lived there officially, was not quite as elegant as it might have been, however.

The house stank of cats' urine. The large garden at the back was left to follow its chaotic devices and duly ran riot. Inspired by the spirit of the age and the copious quantities of marijuana he was smoking, he set about constructing a domed building at the bottom of the garden 'for meditation'. Cushions were strewn over the floor which was supposed to rise electronically into the glass roof. The project never got off the ground, largely because McCartney refused to accept any professional advice. The plans kept being changed, the south London contractor became confused. And when the cost, the only thing that did rise, reached £7,000 (a rich man's annual salary in the mid-1960s) McCartney became 'hysterical'. The dome was a folly, evidence of McCartney's grandeur, but still the gentrification continued.

On Jane's prompting, he bought High Farm, a 183-acre farm in Scotland near the Mull of Kintyre. His success had lifted him out of his background and he acquired a new and appropriately exalted circle of acquaintances who were far more worldly and cultivated than anyone he had known in Liverpool or Hamburg.

Like his parents before him, McCartney has never enjoyed a close relationship with anyone who was not 'family' or, in his case, employee. But if he was reluctant to make the emotional concessions necessary to form real friendships, he still enjoyed mixing with the famous and went out of his way to cultivate them, sometimes to the neglect of the people he was supposed to be close to. Producer Walter Shenson recalls attending a dinner party with McCartney. 'Joan Sutherland, the opera singer, just happened to be there. Paul zeroed in on her at once as the big star.' Shenson and his wife and Jane Asher were ignored for the rest of the evening.

As irritating as McCartney's fondness for the eminent could be, it did have its occasional advantage. It was always Paul who was prepared to shake hands and make the appropriate noises. He did just that when the Beatles went to Rome and Noël Coward, who was on holiday there and staying in the same hotel, informed Brian Epstein that he wanted to meet them.

Epstein was very excited about meeting the famous playwright – and mortified when Lennon declared that he had no interest in meeting 'that old poofter'. Ringo and Harrison sided with John. Paul, well aware of the embarrassment their no-show would cause, quickly agreed to go up to Coward's suite where he was his usual cute, engaging self. Coward declared himself 'charmed' by McCartney and told him to pass on to the others his congratulations on their international success.

He was perfectly well aware, however, that he had just been

George Martin, the musical genius who created the Beatles sound. He wanted to rename the group 'Paul McCartney and the Beatles'. *(Topham)*

The launch of *Sergeant Pepper*, the most influential rock album of all time and the apogee of McCartney's creativity. *(Pictorial Press)*

Jane Asher with her fiancé in October 1967, not long before the final break-up. *(Pictorial Press)*

John, Jane and Paul in search of Nirvana, 1968. *(Pictorial Press)*

Yoko and John with son Julian, 1968. *(Topham)*

snubbed. 'The message I would have liked to send them was that they were bad-mannered little shits,' Coward wrote. Appearances, though, had been maintained – and that has always been a vital consideration to the PR-minded McCartney.

This element of social acquisition carried through into his life. He started mixing with a set of rich young sophisticates, the most renowned of whom was Tara Browne, a cousin of the Guinness clan chief, the Earl of Iveagh. A handsome, high-living young man barely out of his teens, Browne owned Dandy Fashions in Chelsea where McCartney had started buying his clothes.

'Tara was startling looking, he was the most elaborate dresser in London and McCartney was transfixed,' says Ireland's premier viscount the 17th Lord Gormanston, who knew them both and often joined them in their carousing.

Dragged around by his mother, Oonagh, Lady Oranmore and Browne, Tara had 'seen more of the world by the time he was a teenager than most people see in a lifetime', and had a self-possession that was aristocratically grand. One famous story about him is an incident that occurred at Claridge's hotel where, at the age of 14, he had haughtily informed the waiter, 'I asked for cold vichyssoise, not hot vichyssoise, you c—'

'Tara was very calm, very laid-back, very confident. McCartney was much more intrigued by Tara than the other way round,' says Nicholas Gormanston.

The Beatle became a regular visitor at Browne's Belgravia mews home where they would smoke marijuana and spend hours listening to music and watching the oil and water 'dream machine' pictures on the wall. This was the drug age and Browne was in the vanguard. There were always drugs on offer at his home. McCartney took the offered cocaine but resisted the LSD, a remarkable exercise in restraint given its ready availability – Michael Holingshead, the 'man who turned on the world' and first acquainted Harvard's Dr Timothy 'tune in, turn on, drop out' Leary with the hallucinogenic drug, was another member of the Tara Browne set. But even without swallowing one of the impregnated sugar cubes that littered the coffee table, McCartney was being influenced by psychedelia – by the clothes and the underground music and use of colour which were starting to make their impression on London, with Browne as one of their leading propagandists.

Lennon was also influenced by the young aristocrat. Browne owned a sports-car dealership in Drayton Gardens in Kensington and had had one of his vehicles – an AC Cobra – painted in psychedelic colours. McCartney was impressed by this example of rich hippy indulgence. So was Lennon. When McCartney told him about the AC Cobra he promptly had his Rolls Royce painted the same way.

The friendship between Browne and McCartney lasted about a year. 'McCartney had a lot of charm and had fitted in well,' says Lord Gormanston. McCartney went so far as introduce Browne to his father. The elder McCartney must have been somewhat taken aback by his son's choice of friends.

Shortly after the Beatles had conquered the United States Paul asked Jim McCartney if he would like to retire. 'Dad, strangely enough, agreed,' Paul's brother recalls. McCartney installed his father and brother in a £8,750 house with three indoor bathrooms 'across the water away from it all' in the salubrious stockbroker belt of Heswall in Cheshire, an area Jim had always admired but could never have afforded. The elder McCartney moved there from Forthlin Road at midnight. 'We don't want any fuss, son,' he explained. The new house was called Rembrandt and its 'extreme luxury, from comparative poverty, remember, was quite a contrast, to say the least,' Michael remembers.

McCartney was a frequent visitor to Rembrandt, the kind of home his mother had always aspired to, and he enjoyed the domesticity it symbolised – the garden, the outlook, Sunday lunches with his father at one of the upmarket pubs in the area. Browne and some of his other fast friends would sometimes drive up from London to visit McCartney at the house. They were not always in sparkling form by the time they arrived. On one occasion a group of them stopped by at Holingshead's 'psychedelic centre' in Pont Street,

Belgravia, to pick up some LSD for the chauffeur-driven drive north. They had an Alsatian dog in the car with them. Somewhere on the M1 someone got the bright idea of feeding an acid tab to the dog. The dog was given a LSD-coated sugar lump – and promptly went berserk. It was a carload of bedraggled people and one freaked-out dog that eventually arrived at Baskervyle Road overlooking the river Dee with views across to the hills of North Wales.

If Jim McCartney had an inkling of what was going on, he never let on. While they smoked their 'funny cigarettes' he would content himself with a fine Montecristo Havana cigar. 'He seemed rather amused by it all – and very proud of his famous son,' says Lord Gormanston.

The son appeared to share his father's easy-going attitude to events. 'Paul was always very civil and jolly,' Lord Gormanston recalls. Even so, there was something about McCartney that did not seem quite right. 'You always felt a little uneasy about him,' says Lord Gormanston. 'What you saw was what he wanted you to see.' The barrier of self-possession that McCartney had constructed around himself remained in place, even in the drug-drenched environment of Tara's Belgravia mews house. In the end Browne got bored with McCartney and started seeing more of Brian Jones of the Rolling Stones who was more his 'speed'.

In 1966 Browne was killed driving a Lotus. The Beatles immortalised him in 'A Day in the Life' in the line, 'He blew his mind out in a car'. He had been a dazzling addition to the Beatles entourage. He was, after all, an aristocrat – still an important consideration in Britain at the time – and McCartney had been flattered by his attention, though exactly what kind of aristocrat he was the lad from Liverpool never managed to work out. As Lord Gormanston says: 'McCartney really wasn't sure if he was from the House of Lords.' Which, as the younger son of a lord whose title was subject to the rule of primogeniture, he wasn't.

By then McCartney had a title of his own. On 12 June 1965, the Labour Prime Minister Harold Wilson announced that the Beatles were to be given Membership of the Most Excellent Order of the

British Empire. It was a typical manipulation of the honours system for political ends. By MBE standards they deserved it. The Beatles had earned millions of dollars for the Exchequer – much more, in fact, given the extortionate rate of tax, than they had earned for themselves – and as Lennon pointed out, 'If someone had got an award for exporting millions of dollars worth of manure or machines everyone would have applauded.'

Not everyone had applauded the Beatles' award. A number of previous recipients returned their medals in protest, including several Army officers, which prompted Lennon to remark that Army officers got their medals for 'killing people. We received ours for entertaining. I'd say we deserved ours more.'

Wilson was not put off by the protest. He has been charged with not merely honouring the Beatles, but also cynically attempting to woo the future votes of the emerging Baby Boom generation.

Lennon, who despised the British class structure, was predictably reluctant to accept the honour. McCartney, just as predictably, was delighted. 'I think it's marvellous – what does that make my Dad?' he asked. The Queen, McCartney commented after their investiture on October 26, was 'like a mum'. Buckingham Palace, he observed, was a 'keen pad'.

Asked if they had been scared, Lennon had replied: 'Not as much as some of the others in there.' That relaxed approach to the occasion had been assured by the marijuana joints he had hidden in his Beatle boot and which they had smoked in the lavatory before they were ushered into the Queen's presence. Even at this ultimate moment of compromise, Lennon was sticking two fingers up at the establishment that was courting him – but only when he was sure no one was looking, like a mischievous schoolboy sticking his tongue out behind the teacher's back. The carefully constructed image which had been forced on him by Epstein and McCartney and which he so resented had still to be preserved. The Beatles depended on it for their livelihood, which was substantially derived from touring the United States. A drug bust then would have ended their North American career and even Lennon, as irritated as he was with the mould he had been squeezed into, was not prepared to risk that.

Behind the public rendering, however, the edifice of Beatledom was starting to crumble. The Beatles had enjoyed playing before a live audience and McCartney had been thrilled with the screaming adulation that greeted them when they went on stage. 'I liked that then because that was that kind of time,' he said. 'I used to feel that that was kind of like a football match. They came just to cheer; the cheering turned into screaming when it translated into young girls. People used to say, "Well, isn't it a drag, because no one listens to your music?" But some of the time it was good they didn't because some of the time we were playing pretty rough.'

Even McCartney was starting to find it a chore, however. Harrison called it 'a nightmare'. Cities came and went in a meaningless blur. They were kept locked in their hotel rooms, rushed out on to stage, then, while the last sobs of adolescent frenzy still hung in the air, they were smuggled away and flown on to the next engagement. They couldn't hear themselves play above the screams and after a while they didn't bother to try; sometimes Lennon would scream obscenities instead of lyrics into the microphone. It never made the slightest difference.

'Every year we were Beatling was like twenty . . . it seemed like an eternity,' Harrison recalled. 'It might have been fun for everybody else, but *we* never saw the Beatles. We're the only people who never got to see us. We were like four relatively sane people in the middle of madness.'

Not as sane as all that. Rock and roll, like steeplejacking and free-fall parachuting, carries an inherent psychological health risk and the Beatles had climbed higher and had further to fall than anyone. Fame isolates, and the Beatles were as famous and as isolated as anyone of their age could be. They were denied the possibility of leading any kind of normal life when they were on tour. It was aeroplanes, marijuana sessions in soulless hotel rooms, ever larger audiences, those brown paper bags of ready cash, hookers.

'There were orgies in every town,' Neil Aspinall recalled. 'It's only a miracle the press didn't get hold of it.' The press did, but as many of its members were enjoying the off-cuts from this sexual banquet they had a personal interest in not bringing such private matters to a wider audience. After all, boys were surely allowed to be boys?

For the 'boys' themselves, however, the early excitement quickly gave way to a corroding feeling of pointless monotony, punctuated by moments of panic. 'We almost got killed in a number of situations – planes catching fire, people trying to shoot the plane down, and riots everywhere we went,' Harrison remembers.

In Japan 35,000 security men were employed to keep the Beatles apart from their fans and, more importantly, the squads of militant right-wing students who objected to the Beatles' 'perverting' Western influence and were threatening them with execution. McCartney and Mal Evans chose to disregard the warnings and, disguised with false moustaches, sneaked out of their Tokyo hotel to spend the night exploring the city. The police commissioner, who had had them tailed by undercover agents, warned that if they again breached security he would withdraw all protection.

In the Philippines the danger became even more focused. The Beatles flew into Manila on 3 July 1966, where they played two shows before a combined audience of 80,000 people. There was more to playing the Philippines than filling a stadium, however, and Epstein misread the situation badly.

The Beatles had received an invitation to a party being hosted by Imelda Marcos, wife of the nation's dictator. Epstein ignored it. When the military police enquired what time the Beatles would be leaving for the presidential palace he said they wouldn't. The British ambassador telephoned him and warned him that it would be very foolish indeed to ignore the invitation. Epstein would not be persuaded. After the humiliating treatment meted out to them at the British embassy in Washington he had vowed that the Beatles would never again accept an invitation unless they wanted to. And they didn't want to accept this one – they were tired, he explained; they needed their rest.

Epstein and his protégés had spent too long in their ivory tower. While they were on stage at the Arañeta football stadium, the television news announced that the Beatles had snubbed Imelda Marcos and the 300 orphans and cripples which she, unknown to the group, had invited along to meet them. It was, a palace spokesman announced, 'a spit in the national eye'.

They awoke the following morning to find that the hotel staff had been withdrawn. They had no help as they struggled with their luggage, no security men to escort them to the airport. When they got there they found an organised mob waiting for them. They were punched and kicked and spat on as they ran the gauntlet to the KLM jet waiting to fly them out. 'We were terrified,' Peter Brown recalls. They'd had reason to be.

On the plane a row broke out between Epstein and fellow NEMS director Vic Lewis who kept demanding, 'Did you get the money?' The money he was asking about was in one of the ubiquitous brown paper bags that contained almost 50 percent of the concert earnings which Epstein had taken in cash to evade the British taxman.

Epstein, by then overdosed on pills as he usually was, and scared to beyond the limit of his courage, screamed hysterically, *'Don't talk to me about money!'* As the plane tore down the runway on its take-off path Lewis grabbed Epstein by the throat and started to throttle him, shouting, 'I'll kill you.'

It was the end of the fantasy, the end of Epstein's dream. He started sobbing. When the plane landed in New Delhi he was so ill that he needed the attention of a doctor. The Beatles were unsympathetic. They blamed Epstein for the fiasco and for every other upset that went with touring.

Their shows had broken all records; it was the Beatles who pioneered the stadium venue with the concerts at Shea in New York. But, given the poor quality of the available sound equipment, trying to play decent music had become futile. They had carried on because it was expected of them – and for the ready cash it earned them. Even the money wasn't worth this, however, and the money wasn't rolling in the way it should have anyway. For as well as having the British revenue to contend with, they were now running into trouble with America's Internal Revenue Service.

For decades American performers had been coming over to England, earning their money, and scuttling off back to the United States with it. When the Beatles reversed the process the American authorities unsportingly cried 'foul', slapped a withholding order on the Beatles, and made them put down a bond of a million dollars which it took them years to get released. So what was the point, they argued among themselves, of carrying on? They weren't earning what they felt was their due. As far as their music was concerned, their concerts were now an irrelevance. They had had enough. They told Epstein on the plane back to London that they were not going to tour again.

Epstein was promptly sick again. 'What will I do?' he kept asking. At that juncture the Beatles didn't care.

There was still one contract to fulfil before the curtain finally came down, however, and if there were any lingering doubts about the wisdom of going off the road, their last tour of America dispelled them.

The Beatles were due in the United States at the beginning of August. Ten days before they flew in, *Datebook* magazine reprinted an interview with Lennon that had first appeared in the London *Evening Standard*. In it Lennon said that he had been reading about religion and had come to the conclusion that 'Christianity will go'. He went on to say that the Beatles were 'more popular than Jesus'.

The comments had excited no reaction in Britain where they had been either ignored or dismissed as another example of Lennon's increasing eccentricity. The Americans were not so tolerant. Dozens of radio stations stopped playing Beatles records. Several large retail chains refused to handle their albums. There were ritual burnings of Beatles merchandise in the Bible Belt states of the south. Death threats were issued against them.

Epstein was convalescing in Wales when the news came through from America. His first reaction was to try to cancel the Beatles' forthcoming tour of the States. When that course of action proved financially prohibitive – it would have cost over a million dollars – he announced that Lennon had intended no sacrilege and was merely expressing his 'deep concern' at the decline in moral values. It was then arranged for Lennon to apologise formally for any misunderstanding at a press conference in Chicago.

Getting Lennon actually to say sorry was no easy task. He kept avoiding the word. 'I'm not saying the Beatles are better than God or Jesus,' he said. 'I'm not anti-God, anti-Christ, or anti-religious.' But was he *sorry*? Round and round it went until Lennon, in desperation, forced the words out. 'I'm sorry I said it, really . . . I apologise, if that will make you happy . . . if that will make you happy then, OK, I'm sorry.'

From the moment he had first put on a Beatle coat Lennon had worried that they were 'selling out'. He felt trapped in what to him was a straitjacket and his cry for *Help!* became the title of the second, less successful Beatle film. But this was worse, far worse. Now even his opinions were being sacrificed on the altar of commercial expediency. Lennon was disgusted – with himself, with the entity he had helped create and which was threatening to devour him. Being a Beatle was still important to him – he was, he would later explain, still 'too frightened to step out of the palace'. But not at that price on those terms. He had started crying before the press conference and all the stardom in the world wasn't worth that.

The furore also had an effect on McCartney. The death threats unnerved him. Says Peter Brown: 'Paul, because of his nature, was always a doer, a workaholic, so he thought more about it than the others – and the possible consequences.' This was the land of the handgun and McCartney took the threat of the assassin's bullet seriously: Brown, Weiss and Benson all recall McCartney, usually the smoothest of live performers, being physically sick with anxiety before the Beatles went on stage in Cincinnati ten days later. McCartney got over the trauma quickly enough. Lennon didn't, and if any single event can be said to stand as a watershed in a relationship, then that last American tour marked the moment of Lennon and McCartney's public divide.

McCartney was his father's self-reliant son. Beatlemania, like life, might be 'arse over tit', in Jim McCartney's favourite expression, but there was no alternative but to get on and make the best of it. Paul isolated his problems, compartmentalised them, and moved on, smile back in place, platitude again poised for delivery.

Lennon did not have that inner resource to fall back on. While McCartney knew roughly where he was going and, more importantly, who he was, Lennon was lost in a no-man's land of self-doubt. 'I know that John Lennon was quite insecure about himself – and *there's* a monster from the twentieth century! John was definitely no slouch,' McCartney observed. 'But he was insecure about himself.'

In the effort to remake himself in a more honest image Lennon did the only thing possible: he rejected the Beatles. Never again would John Lennon apologise for anything.

On 29 August 1966, the Beatles played their last concert before 25,000 fans at Candlestick Park in San Francisco. McCartney, with his eye on history, ordered NEMS press officer Tony Barrow to make a recording of the show.

It was the end of an era and it came at a fitting time. For three glorious years they had reigned supreme and they had brought freshness and originality, not just to popular music, but to a whole generation's perception of itself and its possibilities. They had been its example. They were also the reflection of its hopes and ambitions and their appeal had transcended age and class and education and ethnic background.

But the world was a' changing. America was plunging deeper into a futile war in South-East Asia. Britain was sinking into industrial chaos and crippling international debt. The Communist empire to the east was clenching its dying fist in a final repression. Cheeky optimism was no longer enough. Harsher voices were needed to reflect the times.

The Beatles, which amongst cognoscenti meant John and Paul,

would adapt to the changing circumstances with the brilliance and instinctive flair that characterised their collaborative genius. Their best work still lay ahead of them. But to achieve it they had to metamorphose themselves. It was time to discard the pupa that had nurtured them – the Fab Four, the Mop Tops, that manipulated, Epstein-constructed personification of mischievous, guileful, guileless youth.

It was time to grow up and both Lennon and McCartney would find the withdrawal from never-never-land a difficult one. Their first reaction, though, was one of joyous liberation. Harrison went on a two-month holiday to Kashmir and declared: 'That's it, I'm not a Beatle anymore.' Ringo threw himself into London's night life.

Lennon retreated to Weybridge to ponder his future. It looked grim. 'It's like a black space out there,' he complained. He spent his days watching television, mindlessly switching channels, his evenings smoking marijuana and, with increasing regularity, dropping LSD which he and Harrison had been introduced to the previous year by a London dentist, making occasional forays up to London in his Tara Browne-inspired psychedelic Rolls. He was stirred from his lethargy to play Private Gripweed in *How I Won the War*, directed by Richard Lester who had made *A Hard Day's Night* and *Help!* He cut off his Beatle locks. In another symbolic renunciation of his old self he started wearing the glasses he had always needed but had been too vain to be seen in. The frames were the old National Health 'granny' style which, to his intense embarrassment, he had had to wear at primary school. But he still didn't know what he was going to do. Was there life after the Beatles? In black moments he would fearfully wonder, 'Where am I going to end up? Las Vegas?'

The transition to 'family entertainer' did indeed seem the only logical step. That was what had happened to Cliff Richard and Tommy Steele, two earlier British pop stars. Even Elvis Presley, the greasy, lip-curling trucker in the gold lamé suit from Tupelo, Mississippi, had succumbed and had reduced himself to churning out rotten films. After all, you couldn't be a rock-and-roll singer when you were 30, could you?

There was another half to the Beatles partnership, however, and Paul McCartney was in no way afflicted by the professional ennui that was consuming Lennon. After a long break on African safari with Mal Evans he returned to announce that a new intellectual movement was stirring and that he, Paul McCartney, intended to be a part of it. His cultural self-improvement became almost frenetic, with saturation visits to art galleries and concerts and cinemas and theatres. He scored the music for the film, *The Family Way*. He produced Cliff Bennett's hit version of his song, 'Got to Get You into My Life'.

Most importantly, although touring days were over, he was anxious to get the four Beatles back into the recording studio and, inspired by the critical success of the *Revolver* album, he started planning the next one. Both Lennon and McCartney were unashamed musical jackdaws, drawing their inspiration from Tamla Motown, rockabilly, even old-time music hall. 'We were the biggest nickers in town, plagiarists extraordinaires,' McCartney cheerfully admitted.

Now it was the turn of the Beach Boys to provide the example and the incentive. 'I'm a competitor, man,' McCartney says. 'It's never stopped; I will never stop competing with every other artist in this business.' The Beach Boys, under the direction of the tortured Brian Wilson who would soon retire to bed in a sandbox for several years, had just brought out an album which had been hailed as a masterpiece. McCartney had been suitably inspired.

'*Pet Sounds* kicked me to make *Sgt Pepper*,' he says. 'It was direct competition with the Beach Boys.'

8

I F *Sgt Pepper* was a beginning, it was also the beginning of the
end. It was the artistic high-point of McCartney's association with
the Beatles. It was the moment when everything blended together to
produce a work that would establish the group beyond challenge as
the most creative musical force of its generation. It expanded the
boundaries of pop and sent rock and roll spinning in uncharted
directions. But behind the psychedelia, the messages of love and
peace, the humour, the promise of a good time, the poignancy, the
sheer joyous nonsense of the Beatles at their creative best, darker
currents were starting to flow.

Harrison, frustrated and disillusioned, was already hinting that
he wanted out of what, for him, had become an artistic borstal for
lost boys, with him cast in the role of third string. And the band's
move away from the strident, simplified rhythms of its infancy into
the electronic sophistications of the studio underlined the irrelevance of Ringo's musical contribution.

Epstein, as Peter Brown mildly recalls, was 'pretty messed up' by
then, existing on a diet of pills, booze and dangerous, often painful
one-night encounters with the rough trade he picked up outside the
military barracks in Knightsbridge.

In late 1966, just before his 'boys' went into the studio to cut
their new album, he attempted to kill himself with an overdose of
sleeping pills. The attempt failed – he was found in time by his

secretary, Joanne Newfield, and his chauffeur, Brian Barratt – but all four Beatles, and McCartney in particular, were becoming disenchanted with their mentor.

And then there was Lennon, deep into LSD and getting deeper, so stoned at times that he could not stand up, with a strange Japanese woman dressed entirely in black starting to follow him around everywhere. Only Paul, full of energy and optimism, was still on the case. And that, as it turned out, proved to be the catalyst for the problems that would soon consume them.

As Peter Brown recalls, 'The Beatles had always been *John's* group.' When the four still young men walked into EMI's Abbey Road studios in St John's Wood a few days before Christmas 1966 it still was. When they walked out again, seven hundred recording hours and $100,000 dollars later, it wasn't. During those four months spent in Studio 2, McCartney had mounted his takeover bid. And he had succeeded. 'It was *Paul's* group now,' says Brown.

Lennon was disenchanted with the persona of rock star he had mantled himself in. Like George, he was looking for some new purpose. But whatever it was, it certainly did not involve handing over to McCartney the leadership of the group he had started and which he still regarded as his own. Yet that is exactly what happened. For *Sgt Pepper* is most assuredly McCartney's album, from concept to final package, and including the many technical detours and breakthroughs on the way.

'It was,' Martin said, 'a time for experiment.' Lennon had his doubts. He was worried that the record was going beyond what the record-buying public would accept. McCartney, in overall charge now, overruled him; he was determined to push the group as far as it could possibly go. And, on this occasion, he was absolutely right. *Sgt Pepper*, he has recalled, 'was an idea I had when I was flying from LA. I thought it would be nice to lose our identities, to submerge ourselves in the persona of a fake group. We would make up all the culture around it and collect all our heroes in one place.'

Popular music, traditionally an industry manipulated by agents and managers and promoters in which the artists were relegated to the role of wind-up, walk-on, disposable marionettes, was growing up. The Beatles were in the forefront of this transformation. The change was commercially led. Record sales were booming; concerts were getting larger; and acts like the Beatles, Dylan and the Stones were generating unprecedented fortunes.

In January Epstein had recovered enough to complete a new agreement with EMI and Capitol which meant that, instead of the risible penny a record they had been earning up until then, they would receive a royalty of 10 percent, rising to 15 percent after 100,000 on single sales and 30,000 for albums sold in Britain. In the United States the figure was even better, going from 10 to 17½ percent.

The money bought them power – not just to write and choose their own material, which they had always done, but to indulge themselves with four-month recording sessions where before a day was deemed quite sufficient (the *Please Please Me* album of only four years before was recorded in under thirteen hours). As if to underline this newfound independence, the names of the bands became self-consciously original. McCartney was in tune with the mood. 'I thought, a typical stupid-sounding name for a Doctor Hook's Medicine Show and Travelling Circus kind of thing would be Sgt Pepper's Lonely Hearts Club Band.'

The original, half-formulated idea had been to make an album about their childhoods in Liverpool and the first tracks were laid down between November and January. But if the Beatles, which meant Lennon and McCartney, had carte blanche to produce whatever they wanted to, and take as long as they wished about it, they were still required to produce a certain number of singles every year. Capitol Records were now demanding one and it was to fulfil the terms of that contract that 'Penny Lane' and 'Strawberry Fields' were rush-released as a double-A side on 13 February 1967 in the United States, and four days later in Britain.

They provided a taste of the banquet being prepared in Abbey Road. The previous Beatles' single, 'Paperback Writer' – the lyrics for which Paul had scribbled in one take, without a word scratched out, on the back of a photograph – had been knocked out in a day. Lennon described it as a typical 'rock 'n' roll song with a guitar lick on a fuzzy, loud guitar'. 'Penny Lane' and 'Strawberry Fields' were dramatically different. It has been called the best two-sided rock single ever released. It was certainly a long, long way from 'Love Me Do'.

Lennon called 'Strawberry Fields' one of his only two *honest* Beatle songs (the other was 'Help'). He had written it in the autumn in Almeria in Spain during a break from filming *How I Won the War*. It look its title from a Salvation Army home near where he had been brought up and where he had attended childhood parties and the name brought happy memories back to him. He first recorded it with only an acoustic car for accompaniment, which George Martin described as 'absolutely lovely'.

At the next session drums and guitars were added. 'It started to get heavy,' Martin said. The song was recorded again, this time with cellos and trumpets. Lennon decided that he liked the beginning of the first version and the end of the second, disregarding the fact that they were in different keys and tempos. 'You can fix it, George,' Lennon replied, with the sublime confidence of someone who took only a superficial interest in the technical complications. 'He was,' Martin says, 'the least technical of the Beatles. John always left this kind of thing to me.'

As it turned out, George *could* fix it. By speeding up one and slowing down the other on a variable-control machine and then cutting the two tapes together at 'precisely the right spot', the ear wouldn't be able to detect the join. It worked, and spectacularly so. As Martin said: 'We ended up with a record which was very good heavy metal. That is how "Strawberry Fields" was issued, and that is how it remains today – two recordings.'

John had been spurred on by McCartney who was the first of the pair to go back to their suburban roots. 'We were always in competition,' McCartney said. 'I wrote "Penny Lane" so he wrote "Strawberry Fields". That was how it was.' The song takes its title from a bus roundabout in Liverpool. 'It's part-fact, part-nostalgia for a place which is a great place – blue suburban skies as we remember it, and it's still there,' McCartney recalled.

Like 'Strawberry Fields', 'Penny Lane' started out as a 'fairly simple song', with some fairly crude lyrics including the reference to 'four-fish-and-finger pie,' a Liverpudlian phrase for what went on in the back seats of the cinema. McCartney, however, and despite his occasional lapses into adolescent humour, was moving on. Consciously, deliberately, he had set about acquiring the intellectual raiments befitting a prince of the cultural revolution. 'Penny Lane' was one of the results.

London in the 1960s was all about experimentation and a new sophistication. Those who were there recall it as a period when every day promised more than the one that had gone before; when ideas, however half-baked and mundane in retrospect, were exciting and stimulating and, not the least of their attraction, a seismic break from the dull, short-grey-trousers and school-blazer conformity that had been everyone's childhood in the 1950s.

Flannel and serge had surrendered to velvet and silks. The Presley sideburns that no one had been allowed to grow now flourished in organic splendour on every cheek. Love, preferably in its physical manifestation, had taken the place of compulsory military service. Drugs, in all their 'mind-expanding' potential, were becoming widely available. Young 'trend-setters' (how dated the phrase now sounds) drank Scotch and Coke in the Scotch of St James's and took their holidays in the hashish beatitude of Morocco or on the hippy trail to India. The parochial accents of the provinces were at last allowed to challenge the official BBC pronunciations. Art galleries and boutiques and discotheques were springing up in every city and magazines and 'alternative' newspapers that catered to these new tastes were being started.

America was at war and sinking deep into South-East Asia but Britain still appeared to be in the dawn of a New Age. And McCartney, the lower-middle-class lad from the Liverpool suburbs transmogrified into cultural high priest, exemplified the change and, at the same time, desperately thirsted to be a part of it. As he declared at the time: 'People are saying things and painting things and writing things that are great. I must *know* what people are doing.'

While Beatle John 'was living on a golf course in bloody *Weybridge*', as McCartney put it, and 'the others were married and living in the suburbs', *he* was the bachelor who was collecting Magritte; watching Bergman films and experimenting with 8mm home movies which he showed 'one frame at a time – flick, flick, flick – which made them last about an hour when they should have been ten minutes'; reading Dylan Thomas and listening to Vivaldi; hanging out with Andy Warhol, gallery owner Robert Fraser, and the Beat poet Allen Ginsberg; putting up the money to help found the quintessential underground newspaper, the *International Times*; helping to start the Indica Bookshop and Gallery where that strange Japanese woman dressed entirely in black would hold her first London exhibition. 'And I was into Stockhausen', the modernist German composer, 'and I used to make a lot of home tape loops and just send them to friends for, like, a buzz. I remember saying to John once, I'm going to do an album of this and call it *Paul McCartney Goes Too Far*, and he said, "Yeah, you've got to do it, man!" So *I* was the one who introduced John, originally, to a lot of that stuff.'

He resents the 'misconception' that he didn't; the suggestion that it was really Lennon who was the cerebral voortrekker who led the group on its cultural explorations; that he was just the 'jolly, cute one' who wrote pretty melodies. 'It's irksome, yes,' he jolly cutely complains, insisting, '*I* was the avant-garde one of the Beatles.' While Lennon was at home in stockbroker-belt Weybridge, playing 'husband and father', *he* was making the rounds, keeping in touch with what was happening. One night he went to a concert of Bach's Brandenburg Concerti. In the studio the next day he asked Martin about the 'fantastic high trumpet' he had heard.

'The piccolo trumpet, the Bach trumpet,' Martin explained. But why was he so interested?

Because that, McCartney said, was the sound he wanted on

'Penny Lane'. He wasn't quite sure how he wanted it used, he just knew that he wanted 'little piping interjections'. David Mason of the London Symphony Orchestra was hired, and, as Martin recalled, 'Paul would think up the notes he wanted, and I would write them down for David. The result was unique, something that had never been done in rock music before, and it gave "Penny Lane" a very distinct character.'

It set the tone of the album to come. When 'Penny Lane' and 'Strawberry Fields' were taken out for the single all that was left in the can was 'When I'm 64'. Other songs were added and developed in that apparently lackadaisical fashion of trial, error and rework that was the Beatles' way. Midway through McCartney came up with *Sgt Pepper*. It was, Martin says, 'just an ordinary rock number and not particularly brilliant as songs go'. Then McCartney brought in the idea he'd had flying from LA. 'Why don't we make the album as though the Pepper band really existed, as though Sergeant Pepper was making the record? We'll dub in effects and things.'

Martin 'loved the idea, and from that moment it was as though *Pepper* had a life of its own, developing of its own accord rather than through a conscious effort by the Beatles or myself to integrate it and make it a "concept" album.'

McCartney became deeply involved in its production. While Lennon was content to throw out a vague idea and leave Martin to get on with turning it into aural reality, McCartney 'would sit down and ask what I planned to do with his songs, with virtually every note'.

It was a commitment that produced a work of genius. It also unveiled an aspect of McCartney's character that had been kept hidden behind the charm and the chirpy smile. Peter Brown bluntly states, 'Paul is a control freak.' *Sgt Pepper* gave him the chance to exercise it.

Martin has said: 'Paul eventually became the one member of the group who always took an active interest in everything the group did. John tended to work very hard at *his* bit, then leave the rest and walk away. George too. Paul got involved in everything.'

At first Lennon, his perception muted by the number of psychologically disturbing lysergic-acid diethylamide (LSD) tabs he was gobbling, didn't seem to notice what was happening. Perhaps, at the time, he didn't care; he once remarked to Apple's press officer Derek Taylor that the happiest time he spent in a recording studio as a Beatle was working on the *Pepper* album.

Yet it was the tensions exposed in *Pepper*'s creation that set in motion the chain of events that, by the following year, had the four musicians at each other's throats and, within three years, had led to the final dissolution of the Beatles. No one outside their coterie knew anything about this. To the rest of the world they were still the lovable Fabs, as Harrison now rather disparagingly calls them.

As Lennon said, in an interview with *Newsweek* published a few weeks before he died: 'I was always waiting for a reason to get out of the Beatles from the day I filmed *How I Won the War*. I just didn't have the guts to do it . . . I was too frightened to step out of the palace. That's what killed Presley. The king is always killed by his courtiers. He is overfed, overindulged, overdrunk to keep him tied to his throne.'

McCartney, unconsciously, unwittingly, would soon give him the reason he was looking for. That strange Japanese woman in black, consciously, determinedly, would give him another. But not yet. For the moment Lennon was happy to get on with doing his own thing – and, no inconvenience for someone consumed by drug-fuelled introspection, McCartney was always there, ready and delighted to take up any slack.

It was Paul who imposed order on the project, gave it its shape, insisted on an early April deadline so that he could fly to Denver in Colorado to join Jane Asher for her 21st birthday. If there weren't enough songs, then Paul, drawing on his prodigious ability to turn out a tune at will and remember the ones he had written years before, would quickly provide some more. 'When I'm 64' was a 'cabaret tune' he had written when he was 15. A hole in the road became 'a good old analogy' entitled 'Fixing a Hole'. A brush with a parking warden named Meta ('Is your name really Meta?' asked

McCartney) Davies near the Abbey Road studios in St John's Wood produced 'Lovely Rita'. A newspaper article about a runaway child provided the inspiration for 'She's Leaving Home'.

There were occasional touches of self-centred arrogance to this virtuoso performance. 'Fixing a Hole', McCartney said, was partly 'about fans'; about the young girls who stood for hours in Cavendish Avenue, waiting for a fleeting glimpse of their smile-on-tap, thumbs-up idol as he drove through the iron gates to the front door of the house their devotion had paid for. In the song he refers to them as the 'silly people' who 'don't get past my door'.

Ringo, too, felt slighted. His contribution to the Beatlemania phenomenon was never properly acknowledged by either Lennon or McCartney. Now he found himself even more on the outside. As he observed: 'With *Sgt Pepper* I felt more like a session man because we were interested in making an *album* with strings and brass and *parts*. Everyone says that record is a classic, but it's not my favourite album.'

Then there was the egotistic insult McCartney delivered to Martin when they were working on 'She's Leaving Home'. McCartney, 'itching to get on with it', telephoned Martin and asked him to come round the next afternoon to help on the song. An orchestra, he said, would be booked, and Martin could write the score. The A & R man explained that he simply wasn't available at that short notice; he was booked to record Cilla Black at two-thirty that afternoon. McCartney suggested two o'clock. Martin replied firmly: 'No, I can't, I've got a session on.' McCartney said, 'All right then', hung up and asked Neil Aspinall to telephone around and find someone else. Aspinall found Mike Leander and the fol-lowing day McCartney presented Martin with the Leander score and told him to get on with recording it.

But Martin was not just another hired hand, available at a moment's notice to service the Pop Prince. Only five years before he had been the one doing the hiring. It was Martin, after all, who had taken the chance no one else was prepared to take and signed the rough, yobbish, musically unsound quartet from Liverpool to

Parlophone; Martin, who, with empathy and technical artistry, had given them musical polish, encouraged their songwriting and been instrumental in creating, on record, the unique Beatles sound. As McCartney concedes, in the beginning Martin 'had a lot of control. We used to record the stuff and leave him to mix it, pick a single, everything.'

As a result of his endeavours the Beatles had become as rich as Croesus and more famous, or so John Lennon would have it, than Christ. Martin, meanwhile, had to make do with a more mundane reward. 'The Beatles,' he observed, 'were never ones for showing concern, or gratitude towards anyone else . . . never the kind of people who would go out of their way to say, "What a great job you've done, George! Take three weeks off."'

Dick James had offered Martin shares in Northern Songs. If he had accepted them he would have been a millionaire but he had rejected the offer on ethical grounds and so remained a salaried employee of EMI earning less than £3,000 a year. He wasn't getting much out of the Beatles' phenomenal success 'from a financial point of view, but at least I was getting satisfaction'. McCartney – thoughtlessly, unconcernedly – had just taken that away from him.

'She's Leaving Home' was the only Beatles' song scored by some-one other than Martin. 'Paul obviously didn't think it was important that I should do everything,' Martin would write plaintively. McCartney, intoxicated by his own creativity – 'I was inspired,' he said – was unaware of the wound he had caused. It was not until Martin emerged from his soundproof control booth to publish his memoirs twelve years later that he discovered just how much he had wounded the reserved, self-effacing, softly spoken Martin.

'It hurt him; I didn't mean to,' McCartney said. He considers 'She's Leaving Home' to be one of his better ballads from that period. Martin remembers it as 'one of the biggest hurts of my life'. To which McCartney coldly replies: 'Well, if that's the only hurt I've done him . . .'

But if the creative process happened to leave a few bruised egos in its wake, McCartney could justifiably argue that, as far as *Sgt*

Pepper was concerned, the end justified the means – and, with the other half of the Lennon–McCartney songwriting partnership on space-cadet training, that he *was* the means.

There are thirteen tracks on the album if you count the reprise of 'Sgt Pepper'. One, the Indian-influenced 'Within You Without You' which Martin, with genteel understatement, described as 'rather dreary', was contributed by Harrison. Lennon managed to turn in three – 'Lucy in the Sky with Diamonds', 'Being for the Benefit of Mr Kite' and 'Good Morning, Good Morning'. Had it not been for Paul's input, it would have been a very short long-player; of the remaining nine tracks, eight were McCartney's.

That left 'A Day in the Life', the psychedelic anthem of the 1960s – and the last genuine Lennon–McCartney co-composition. John and Paul still continued to influence each other's works, adding a line, taking one away, changing a riff, contributing a break, suggesting a different arrangement. It was John, for instance, who contributed the lines about being 'cruel to my woman' – 'I used to be cruel to my woman and physically – any woman / I was a hitter / I couldn't express myself and I hit' – to 'Getting Better', the song Paul had written based on the phrase, 'It's getting better', which drummer Jimmy Nichols had used when he was asked what it was like standing in for unwell Ringo on the Australian tour of three years before. It had been a long time, however, since the pair had sat down and written together. Effectively, the partnership was dead. In 'A Day in the Life' it reconvened for one glorious final flourish.

Lennon had been amused by the stories he had read in the newspapers about the number of potholes in the streets of Blackburn and about a lucky man who'd made the grade and was pictured in his big new car. The death of Guinness heir Tara Browne, going through a red light in Earl's Court at 110 mph in his Lotus Elan, was still fresh in the memory. That gave him three verses but no connection. McCartney produced an unfinished song he had written about his childhood memory of catching 'my school bus, having a smoke, and then going into class. It was a reflection of my school days – I would have a Woodbine then, and somebody would speak and I would go into a dream.' Then he threw in what Lennon called 'the beautiful little lick in the song, "I'd love to turn you on", that he'd had floating around in his head and couldn't use'. The two parts, as McCartney noted, 'happened to fit well'.

But how to join them together? Martin asked Lennon. Lennon rummaged through his hallucinated mind and replied: 'What I'd like to hear is a tremendous build-up, from nothing up to something absolutely like the end of the world.' Hire a symphony orchestra, he suggested. Martin objected. A symphony orchestra, Martin pointed out, needed a score more precise than 'the end of the world'. 'Why?' Lennon asked. An orchestra was duly hired. At which point McCartney, ever the master of Beatle ceremonies, took charge.

The giant Studio 1, the only one large enough to accommodate a full orchestra (though, for cost reasons, Martin managed to keep the number of musicians down to forty-two) was booked. McCartney issued the instruction that everyone, Martin included, had to come in full evening dress because it would be 'fun'. The mainly middle-aged musicians, as Martin recalled, 'thought it was all a stupid giggle and waste of money', but they entered into the spirit of the occasion.

Mick Jagger and Marianne Faithfull came along. The Fool – Simon Posthuma, Josje Leeger and Marijke Koger, the dreamy-eyed wardrobe master and mistresses at the court of the Beatle kings, whose ingenuousness made them no Fool when it came to parting their patrons from their money – handed out sparklers, funny hats and party novelties to the orchestra. David McCallum, once the leader of the Royal Philharmonic, ended up wearing a bright red clown's nose and paper glasses. Eric Gruenberg, formerly the leader of the BBC Symphony Orchestra, held the bow of his violin in a giant gorilla's paw. The effect, Martin recalled, 'was completely weird'.

So too was the sound the orchestra had to produce. Instead of working as a unit, the musicians were ordered to forget a lifetime's professional training and play as individuals. If Lennon wanted the end of the world, then McCartney was going to give it to him. 'The orchestra crescendo,' McCartney recalled, 'was based on some of the ideas I'd been getting from Stockhausen and people like that, which is more abstract.'

Paul gave the order: 'Start on your lowest note and eventually, at the end of the fifteen bars, be at your highest note.' How they got there was up to them, but it all resulted in a crazy crescendo. 'It's interesting because the trumpet players, always famous for a fondness for lubricating substances, didn't care, so they'd be there at the note ahead of everyone. The strings all watched each other like little sheep: "Are you going up?" "Yes." "So am I." And they'd go up. "A little more?" "Yes." And they'd go up a little more, all delicate and cozy, all going up together. You listen to those trumpets . . . they're freaking out!'

Afterwards, the four Beatles with George Martin hit the keys of three pianos simultaneously while the sound engineer pushed the volume input faders as high as they would go to catch the last withering sounds (you can just hear the studio air-conditioning whirring in the background). To round it off McCartney got the others to chant any nonsense – 'yum tum, tim ting sort of sounds' – to place on the run-out groove. Finally and because, as McCartney pointed out, the Beatles had never done anything for dogs, a 20,000-hertz note audible only to canine ears was added.

The ungrateful curs did not appreciate McCartney's thoughtfulness and continue to whine fearfully whenever they hear it. The dogs were a species alone. Just about everyone else was dazzled. Self-indulgent it may have been – they spent an hour getting the 'funny noises' made with a metal comb and tissue paper on 'Lovely Rita'. A technical nightmare to produce on the old sound machinery it certainly was – Martin was laying down nine tracks on a machine only capable of taking four.

The finished article, however, was 'bloody marvellous!' As Martin said: 'It was the album which turned the Beatles from being an ordinary rock-and-roll group into being significant contributors to the history of artistic performance. It was a turning point – *the* turning point. It was the watershed which changed the recording art from something that merely made amusing sounds into something which will stand the test of time as a valid art form: sculpture in music, if you like.'

There may have been better Beatles' albums (*Revolver* contains a superior collection of songs and the *White Album*, in retrospect, is more interesting). But no record, before or since, so encapsulated the spirit of an age. Kenneth Tynan, not one much given to hyperbole, summed up the critical reaction when he called it 'a decisive moment in the history of Western civilisation'.

And McCartney wanted it made known just where the credit belonged. 'That album,' he states, 'was largely my influence. *I* thought of the idea, the concept of pretending we were another group. I was trying to get everyone in the group to be sort of farther out and do this far-out album.'

Not everyone agreed with McCartney's recollection. According to Pete Shotton, Lennon's friend from school days, it was actually the Beatles' road manager and bodyguard, Mal Evans, who not only coined the name, Sergeant Pepper's Lonely Hearts Club Band, but also suggested that 'this fictitious ensemble be presented as the Beatles' alter egos'. Evans, however, was only a hired hand. McCartney was a prince of the New Age. If the prince chose to claim it as his own, no lowly courtier was going to contradict him. And besides – regardless of whose original phrase or thought it was – it was McCartney who had got it down on tape.

Lennon harboured more subtle reservations. He was not overly impressed by the elaborate production. And for all McCartney's talk of 'concept', the record doesn't have one: '*Sgt Pepper* is called the first concept album, but it doesn't go anywhere,' Lennon said. 'All my contributions to the album have absolutely nothing to do with this idea of Sgt Pepper and his band. But it works – because we *said* it worked.'

After the first tracks had been recorded, McCartney became convinced that the album was going to more than just work – it was going to be a great artistic achievement. To complement what was inside, he insisted on an equally spectacular cover for the outside.

The aptly named Fool produced a 'swirly orange and green and purple' version. It didn't work – not least because the centrefold design was too small for the space it had to fill. 'What are we selling here?' Neil Aspinall wanted to know. 'A Beatles album or a centrefold with a design by the Fool which isn't even ready?'

On the recommendation of gallery owner Robert Fraser, pop artist Peter Blake was employed. He recalled: 'Paul explained that it was like a band you might see in a park. So the cover shot would be a photograph of them as though they were a town band finishing a concert in a park, playing on a bandstand with a municipal flowerbed next to it, with a crowd of people around them.'

To make up the 'lovely audience', McCartney recalled, 'we came up with a list of our heroes, like Oscar Wilde, Marlon Brando, Dylan Thomas, Aldous Huxley, Lenny Bruce. Everyone had their choice.' Harrison, in his Indian phase, suggested a number of gurus and Gandhi. The iconoclastic Lennon suggested Hitler and Jesus. Ringo didn't suggest anyone.

Blake said: 'I think my main contribution was to decide that if we made the crowd a certain way the people in it could be anybody. I think that that was the thing I would claim actually changed the direction of it: making a life-sized collage incorporating real people, waxworks, photographs and artwork.'

They couldn't, as it turned out, have just anybody, and certainly not everybody they wanted. If Epstein had had his way they wouldn't have had anybody at all. He was convinced that the idea would lead to lawsuits. EMI agreed with him and insisted that written permission be obtained from everybody they intended to include in the photograph or, if they were dead, like Marilyn Monroe, from their estates.

'There's no risk whatsoever,' McCartney assured EMI Records managing director Sir Joseph Lockwood. 'Everybody will be delighted.'

EMI did not share McCartney's optimism and demanded an indemnity of 'several million pounds'. Epstein, by now in a panic but unable to change McCartney's mind about the cover, frantically ordered his personal assistant, Wendy Moger, to get legal clearance from everyone mentioned. She couldn't, of course.

Leo Gorcey of the Bowery Boys demanded payment and was dropped. Mae West refused – what would *she* be doing in a lonely hearts' club, she demanded to know – and was only won round after each Beatle wrote her a personal letter. EMI vetoed Hitler and Jesus. They also ordered Gandhi to be removed because, as Lockwood told McCartney, 'We can't offend the Indians . . . lots of trouble there, you know . . . EMI India', which enjoyed a virtual monopoly in the subcontinent.

Despite the problems, and with agreement obtained from only half the people, and over Epstein's continued protests – one of his last acts was to tell his American lawyer, Nat Weiss, to issue the album in a brown paper bag – the cover appeared as Paul, with Blake's help, had visualised it. Blake's name, regrettably, did not appear on the credits.

The cover caused almost as much comment as the record itself. Its celebration of pop art and pop culture set new standards in design which had an important influence, not just on the record industry, but on all the visual arts including clothes, furniture, and magazine lay-out.

'We realised for the first time,' said McCartney, 'that some day someone would actually be holding a thing they'd call "the Beatles' new LP", and that normally it would just be a collection of songs or a nice picture on the cover, nothing more. So the idea was to do a complete thing that you could make what you liked of: a little magic presentation . . .'

Given the Beatles' increasingly well-known propensity for nefarious substances and the widely held belief that everything they did contained some cryptic meaning, it was inevitable that people started reading more into the cover than was actually there. One myth was that, hidden among the flowers in the photograph, were marijuana plants. They weren't – the plants, as Blake pointed out, came from a local nursery of good repute. Another was that the sleeve insert was impregnated with LSD. Nonsense, of course. As

Harrison dismissively remarked: 'As if EMI would impregnate every album insert!'

The legends that surround the album are not entirely without foundation, however. *Sgt Pepper*, Lennon pointed out, may not be hermetic in a musical sense, but it certainly has a theme and one that runs right through the album. Drugs. As Martin has observed: '*Pepper* would never have been formed in exactly that way if the boys hadn't got into the drug scene, and if I hadn't been a normal person. If they hadn't been on drugs, it's possible something like *Pepper* would have happened but not quite so flowery, maybe.' By 1967 all four of the Beatles were heavily into marijuana. Harrison and Lennon had acquired a taste for LSD. McCartney, the 'avant-garde one', had discovered cocaine through his friendship with Tara Browne.

EMI took an indulgent view of their most important artists' criminal indulgence. 'I knew there was some possible connection with cannabis in the studios – "smells" were noted – but I never pursued it,' Sir Joseph Lockwood said. The Beatles were big money. 'I had a pretty close relationship with the Beatles, largely because they were so successful,' Lockwood observed. If they wanted to get stoned while they made EMI even more money, the attitude was: 'Let them.' Brian Gibson, the technical engineer who worked on the *White Album*, observed: 'Everyone knew what substances they were taking, but they were really a law unto themselves.'

In deference to laws less compromising than those in force in Abbey Road, they tried to keep their toking secret, taking it in turns to sneak off to the canteen where Evans would have a joint rolled and ready. No one was fooled.

Martin knew, Lockwood knew and when the album was released, everyone else knew too. The lyrics to every song, which were published, in full and for the first time on a pop album, seemed to hint at it. 'With a Little Help from My Friends' was taken to endorse drug use. Henry the Horse in 'Mr Kite' was supposed to be a reference to heroin. And it didn't take much to work out that the initials of 'Lucy in the Sky with Diamonds' were LSD.

In truth, none of those songs had anything to do with drugs. 'With a Little Help from My Friends' was just another McCartney song, drawn from his seemingly bottomless well of inspiration. 'Mr Kite' took its lyrics from an 1843 poster advertising a fairground troupe he had bought in an antique shop. Its composition gave Lennon no pleasure. 'I hardly made up a word, just connecting the lists together. I wasn't very proud of that. There was no real work. I was just going through the motions because we needed a new song.' 'Lucy', despite its acronym, was equally innocent in origin. It was inspired by Lennon's son Julian, then aged four, who brought home from school a painting he had done of his classmate, Lucy, set in a sky of exploding stars. Lennon maintained that the images, of tangerine trees and marmalade skies observed through kaleidoscope eyes, were from *Alice in Wonderland* and not from the head shop in Belgravia's Pont Street.

Yet however ingenuous the individual songs may have been, the album as an entity reeked of reefer smoke. McCartney confirmed: 'Until this album we'd never thought of taking the freedom to do something like *Sgt Pepper*. Marijuana started to find its way into everything we did. It coloured our perception, and we started to realise there weren't as many barriers as we thought.'

When it came to breaking down mental barriers, Lennon was in a class of his own. He was dropping acid almost every day. Alone in his psychedelic gloaming, he would spend his hours stretched out on a sofa in his loggia in Weybridge, sometimes getting up to bang away at his piano painted in psychedelic colours by the Fool's Simon and Marijke, always with the television on. In ironic contradiction of the wholesomeness the advertisers were hoping to convey, a cornflakes commercial stimulated one drug-saturated viewer, not to buy their product, but to write 'Good Morning, Good Morning'.

In 'bloody Weybridge' – 'dope-smokers' belt' as Harrison called it – Lennon's problems were his own and his family's. In the studio they became the group's. On March 21, when they were overdubbing the vocals for 'Getting Better', it got decidedly worse for Lennon. John, who kept up the habit acquired in the band's Hamburg days of feeding himself uppers, had mistakenly taken the wrong pill out of his pocket. Instead of an upper, he had swallowed another acid tab. 'I'm tripping,' he started saying. The trip was a bad one. Studio 2 suddenly became a dangerous place. Lennon felt scared. 'I thought I was going to crack,' he recalled. Martin, from the control box, asked if he was feeling unwell. He replied that he wasn't, that he was 'feeling very strange', that he needed some air.

With the usual five hundred or so screaming fans camped outside in Abbey Road, taking the tripping Lennon out of the front door was clearly impossible. As it was a clear, starry night, the 'headmasterly' Martin, innocently unaware at that stage of what drugs his pupil was into, foolishly led him up on to the roof. But the roof had only a six-inch parapet with a sheer 90-foot drop on the other side which Lennon, in his bemused state, was in danger of taking.

'Don't go too near the edge, there's no rail there!' Martin pleaded.

When Lennon had recovered his equilibrium, he went back down into the studio. He was too ill to resume work, however, and Paul volunteered to take him home. Until then McCartney, self-righteously and feeling 'really goody-goody' about it, had resisted the peer pressure of his fellow Beatles, all of whom had been urging him to try LSD. When he got Lennon home, however, his resolve dissolved and he took his first acid trip – to keep company with Lennon who was zooming.

'I figured, you know, I can't leave the guy on his own,' McCartney explained. This affection for illicit substances found its musical expression in 'A Day in the Life', the one track on the album that *was* about drugs.

Said McCartney: 'This was the only one of the album written as deliberate provocation to people. I remember being very conscious of the words, "I'd love to turn you on", and thinking, Well, that's about as risqué as we dare get at this point.'

The drug-inspiration, whether conscious or otherwise, was duly noted by officialdom. The BBC banned 'A Day in the Life', as they did 'Lucy in the Sky with Diamonds'. It would not be long before action was taken to prove that, whatever the Beatles may have thought, they were not a law unto themselves – though the ever-cute McCartney, whose line about wanting to turn people on was what so focused police attention to their substance-abuse, would ironically, predictably, be the one to get away with it longest. Why bust Mr Goody Goody when there was big bad John available to take the fall?

For the moment, however, the Beatles, MBE, remained the sacrosanct personification of popular British culture. It was the summer of peace, of hippy beads and crushed velvet and love-ins. It was a happy time and when Harrison, on 'Within You Without You' sang, 'With our love – we could save the world', the world, or that part of it aged under 30, believed him.

There were ominous portents of the troubles to come, however, and John, George and Ringo would have been well advised to have paid closer attention to Paul McCartney when he sang the allegorical line, 'When I'm wrong I'm right'.

A moment of sanity in the madhouse of
Apple, that glorious, extravagant,
freaked-out experiment in what
McCartney called 'Western
communism'. *(Pictorial Press)*

John and Paul at London Airport, 1968,
shortly before the core of Apple turned
rotten. *(Hulton Deutsch)*

Allen Klein, of whom John Lennon said, 'I've got my own dog to go after McCartney's dogs.' *(Topham)*

Winona Williams, who asked McCartney: 'What is *she* doing here?' The 'she' was Linda Eastman, and she was here to stay. *(Harry Benson)*

9

On the night of 26 August 1967, Brian Epstein at last succeeded in doing what he had tried to do before and killed himself. His death was not unexpected. Insecure, dependent on drugs and alcohol, desperately lonely, homosexual but terrified of coming out, he had been balanced precariously on the precipice for months.

In October his five-year management contract with the Beatles came up for renewal. His mental state was not helped by the fear, imaginary or not, that the Beatles were planning to dispense with him.

Peter Brown maintains this was never mooted. 'I don't think they ever would have fired him,' he says. 'After all, it was Brian who first showed faith and belief in them. There was nobody else they could have turned to. And the fact that he was a bit of a mess for the last eighteen months didn't really matter. The record contract had been signed for a further nine years and that was in place. They weren't going to tour. So there was no business to be done, except day to day things which I did. People were concerned about Brian but I don't think it ever entered their minds – at least that I am aware of – that he was such a mess that they had to get rid of him.' Not everyone agreed. George Martin believed it was 'inevitable' that Epstein would lose the Beatles: 'There was absolutely no question about it,' he wrote.

Epstein himself was convinced that there was a plot afoot to deprive him of the only real role he had in life, which was looking after his 'boys'. He had good reason to be worried. The merchandising contracts he had signed had lost the Beatles a fortune. McCartney, who was now taking an increasingly active interest in every aspect of the group's empire, was furious. As he bitterly pointed out: 'We got screwed for millions. It was all Brian's fault. He was green. I always said that about Brian. Green.'

There was another cause for contention. Epstein had indeed renegotiated the Beatles' contract with EMI. But the Rolling Stones were doing even better with the same company. In private the Beatles and the Stones were the best of friends, and in 1967 Mick Jagger had suggested that for convenience's sake the two groups should set up a joint office to handle such things as insurance, bookings and their daily needs. Isolated by their fame, they turned to each other for companionship, meeting up in nightclubs, attending each other's recording sessions, taking drugs.

When it came to the rock and roll, however, the Beatles, and Paul especially, maintained that they were number one. And so they were, by any yardstick – record sales, size of audiences, worldwide adulation. Yet it was the Stones, not the Beatles, who were ahead in the financial stakes.

In 1965 the Stones' manager, Andrew Loog Oldham, had placed the group's financial affairs in the hands of a rough New Yorker named Allen Klein. Abrasive, uncouth and with a vocabulary to match, Klein had made his reputation by legally strong-arming fortunes out of the record companies for people like Bobby Darin and Connie Francis.

He had introduced himself to Darin at a party with the question: 'How would you like a hundred thousand dollars?' For what? Darin asked. 'For nothing,' Klein replied. 'Just let me go through your accounts.' Darin said yes, Klein duly went through the books – and came up with the money he had been promised in royalties which the record companies seemed to have forgotten they owed.

This 'I can make you rich' approach was persuasive – and, if you happened to be Paul McCartney, very annoying. While the Beatles were still making do on a penny a record, Klein had stormed in on the Stones' recording labels and emerged with an advance on royalties of $1.25 million – an unheard of sum at the time. Why, McCartney wanted to know, could Klein succeed where Epstein failed?

Klein fuelled McCartney's exasperation. He could, he said, do the same for the Beatles. It started to look as though the Beatles were prepared to let him. Leaked stories that two of the Beatles – 'one of them certainly Paul', according to biographer Philip Norman – were keen to employ Klein started appearing in the newspapers. Klein openly declared that he would have the Beatles 'by Christmas'.

Epstein was shaken enough by this naked challenge to his position to issue an official statement dismissing Klein's boast as 'rubbish'. He may have been right but neither McCartney nor the others did anything to reassure him; McCartney bombarded him on an almost daily basis with enquiries and complaints which Epstein, who by this stage couldn't drag himself out of bed much before five o'clock in the afternoon, was usually incapable of answering. And when he could have been of help, he got it hopelessly wrong.

In the summer of peace Paul McCartney was at his zenith. *Sgt Pepper* had been greeted with praise unprecedented in the history of popular music and McCartney had basked in it. *All You Need is Love*, the Beatles 'message to the world', was about to be broadcast to an audience of over 200 million people in the first live, worldwide, television programme. The Beatles, it seemed, could do no wrong. At which point McCartney – in an act of naïvety or hubris, according to taste, but certainly in the grand tradition of Greek tragedy – put his foot right in it.

In an interview with *Queen* magazine that was quickly picked up in the United States by *Life*, he went on record and admitted that, yes, he had taken LSD. 'It opened my eyes,' he said. 'It made me a better, more honest, more tolerant member of society.' Society proved itself less so and McCartney, so used to praise, now found himself buried under an avalanche of criticism. His house in

St John's Wood was besieged, not by fawning fans, but by hard-nosed journalists and camera crews demanding, not autographs, but answers.

Was he endorsing drug abuse? As a public figure, did he not have certain responsibilities to people who looked up to him? Who had supplied him with this now-illegal drug? And, just to fill in the technical side of the story, how many times had he taken it?

McCartney fended off the questions as he best knew how – with smiles and evasions. He had simply given an honest answer to a question, he explained. And, no, he didn't think that millions of Beatle fans were going to rush out and take LSD just because he had (on four different occasions, he admitted).

The journalists persisted. 'As a public figure, aren't you respon-sible?' The smile vanished. Fractiously he replied: 'No, it's you who've got the responsibility not to spread this now. You know I'm quite prepared to keep it as a personal thing if you will too. If you'll shut up about it, I will.' At which point Epstein added his voice.

When Paul informed him of what had happened he was, he said, 'very worried'. In an effort to deflect the criticism, Epstein announced that he too had taken LSD. All he succeeded in doing, of course, was fanning the controversy. Questions were asked in the Houses of Parliament. The Home Office issued an official statement saying it was 'horrified' by Epstein's attitude to dangerous drugs.

McCartney was furious. Whatever mistake he had made had now been compounded by Epstein's indiscretion which had served no purpose other than to attract even more attention to the folly. He telephoned Epstein and berated him. He telephoned again – and again – until in the end, Brian stopped taking his calls.

In a last determined effort to catch the dying rays of a summer that was becoming fatally overcast, Epstein threw a lavish party at Kingsley Hill, his country home outside London. It was a futile attempt and McCartney added to his gloom.

The best LSD available, prepared in San Francisco by a renegade chemist called Owlsley, had been specially smuggled into England in the camera lenses of a crew the Beatles had sent to California ostensibly to film the Monterrey rock festival. Procol Harum's 'A Whiter Shade of Pale' and 'Sgt Pepper' played endlessly through the afternoon and into the night. Flasks of tea laced with acid were passed around. The Fool played the role of court jesters, dancing around the garden in their chiffon robes, embracing everybody. One of Epstein's over-drugged female assistants threw up over Nat Weiss's shoes. Cynthia Lennon, on her second trip and consumed with anxiety, stayed locked in a bedroom, her marriage fading away from her in technicolour paranoia.

The guests included Mick Jagger and Marianne Faithfull, composer Lionel Bart and, more unusually, John Pritchard, conductor of the London Philharmonic Orchestra and the representative of an older and decidedly more sedate musical heritage.

'John loved the party,' Peter Brown says. Epstein didn't. Lennon, Harrison and Ringo were there. McCartney wasn't. At the last moment he had telephoned and made some excuse. Epstein was 'devastated'. The other Beatles tried to comfort him, but without much success. The LSD he had taken did nothing to soothe him. Quite the contrary: he shuffled around the drawing room mumbling, 'Paul didn't come . . . this of all days . . . he should have come.'

There wasn't much love left now and if that was what Epstein needed, then he wasn't getting it from McCartney. But if Paul had decided, after the cautionary tale of the *Queen/Life* interview, that it was not in his best interests to be publicly connected with LSD, he remained a resolute proselytiser of marijuana. It was a fashionable thing to be and McCartney was nothing if not fashionable.

It is sometimes tempting to view McCartney as a social navigator, forever trimming his sails to the wind of fashion; picking up ideas at the appropriate time, then jettisoning them when the breeze changed. But if it is true that of all the Beatles he was the one who responded most readily to fame, there was more to his actions than mere self-interest. Extraordinarily talented himself, he had a perfectionist's interest in getting the very best out of and for the group.

Certainly he can be hurtful when occasion takes him. Lennon, it is true, had the reputation for delivering scathing remarks (when Epstein said he was thinking of writing an autobiography and asked what he should call it, John replied, 'The Queer Jew'). But as McCartney acknowledges in a *Playboy* interview, 'I could be wicked, too.'

His unsympathetic treatment of Epstein, however, stemmed not from any belief that the unfashionably pinstripe-suited or ridiculously floral-shirted Brian was out of touch with what the Beatles had become and where they were going (or, at least, where they *thought* they were going); nor, as it did with Lennon, from a vicious sense of humour. It was all about money and commitment.

A workaholic himself, he took exception to Epstein's increasing inability to get to the office until everyone else was getting ready to go home, while the money problems really grated. A sizeable share of the riches Epstein had so foolishly signed away would have belonged to McCartney. Lennon, aimlessly staring at his television set in Weybridge, might not care. McCartney, the lower-middle-class lad from Liverpool, most decidedly did.

Similarly, McCartney's espousal of marijuana sprang from his sincerely held belief that 'pot is milder than Scotch' – an opinion he still holds. That year, 1967, he put his views on record and joined dozens of other well-known people in putting his name to a petition published in *The Times* calling for the legalisation of marijuana. It was the fashionable thing to do. Paul, however, did more than put his name to the petition. He also, indirectly, affixed it to the cheque. The advertisement was the brainchild of Steven Abrams, president of the quintessential 1960s Society of Mental Awareness which the 'avant-garde' McCartney supported. He promised Abrams that he would pay for the advertisement and when *The Times*, on the day before publication, demanded payment in advance for this controversial use of one of its pages, a taxi was dispatched to Peter Brown to pick up the cheque. The £1,800 the advertisement cost was eventually debited to the Beatles' advertising account.

Epstein, desperate to keep up with his 'boys', was one of the signatories, as were Graham Greene, the television presenter David Dimbleby and Brian Walden, MP, now the formidable television political interviewer. The pace was telling, however, and Brian was getting left a long way behind. While he stayed hidden away in his house in Belgravia's Chapel Street, hoping and dreading that McCartney – the only one of the four, as Brown has pointed out, he 'truly needed to fear' – would telephone, the Beatles were spinning off in other directions.

They flew to Greece with the grandiose idea of setting up a hippy commune and flew back disillusioned when the right-wing government then in power tried to turn their visit into a tourist promotion. The next inspirational stop was India.

On the Harrisons' trip to the sub-continent the previous year Patti had become fascinated by Hinduism. She had bought books on Transcendental Meditation and mysticism and, on their return to England, had enrolled in another 1960s organisation, the Spiritual Regeneration Movement, where she had been given her own mantra, a sacred, secret text used as an incantation. George, sceptical at first – 'What kind of scene is this if they make you keep secrets from your friends?' he asked – had come to share her interest. When Patti learned that the Maharishi Mahesh Yogi would be giving a lecture at London's Hilton hotel on August 24, she persuaded Harrison to attend. Paul and John – Ringo was with his wife, Maureen, who had just given birth to their second child – were whipped along by Patti's enthusiasm and decided to go too. Paul took along Jane Asher and his brother, Mike McGear.

The Maharishi, a physics graduate who was rather more streetwise than his saintly image might have suggested, delivered his usual speech about the sublime consciousness, peace and eternal harmony, and then invited the Beatles and their entourage up to his suite for a private audience. Nirvana – that blissful state where the individual becomes part of a greater whole – he promised, could be achieved through meditation, without resort to drugs. McCartney was intrigued. Lennon was bowled over and declared himself 'in a daze'. The Maharishi invited them to attend a ten-day seminar he was holding in Bangor in Wales. The Beatles accepted and the following day, suitably attired in beads and robes and with the ubiquitous Mick and Marianne in tow, they set off from Euston station (Cynthia, with heavy symbolism, missed the train).

They spent the night in a dormitory at the inappropriately named Normal College where, according to Brown 'a warm wave of camaraderie from the old times washed over them'. The next morning Paul called a press conference and announced that they had given up drugs. 'It was an experience we went through,' he declared. 'Now it's over. We don't need it any more. We think we're finding new ways of getting there.'

The Beatles off drugs? There was a news story for the British papers to plaster across their front pages as an antidote to the pro-drug pronouncements of the previous months. The story, however, would soon be overtaken. For if John, Paul, George and Ringo had forsworn their intemperate ways, if only briefly, Epstein had not.

Harrison and McCartney had 'half-heartedly' asked him to join them in Bangor but he declined, saying he had arranged to spend the Bank Holiday weekend with friends at Kingsley Hill. When the 'friends' failed to turn up, he telephoned around to see if he could round up a second contingent. He couldn't, and in a black despair left his house-guests, Peter Brown and Geoffrey Ellis, another old chum from the early Liverpool days, who had become chief administrator of NEMS, and drove back to Belgravia.

That was on Friday. On Saturday evening he telephoned Kingsley Hill and said he would drive down later that night. Brown suggested he took the train. Epstein agreed and said he would ring back and let them know what train he would be on.

He never phoned. On Sunday afternoon, on Brown's telephone instruction, his manservant, Antonio, and chauffeur Brian, broke down the double oak doors to his bedroom. They found his body, dressed in pyjamas, curled up in the foetal position on the bed. The coroner's verdict was that he had died from 'incautious self-overdoses' of Carbrital sleeping pills.

Brown telephoned Bangor and got hold of Jane Asher. 'I didn't tell her anything; I told her to find Paul and phone me back,' says Brown. McCartney rang back on a public pay phone. Brown broke the news to him. 'He was clearly stunned. They all knew Brian was pretty messed up but nobody expects someone, even if they are messed up, to die at thirty-two years old – particularly if you are in your twenties and consider yourself immortal.'

The ten-day meditation session was over almost before it had begun. Lennon, echoing the Maharishi who was saying that of course Epstein hadn't really died, he'd just gone to another place, said: 'Our meditation has given us the confidence to withstand such a shock.' McCartney, reacting appropriately to death, said: 'It is a great shock and I'm very upset.'

Epstein was buried two days later at the Longlane Jewish Cemetery in Liverpool. None of the Beatles attended. Aware that their presence would have turned the service into a circus, they had decided it would be wiser to stay away.

Brown and Cilla Black were among the mourners. Epstein, in what was left of his bodily form, very nearly didn't make it. Always late in life, his corpse got delayed on its motorway journey up from London. 'He can't even make it to his own funeral on time,' Brown whispered to Cilla. In her distraught state Cilla burst into a fit of uncontrollable nervous giggles, much to the puzzlement of Epstein's grieving relations.

McCartney's reaction was to throw himself into work. Three days after the funeral he ordered Peter Brown to summon the other three Beatles to his home in St John's Wood. They must start work, he declared, and the project they were to embark on was the one they had been toying with and putting off since April.

It was, predictably enough, another McCartney idea. Like *Sgt Pepper*, it had come to him on an aeroplane flight from LA. He had flown to America the day after the album was completed to join Jane Asher for her 21st birthday. On the flight he had read about writer Ken Kesey's troupe of Merry Pranksters who had driven across the US in a psychedelic-painted bus, filming as they went.

He decided that anything Kesey could do, he could do better. Letting his imagination run away with him, McCartney, comfortably installed in first class, started drawing pictures in a notebook of clowns and dwarfs and fat women. He decided on the title, 'Magical Mystery Tour', hummed out a tune and wrote the opening line. Back in the Abbey Road studio later that month, the song was recorded, with any old thoughts anyone could come up with making the rest of the lyrics. And that had been that. But now Epstein was dead and McCartney was desperately anxious to get back to work.

'It was part of Paul's reaction to Brian's death – to immediately start doing something,' Brown recalls. 'He kept saying, "Let's not waste a minute, let's get on with something, we can't be seen to be sitting around."'

Lennon was sceptical. 'I knew we were in trouble then,' he remarked. 'I didn't have any misconceptions about our ability to do anything other than play music.'

McCartney is a considerable force when he has the bit of an artistic idea between his teeth. He goes on and on about it until, in the end, it is easier to agree with him than submit to any more of his haranguing. John and George, against their better judgement, eventually went along with the project on the grounds, as Lennon said, that 'we felt that we owed it to the public to do more of these things'. What they got was a whole lot less than they had come to expect from the Fab Four.

At 10.45 a.m. on September 11 the blue and yellow coach with forty-three assorted freaks aboard set out from Allsop Place in London – without any idea where they were going, without a script except the one in McCartney's head.

They got caught in traffic jams. Fights broke out between the dwarfs and the fat ladies. Lennon lost his temper at one stage, leapt out of the bus, and tore down the Magical Mystery Tour banners. They were turned away from Shepperton Studios where Paul wanted to film the top-hat and cane finale because no one had thought to book a sound stage. When Paul flew to France to film

The Fool on the Hill he forgot his passport and his wallet, he didn't have the right lenses for the camera, and the sequence of two and a half minutes ended up costing £4000 (£35,000 in 1991 money). Disagreements broke out in the cutting room, with McCartney countermanding Lennon's suggestions.

McCartney's 'flick, flick, flick, one frame at a time' approach may have been all right for a home movie. For a television special it was a disaster; the only memorable 'flicks' in the whole fifty minutes are during *The Fool on the Hill* when McCartney's penis is exposed as he dances over the crest of the knoll, though it was not until the advent of home video and the pause button that the audience was able to share the adolescent joke. The staff at NEMS urged McCartney to forget it. 'Better to junk it than be embarrassed by it,' Brown advised.

McCartney wouldn't hear of that. *Magical Mystery Tour*, he insisted, was going ahead as scheduled. As usual he got his way. He had devoted fifteen weeks, day and night, to putting the *Magical Mystery Tour* together. 'When you've spent a long time on something, even when it's not good enough, you begin to feel perhaps it's better than you know it is,' he said, with a remark that explains many of his later failures.

When it was shown on British television on Boxing Day it was greeted with derision. In a front-page review the *Daily Express* aptly described it as 'blatant rubbish'. At one point on the tour Ringo screams, 'I've had enough of it, I can't stand anymore, I'm getting off' – sentiments shared by most of the 15 million people who had tuned in to watch it and quickly tuned out again.

McCartney, never good at taking criticism, was deeply wounded. And it wasn't just the newspaper critics he had to contend with. Lennon, too, was indignant. He was irritated by the way McCartney had bullied him into taking part in a project which, from its inception, he had had no faith in. He was disturbed by the control McCartney had assumed over the group, over him – a domination that drugs made him increasingly powerless to resist. He was angry at the way £40,000 of Beatle money, which is what it cost to make, had been squandered. He called the disaster 'the most expensive home movie ever made'.

McCartney, stung by Lennon's reproaches, said: 'John said *Magical Mystery Tour* was just a big ego trip for Paul. God. It was for their sake, to keep us together, keep us going, give us something new to do . . .'

Peter Brown believes that if Epstein had been alive and in control the fiasco would never have been allowed to happen. But Epstein was dead . . . Despite the coroner's verdict of accidental death, rumours continue to surround Epstein's demise – that he was suffocated in a rubber mask during a sado-masochistic ritual; that he was killed by a rent boy he had hired for the night.

There was also the big question mark over those licensing contracts Epstein had messed up. It wasn't just Paul McCartney and the other three Beatles who had been 'screwed'. In the legal confusion contracts for $80 million worth of Beatle merchandising had been cancelled and a lot of dangerous people stood to lose a lot of money.

A few weeks after Epstein was found curled up like a baby in Chapel Street, his solicitor, David Jacobs, was found hanging in his garage. The cause of death was determined to be suicide. But Jacobs had been a signatory on some of those contracts and friends had noted that he was running scared in the last few days of his life. Maybe Epstein was, too.

'The idea of Brian's murder is crazy, but all that merchandising trouble is true,' said McCartney. But dead Epstein certainly was. And with him went Lennon's last hold on the Beatles.

John had resented the way Epstein had repackaged the Beatles as nice, cute, would-be middle-class boys. He had gone along with it because, like Paul, he wanted to be a star. And because of his unspoken affinity with Epstein, he believed he would always be able to exercise control over what the Beatles did. But now Epstein was gone and Lennon was going – deep into the drug-induced chasm he had made for himself. The restraints were off the 'control freak'. The group was now Paul's. Except, of course, that it wasn't. Two women had entered the Beatle court, two Guineveres destined to break forever the enchantment of Pepperland. One was the strange Japanese lady dressed all in black. The other was Linda Eastman. Ironically, McCartney was responsible for the introduction of both.

10

THERE was never any doubt in the mind of either John Lennon or Paul McCartney about who was responsible for the success of the Beatles. 'Whether George or Ringo joined was irrelevant, because Paul and I created the music, OK!' Lennon once coolly remarked.

Ringo, the luckiest drummer in Liverpool, had been content to live with that, collecting his share of the money, indulging himself with his expensive cars and electronic toys, ready to fall in with whatever plans the team bosses came up with.

Harrison, brooding sullenly at the back of the studio, was not so sanguine. Neither Lennon nor McCartney paid any attention. Nor did George Martin. 'I never used to give George a great deal of time,' he admitted. 'George was kind of tolerated.' He concentrated 'on the two winners – John and Paul'. When, for instance, Lennon and McCartney were playing around with different riffs on the piano, it was Harrison who said that the tune they had knocked out a few minutes before was interesting. Without even a nod of acknowledgement, they went back to the one Harrison had suggested and turned the riff into 'I Feel Fine'.

Harrison was becoming increasingly frustrated by this secondary role he had been assigned. Harrison recalled: 'My problem was that it would be very difficult to get in on the act because Paul was very pushy in that respect. When he succumbed to playing on one of your tunes, he'd always do good. But you'd have to do fifty-nine of Paul's songs before he'd even listen to one of yours.'

McCartney, revelling in his role of musical auteur seemed unaware of the problems that were welling up. Singleminded to the point of tedium, he saw it as his responsibility to keep the group together and hard at work. 'I *loved* being a Beatle,' he recalled. And he still drew a great part of that pleasure from his association with Lennon. John may have been teetering on the edge, increasingly disenchanted with the way McCartney was usurping his position, but McCartney didn't see it that way, not yet. 'John and I were perfect for each other,' he said.

It was a partnership that succoured and sustained him. He has always looked to others to help give shape and definition to his ideas and his personality. The leader of the band he may be – but he always needs the band. It is only in association with other people that he is able to be himself. His life has been underscored by his relationships, be they mother, father, wife or Lennon. They have provided the sounding-board for what he wants to say and be, and back then what he wanted to continue to be, more than anything, was John Lennon's partner.

'One of the best things about Lennon and McCartney,' he said, 'was the competitive element within the team. It was great. I could do stuff he might not be in the mood for, egg him in a certain direction he might not want to go in. And he could do the same for me. If I'd go in a certain direction he didn't like, he'd just stop it like that,' with a snap of his fingers. McCartney would have been happy to have made it a lifetime's association. But the poignant truth was that, music apart, the two were very different kinds of people.

Peter Brown says: 'They hardly had anything in common except their music and the fact that they both realised that if Paul wrote a song and they went into the studio, John had a way of putting an edge on it while Paul had a way of softening a John song. It worked for both of them and they both got a lot out of it.' The relationship, however, was based more on habit than affinity. 'It had become a

178

family thing,' says Brown. 'They had been together since they were teenagers. If they had met later they would have had nothing in common.'

The looming divorce had yet to degenerate into open warfare, however. The Beatles were still doing things together. They were still on their transcendental kick and George and John had become vegetarians. ('That dreadful food they eat – it's no wonder they get high,' Jane Asher's mother remarked.) In February 1968 they all flew off to India for a family outing to the Maharishi's transcendental meditation centre at Rishikesh.

It was not a happy experience. The Maharishi turned out not to be the aesthete they had first imagined. Ringo, who missed his egg and chips and never really grasped what it was all about anyway, was the first to be disillusioned. He was soon flying home with his wife Maureen to complain that Rishikesh was similar to a Butlin's holiday camp.

McCartney and Jane Asher were the next to pull out. They had expected to find a simple retreat where they could search for the Word in beatific solitude. What they found was an expensive holiday camp with four-poster beds, a helicopter pad, an international chef, and a clientele of middle-aged Scandinavian women. They had not flown halfway round the world for this. Paul had never been that taken with it, in any case. He had only gone along with the Maharishi because first George and then John were so enthralled by him. He wanted to be open-minded. He wanted to see what was in it. But at heart the 'avant-garde one' (Paul's description) was really 'too bourgeois' (Brown's description) to play acolyte to an Indian guru of unknown provenance who was clearly intent on getting as much out of the Beatles as they could ever get out of him. After six weeks they had had enough and followed Ringo home to England.

Three weeks later Lennon, Harrison and their wives finally fled the ashram. The Maharishi let it be known that he expected the Beatles to tithe as much as 25 percent of their income to him which was to be deposited in a Swiss bank account. What finally brought the Eastern idyll to its inglorious conclusion was the suggestion that the Maharishi was using his ethereal position to take physical advantage of the young women in his holy care.

According to Brown, McCartney adopted a 'smug, I told you so' attitude to the whole episode. In fact he was very angry. Always concerned about his image, which at that time was inseparable from the group's, he believed that they had been made to look foolish. He blamed Harrison. So did Lennon. By now, however, other, more serious problems had appeared on their collective horizon. They would prove to be insoluble.

On 9 November 1966, on the day Brian Epstein publicly announced that the Beatles would no longer be touring, John Lennon had met that Japanese woman dressed in black. Her name was Yoko Ono and she was an anti-artist. It was the beginning of the rock era's most spectacular, most publicised, most indulgent love affair. Paul McCartney had organised the introduction – an act he would come to regret bitterly.

Yoko had turned up one night at McCartney's house in St John's Wood. 'There was a charity thing – it was rather avant-garde, something to do with John Cage,' he recalled. Born in 1934 and six years older than Lennon, Ono was the daughter of a Tokyo banking family. Her childhood was spent shuttling backwards and forwards between Japan and the United States. At 23, she eloped with a composer named Toschi Ichiyananagi and was disinherited for her rebellion. In retaliation she sent her parents a bottle filled with urine. The marriage, which lasted seven years, took her to New York where she started mixing with experimental musicians like John Cage. When they returned to Tokyo she left Ichiyananagi and married artist Tony Cox. She bore him a child they named Kyoko but motherhood did not come easily to her.

'Society's myth is that all women are supposed to have children, but that was a myth,' she said. 'I did become attached to her and had great love for her, but at the same time I was still struggling to get my own space in the world.'

To find it, the Coxes moved back to New York. The New York

art crowd remained singularly unimpressed by her work, however, and in 1966 and almost penniless, the Coxes arrived in London. With the same determination she had shown in New York but with a little more success, she moved in on the London art scene, started staging exhibitions and eventually ended up in McCartney's home.

'She wanted lyrics, manuscripts,' McCartney recalled. He had never made a habit of giving anything away. He wasn't going to start now. 'I really didn't want to give her any of my lyrics – you know, selfish, or whatever, but I just didn't want to do it. So I said, "But there's a friend of mine who might want to help – my mate, John." I kind of put her on to John and then they hit it off – it was like wild fire.'

The blaze which would engulf the Beatles took a while to get started. Their first meeting took place at the Indica gallery at an exhibition entitled 'Unfinished Paintings and Objects by Yoko Ono'. Lennon had been invited by John Dunbar, once the husband of Marianne Faithfull. When he arrived in his chauffeur-driven Mini, Dunbar told Yoko, 'Go and say hello to the millionaire.'

Yoko's art, even by the experimental standards of the 1960s, was unusual. The exhibition included an apple on a stand, for sale at £200. Patrons were invited to climb a ladder and look at the word, 'Yes', written on the ceiling. She handed Lennon a card with the word 'Breathe' printed on it. She invited him to hammer a nail into a board of wood for five shillings (25p). Lennon replied that he would hammer an imaginary nail for an imaginary five shillings. Yoko smiled. Lennon left and went home to Weybridge and the mortar board on which he kept his mixture of uppers, downers and LSD.

It was an unremarkable beginning. But Yoko had made an impression on Lennon – and he on her. She tried to see him to persuade him to subsidise another exhibition but didn't get past the Beatle minders. More successfully, she sent him a copy of *Grapefruit*, a book she had written three years before, which contained lines such as, 'Kill all the men you have slept with. Put the bones in a box and send it out into the sea in a box with flowers'; and 'Stir inside of your brains with a penis until things are well mixed.'

Lennon's brain didn't need any more mixing. It was well mixed already. He had, he said, taken over a thousand LSD trips. So devastating was the effect of the acid that on some days, he admitted, he lost the ability to see in colour – everything appeared in stark monochrome. Cynthia, ever the loyal northern wife, was desperately miserable. 'The rot began to set in the moment cannabis and LSD seeped its unhealthy way into our lives,' she observed. She cooked him food he didn't eat; spoke to him and got no answer; waited up for him when he didn't come home. She continued to believe that he still loved her but it was a sad self-deception. John was entranced by Yoko and her weird, discordant ideas which seemed so neatly to match his own.

All the time he had been in India he had written, on an almost daily basis, to Yoko and she had faithfully written back. 'I started thinking of her as a woman and not just as an intellectual woman,' Lennon recalled. On the aeroplane home he brutally, unnecessarily, spelt out just how irrelevant Cynthia had become to his life. Fortified by a succession of rum and cokes, he started listing the women he had slept with during their marriage. Cynthia screamed that she didn't want to know but Lennon persisted (singers, film stars, Playboy Bunnies, groupies, the wives of friends . . . the tally came to over 300). In May yet another name was added to the list. Yoko's.

Two weeks after they had returned from India Lennon had retired into psychedelic seclusion and Cynthia had gone on holiday to Greece. When she arrived back in Weybridge she walked in to find Yoko comfortably installed – in *her* house, in *her* bed.

'It was as if I didn't belong anymore,' she said. She didn't. Neither did McCartney. Lennon had found what he was looking for. And so, as it turned out, had McCartney.

Like Lennon with Cynthia, McCartney appeared to have a happy, settled relationship. He had been going out with Jane Asher since the 'She Loves You' days of early Beatlemania and everyone – including Paul himself – believed that they would one day get married. In December 1967 they had even got as far as announcing their engagement. It was a popular union. Jane – bright, attractive – appeared to be everything a Beatle's consort should be. Behind the gilded image, however, the affair had been in difficulties for some time. Drugs still had an influence. When Jane returned from her five-month theatre tour of the United States, 'Paul had changed so much. He was on LSD which I knew nothing about. The house had changed and was full of stuff I didn't know about.'

The problem ran deeper than that. McCartney, young, rich and famous, and a self-confessed womaniser – 'I was the biggest raver out' – had never forsaken his bachelor ways. And in cruel summation of his time with Jane he would later say, that of all the women he had been with during that period, 'I didn't have one girl I could really call a pal'. Not even, or so he seemed to be implying by that remark, the girl who had shared his life for five years. It had been to fill the emotional void that McCartney had turned to drugs – though never to the self-destructive extreme that Lennon did. McCartney, always determined to be in charge of everyone, including himself, held back.

He had smoked marijuana on an almost daily basis ever since Dylan had rolled him his first joint. During the making of *Sgt Pepper* he snorted cocaine. But always with restraint. One of the reasons for taking drugs is to release yourself, find yourself, get out of yourself. But that can be contradicted by the *fear* of losing yourself. You may be interested in seeing what happens but at the same time you don't want to lose control. Lennon fell into the first category; McCartney was firmly in the second. His LSD use, in comparison to Lennon's, was modest, and he never joined John at his mortar board. And when Lennon suggested that they should have holes drilled in their skulls in an operation called trepanning, he firmly declined.

Recalling Lennon's self-destructive ways, McCartney said: 'He would often say things like, "If you find yourself at the edge of a cliff and wonder whether you should jump off or not – try jumping."' McCartney, still able to see things in colour and three dimensions, said, No, he wouldn't. He was afraid. That worried him sometimes. 'I felt bad about saying no. I thought, Oh, here I go again, look at me, unadventurous. But unadventurous – by the extravagant standards set by Lennon, that is – he remained. For McCartney, being in control was always more important than freaking out. He gave up cocaine, for instance, almost as soon as he took it up. Heading for the lavatory for another snort he suffered 'the plunge . . . the drop', the depression that can follow the high, 'so I knocked that on the head'.

That incident took place in a nightclub. So did another, more fateful event. One evening in the summer of love, recording finished early and Peter Brown and McCartney hit the club circuit. They ended up in the Bag of Nails where Georgie Fame was playing with his Blue Flames. A tall, blonde with an American accent came over to say hello to Brown. Brown introduced her to McCartney: 'Paul, this is Linda Eastman.'

McCartney remembers: 'I saw this blonde across the room and I fancied her. So when she passed my table I said something stupid like, "Hello, how are you? Let me take you away from all this."'

'It was,' so Linda insists, 'like a cartoon. It sounds silly, but our eyes met and something just clicked.'

Brown laconically observes: 'They certainly established some kind of relationship that night – they went off together.'

Linda Eastman had been down rock's fast lane in a stretch limousine. Brought up in Scarsdale, the Weybridge of New York, her family, as she has proudly pointed out, is 'very academic. My father was brilliant. My brother was brilliant. They both went to Harvard Law School and did very well.' Linda did not echo their success. Her Scarsdale High School Yearbook described her as a 'strawberry blonde' with a 'yen for men'. And what else? There wasn't much else to say.

'I wasn't a very good student,' she concedes.

By one of those coincidences which mark Lennon and McCartney's lives, she attended Sarah Lawrence College where Yoko Ono had been a student for three years. Linda's stay was a brief one. 'All I ever cared about were animals, rock music and photography – it was a great disappointment to my family,' she says.

There was more to her background, as Lennon, with the assistance of Allen Klein, would discover. For the moment, though, Linda was regarded as just another blonde, sexy WASP from the right side of New York's social tracks, captivated by rock and roll and its glamour and always willing to make the true fan's ultimate sacrifice. Rock and roll had quickly become more than a dance track on the turntable. It became a physical part of Linda's life. She took a participatory interest in the business.

When Linda was 18 her mother died and her father remarried. She moved to college in Denver, married geology student Bob See, gave birth to a daughter they named Heather, left her husband and moved to Tucson. After a year in Arizona she returned to New York and got a job working at *Town and Country*, America's leading social magazine. One invitation that came into the magazine was for a press reception to meet the Rolling Stones on a private yacht sailing around Staten Island. Linda went along with her camera. She was on her way.

Using her looks and her modest skills as a photographer, she made it her business to get to meet the rock stars that rolled in and out of town and she was successful at what she did. Her friends included the Animals' Eric Burdon who liked breaking eggs on the women he was making love to. According to Brown: 'Linda once bragged that her babysitters included Mike Bloomfield, Stephen Stills and Al Kooper.' It was Chas Chandler, also once of the Animals and the man who 'discovered' Jimi Hendrix, who took her to the Bag of Nails the night she met McCartney.

Brown knew Linda from New York. 'She had sent me her portfolio and asked me if I could get her some work in London,' he recalls. Included was a series of pictures of the Stones. Brown was particularly taken with a photograph she had shot on the yacht of Brian Jones, the band's troubled and soon to be dead guitarist.

'I adored Brian and when I saw the ten by eight picture of him I took it,' he says. 'I sent the portfolio back to her and told her,

"You'll find one picture missing." She said to me, "The one of Brian." She knew exactly the one I would want. So I owed her one, in a way.'

Brown was to repay her favour with interest. While Epstein was on a drug cure in a rehabilitation home, Brown was busy organising the *Sgt Pepper* launch. A dozen 'key' journalists were invited to a dinner party at Epstein's Chapel Street house and a dozen photographers were also asked along. In May of 1967 Linda flew to London intent on meeting the Beatles (she had her romantic eye set on John, she admitted later – and John did once give her his brief, passing attention). She telephoned Brown.

'It was the first time I ever did it. I broke the rules and let Linda in,' says Brown. 'She never got to talk to him then because she was brought in and they posed for photographs and then she left. But he noticed her.' He noticed her again at the Bag a few nights later. When Linda returned to America they kept in touch and when Paul went to New York he would spend his nights with her. And when he went to Los Angeles with Ron Kass to address a convention of record company executives, Linda flew out, at her own expense, to join him. She went there to play the most obvious card in the female deck.

McCartney had been enjoying himself in LA. He had what Kass dubbed his black and white minstrel show – a white actress and black Winona Williams, an extraordinarily beautiful girl who enjoyed a long relationship with rock superstar David Bowie and was friendly with Jimi Hendrix. He had installed them in a bungalow suite at the Beverly Hills hotel.

Winona had met the Beatles on a visit to London the previous year. She shared the same birthday as Lennon – October 9 – and she says that John told her that the song 'Birthday' was written for her. It was with McCartney that she formed an attachment, however, and when he arrived in Los Angeles where she was then based, 'I organised a party for fifty to seventy-five people for him at a nightclub.'

Their relationship had not been a smooth one. At the Speakeasy in London McCartney had kicked her under the table when she admonished Lennon for making cruel fun of Ringo. He told her: 'Shut up – you're asking for it.' In Los Angeles she had had a row with him ('I was jealous,' she explains) and he had left her to make her own way back to the Beverly Hills hotel. She was given a lift back by a girlfriend who was stopped by the police en route and arrested for drunk driving. 'I went on to the hotel to ask Paul for some money to bail her out,' she recalls. 'I knocked at the door and Linda answered.'

Winona knew Linda Eastman and didn't like her. 'Her main focus had always been Mick Jagger but he didn't want to know,' Winona says. 'She just didn't have it – not everyone goes for women who don't shave their legs or their armpits. Plus she had a little daughter, Heather.' Winona had a different view of how to bring up a daughter, and had little respect for Linda's way.

Now she was faced with Linda on the proprietorial side of McCartney's doorway. 'I coolly said: "I need to speak to Paul,"' Winona recalls. 'He came to the door with a little smirk on his face. I told him what happened and that I needed some money. He told me that he never carried cash. I pulled him aside and asked him, "What's going on, what's *she* doing here? I thought we had a date tomorrow." He said, "I'll explain it to you later." I left to go and get the bail money to get my girlfriend out of jail from John Phillips of the Mamas and Papas.'

The following day Winona and McCartney met up in the lobby of the Beverly Hills hotel. McCartney had Linda in tow and Winona, as she recalls, 'went into a pout. Paul said, "Come on love, don't be like that." I asked, looking at Linda, "What's the deal here?" He said: "I've just been informed that I'm going to have a baby." Linda had come out to Los Angeles to tell Paul that she was pregnant!'

This was a false alarm: it would be another fourteen months before Linda eventually gave birth. Her relationship with McCartney gestated rather more quickly. The other girls who provided the top rock stars with companionship never understood

McCartney's interest in Linda. She was pretty certainly but there were prettier girls around – and unlike Linda, they shaved their legs.

Linda had other things going for her, however. First and foremost, she was a fan and McCartney was too savvy and too egocentric to miss that. Like McCartney, she had an addiction to marijuana. She was also a girl from a good background, and that was important, too. As Brown drily observes: 'Paul was very flattered by her attention because he saw her as a class girl coming from an intellectual, successful, New York family. Paul was attracted by that.' She was socially acceptable, intelligent, and McCartney could be proud of her. Coming from an affluent background, money didn't particularly matter to her – she was not interested in jewellery or material display and that too suited McCartney.

There was also something else and it was this that really separated her from the other women in the higher echelons of rock. When McCartney visited her in New York she introduced him to her daughter and left him babysitting while she went off to photograph a band at the Fillmore East. When he returned to London she sent him a blow-up picture of himself with little Heather kissing him superimposed on the top. McCartney, who retains the warmest memories of his own, idealised childhood and is forever trying to recreate it, responded to the gesture. It was a love match in the making – and one that McCartney believes was predestined.

When Lennon wrote 'Lucy in the Sky with Diamonds' the girl with kaleidoscope eyes was, he said, 'the female who would one day come to save me. It turned out to be Yoko'. McCartney had also had a forewarning.

'Before I met Linda,' he recalled, 'I had been to a clairvoyant in Brighton and she told me, "You're going to marry a blonde and have four children." "A blonde? My girlfriend's a redhead and we surely don't intend to have four children." Most people thought I was due to marry Jane Asher – I rather thought I was, too. But I just kept remembering Linda, this nice blonde American girl.'

The redhead was still in situ, however. Jane Asher was intelligent, talented, and at least as well-bred as Linda. She was a fixture in his life. As Winona Williams recalls: 'He was very hung up on Jane. When any conversation between us got really serious it was always about how much he cared about Jane, how she was the one love of his life.'

Jane was certainly no groupie who could be ordered out into the night. She was the girl he came home to. It was a relationship that looked as though it would struggle on indefinitely. And so it might have – except that one day Jane came home when she wasn't expected.

A successful actress in her own right, Jane was frequently away on tour. McCartney resented her absences, though not so much that he didn't use them as an opportunity to go out playing with whoever happened to be available – and for one of the world's most eligible bachelors there were plenty of women who were. Jane either didn't know about it or pretended she didn't. But she could not ignore Francine Schwartz.

An advertising copywriter from New York, Schwartz had come to London to try to persuade McCartney to help her produce a film script she had written. She went round to the Beatles' offices and took her place in the queue. The reception was awash with hopefuls trying to interest one or other of the Beatles in every kind of half-baked idea imaginable. The receptionists used to turn away almost everyone and threw out a lot of good ideas along with the bad. Schwartz was one that got through, to McCartney's embarrassment. For some inexplicable reason Barbara Bennett, the secretary on duty at the time, told Schwartz to come back after lunch when McCartney would be there.

It was a transformed Schwartz who reappeared that afternoon. The prospect of meeting the great prince of rock and roll had that effect on women. When Linda Eastman had arrived in London she was a scruff. When she attended the *Sgt Pepper* party in Belgravia she was washed and combed, wearing false eyelashes and dressed in the height of Chelsea fashion. So it was with Schwartz. She had bought herself a new dress and had her hair cut at Vidal Sassoon. She was introduced to McCartney who said he was busy but would get in touch later. A month later he telephoned her and invited her to the Abbey Road studios where she claims she met Lennon and Yoko and sang backing vocals on *Revolution*.

When nothing much else happened she sent McCartney a note which read: 'Dear Mr Plump, I think I'm going to have to go home soon. When am I going to see you?' McCartney replied with a note of his own which was delivered with the Sunday morning milk to the flat she had rented in Chelsea. It read: 'Make it Monday, Mr P.'

The next day McCartney bounded in with his sheepdog, Martha, and went to bed with her. After that he started dropping round, sometimes at five o'clock in the morning, shouting, 'It's F-Day!' He got her a job in the Beatles' press office. Eventually he moved her into Cavendish Avenue. He was, he told her, looking for a woman who could take care of him in the way that Jane, who was again away on tour, couldn't.

According to Schwartz he complained: 'Jane is obviously confused as to her priorities and is too caught up in her own career and doesn't see the obvious need to give it all up for me.' He added: 'True love should mean total devotion.' Could she give it? 'I sure would like to try,' she replied.

She cooked his food – baked beans on toast was a favourite – cleaned up after the household pets which weren't house-trained, dealt with the dope dealers, made love to him. It wasn't all she had hoped for – especially the sex. McCartney, she later wrote, 'felt sometimes that he wasn't manly enough.' As a lover, she observed, he had a tendency to rush things. He was neither 'terribly good or terribly bad'. But sex, she reasoned, wasn't everything. They had, she said, 'the ephemeral thing we substituted for lovemaking'.

There was nothing ephemeral about Jane Asher's reaction when she arrived home unannounced one night. As she disappeared through the iron gates the fans outside tried to warn Paul of the rapidly approaching disaster, frantically buzzing the intercom and screaming, 'Look out, Jane's coming!'

Paul shouted back: 'Pull the other one.'

Jane let herself in with her key, walked up the stairs, and found the bedroom door closed. Intuitively she knocked. McCartney leapt out of bed, opened the door, and tried to squeeze out without letting her see into the bedroom. But Jane had seen enough. It was an awful repeat of what had happened to Cynthia Lennon when she came home from Greece to find Yoko Ono installed in her place.

Jane left the house, never to return. It was Jane's mother who came round to pick up her things. It was Schwartz who helped her pack them up. It was the end of a five-year affair. It was also the end of Schwartz who was quickly on her way back to America. She left with the parting observation that McCartney was 'petulant, outrageous, adolescent, a little Medici prince, powdered and laid on a satin pillow at a very early age.'

With Jane gone and Schwartz dismissed, there was now a vacant space on that satin pillow. Linda Eastman would soon be on her way over from America to fill it. She was not a popular choice. The Beatles' fans resented her. Margo Stevens, one of the girls who kept daily vigil outside the Cavendish Avenue place, was quoted as saying: 'She was hairier than he was.'

McCartney's friends also had their doubts. Hunter Davies, the Beatles' official biographer, wrote: 'It seemed at first to us that Linda was very much a yes-girl, who was overdoing her adoration for Paul, clinging on to him all the time, hanging on his every word. We couldn't see it lasting. We couldn't see what she was giving Paul.'

Peter Brown could. 'She played the happy family card,' he says. As one relationship approached its breaking point, another was being created. The transition would be painful, drawn-out, brutal.

11

THE Beatles were always into money. But by the end of 1967 they were being taxed up to the hilt of their earnings. Harrison underestimated when he wrote about 'one for you, nineteen for me' in *Taxman*. The revenue were actually taking 96 percent.

They still lived well; by June 1967 they had spent upwards of £750,000 on houses, cars and all the other accoutrements of rock stardom. The money supply seemed endless. In hard fact, however, they were living beyond their means. There were more tax demands in the pipeline and, as financial matters stood, they were going to have trouble meeting them. The solution, paradoxically, was to spend more.

In 1965, Epstein, growing uneasy at the mess the Beatles' finances were becoming, had investigated the possibility of taking the group offshore into a tax shelter in the Bahamas, beyond the voracious grasp of the British and American authorities. Prime Minister Harold Wilson's lawyer, the imposing (in both the legal and physical sense) Arnold Goodman, was consulted. Goodman said that to do so was certainly not illegal but he advised caution. Because of their enormous fame and the enormous sums of money they were earning, Goodman warned that attention would inevitably be drawn to any overt attempt at tax avoidance. It would, he said, be wiser to look for another way out of their problem. Epstein duly dropped the scheme.

Now the accountants came up with another suggestion. Expand, they said. Invest in related businesses and property with the eventual objective of going public. It was sound advice and McCartney was enthusiastic. With Paul pushing, a new company was formed. The name Apple was chosen for its symbolic association with childhood innocence. McCartney punningly insisted on it being called Apple Corp.

It was an opportunity for the Beatles to take charge of their own affairs. Shortly before he died, Epstein, who only the previous year had been offered £20 million for NEMS, had been negotiating to sell his organisation to Robert Stigwood, the brash Australian pop entrepreneur who launched the Bee Gees, for the ludicrously low sum of £500,000. With Epstein dead, Stigwood moved to take control. McCartney blocked the move.

'We're not about to be sold like some sort of chattel,' he declared. 'Not to Robert Stigwood, not to the Queen Mum.' From now on the Beatles were going to manage themselves.

As the vanguard of the New Age, however, McCartney had no intention of appearing to join the 'men in suits', as the Beatles disparagingly called all businessmen, including those who worked for them. Even if the object was to make money, appearances had to be maintained. 'If the Beatles have to go into business then we want to have fun with it,' he declared. And everyone, he insisted, was invited to join in the frolic.

Lennon would later deny McCartney's involvement in Apple's inception, with all the divorcé's venom that marked just about everything else he had to say about his ex-partner. 'It was certainly never Paul's idea, as he has gone on about,' he said. 'Apple was presented to us as a reality by the Epsteins in 1967, before Brian died. Brian and his furniture-salesman brother Clive. And they hadn't the slightest idea what they were doing. It was really just a loony tax scheme. Our incomes would be hidden inside Apple. Then the money would be moved around.'

Lennon's disclaimer notwithstanding, it was McCartney's energy that got the company up and operating. 'Apple was largely structured

On 12 March 1969, James Paul McCartney married Linda Louise Eastman in mayhem at Marylebone Register Office. Pete Brown is on the extreme left. *(Hulton Deutsch)*

The McCartneys leaving the Law Courts in 1971, during the hearing of the case in which Paul set out to dissolve the Beatles partnership. *(Topham)*

The fulfilment of all his dead mother's ambitions: McCartney's house in St John's Wood, 1970. *(Hulton Deutsch)*

Paul, Linda, Heather and Ringo on the set of Ringo's film *The Magic Christian*, 1969. *(Pictorial Press)*

in the way Paul wanted to do it,' Peter Brown says. 'Paul was the one who came into the office every day, Paul was the one I and Neil Aspinall would mainly talk to about how we should do this or that, how we should structure a deal. It was Paul who made the decisions. And he liked to do this. He liked to see himself as a businessman.'

He played the part with relish, wearing a black overcoat, walking from his home in Cavendish Avenue where Linda was installed from October 1968, and travelling to the office by underground or bus.

It was also McCartney who set the company's altruistic tone. He flew to America with Lennon, saw Linda Eastman, and appeared on the Johnny Carson Show to announce that Apple would be a 'kind of Western communism . . . We want to help people, but without doing it as a charity. We always had to go to the big men on our knees and touch our forelocks and say please can we do so and so. We're in the happy position of not needing any more money, so that for the first time the bosses aren't in it for the profit. If you come to me and say, "I've such and such a dream", I'll say to you, "Go away and do it."' Said Harrison: 'We wanted to let serendipity take hold.'

To underscore the point an advertisement was placed in the music press. It showed a photograph of Alistair Taylor, an old friend of Epstein's who had risen to be office manager of NEMS, in which he was dressed as a street busker. The caption announced: 'This man had talent. One day he sang songs to a tape-recorder (borrowed from the man next door) . . . sent the tape, letter and photograph . . . if you were thinking of doing the same thing yourself, DO IT NOW! This man now owns a BENTLEY!' The Apple offices were besieged. There were a lot of would-be Bentley drivers out there.

Apple had moved into a £500,000, five-storey Georgian house in Savile Row, the road whose name is synonymous with the finest bespoke tailoring. Discretion had always been its characteristic. Now its pavements were clogged with queues of hippies and Hell's Angels trying to get into number 3.

Several Christs turned up. So did at least one Adolf Hitler. A donkey made it past the doorman, in his dove-grey Tommy Nutter morning coat, and up in the lift to the press office. A clan of Californians moved in and their naked children ran around the reception area. A man called Stocky sat in one of the offices drawing pictures of genitalia.

The post brought sackloads of home-recorded tapes and illiterate film scripts. They were unceremoniously dumped in a cupboard, never to be heard or read, a testimony to the truism that communism, even of the Beatles' kind, was only as good as its bureaucracy which, at Apple, wasn't very good at all.

The Fool had lost the Beatles £200,000 of their money in the Apple boutique in Sherlock Holmes's Baker Street. It is estimated that 'Magic' Alex Mardas, the Greek Lennon was very attached to, spent another £160,000 of Apple funds producing little of any discernible value (some 100 patents applied for on his behalf by the EMI lawyers were turned down).

There was an element of public show to the craziness, however. As prophets of flower power, the Beatles were very self-conscious about being seen as becoming too grand, too Establishment. They were wary of being accused of selling out. The craziness had to be absorbed which was why even the obviously deranged were sometimes given houseroom in Derek Taylor's press office.

There was another, more intrinsic fault in the organisation and that was the Beatles themselves. Epstein, for all his incompetence, had protected them from the harsh realities of business. They had been kept emotionally cocooned and had never had to deal with household bills or mortgages, never mind millions. As Lennon said, they didn't even know how to check into a hotel. Now they were in control of their own financial destiny and there were moments, Apple's administrative director Peter Brown recalls, when it became a 'nightmare.

'Ultimately all the decisions had to have the approval of the four owners, of the four Beatles. They had no way of making the necessary judgements. We all learn things as we grow up in our transition from school to starting a job. They didn't have that experience. They had either been poor or very rich. We would say, "Do we want to make this deal with 20th Century Fox?" They would say, "Why do we have to go with those arseholes from 20th Century Fox, why can't we do it with some bright young guy just developing in Soho?" We would say, "You can't do it like that because we need 20th Century; we need their distribution, we need their money." We were writing the rules as we went along.'

But if the lingering impression of Apple is that of uncontrolled hippy insanity, some serious work was going on behind the scenes. McCartney proved himself a fast learner who was smart enough to hire talented people. The eminently competent Ron Kass, later the husband of Joan Collins, then the vice-president of Liberty Records, was lured away to set up Apple Records. On the prompting of McCartney, Jane's brother Peter Asher had switched from being a pop star and was appointed head of A & R and repaid the company by signing a young singer named James Taylor. A film section, under the direction of Richard Lester's former associate Dennis O'Dell, was started. McCartney himself, on the advice of Twiggy, had signed a singer called Mary Hopkin and produced her first record which became an immediate number one.

Apple was also the releasing arm for new Beatles records. The first was 'Hey Jude', a song McCartney had written for Julian when John and Cynthia finally broke up, which became their biggest hit, selling over seven million copies. Between them 'Hey Jude' and Hopkin's 'Those Were the Days' sold a mammoth thirteen million records, a magnificent financial springboard for any new company.

Says Peter Brown: 'The greatest chaos seen by the media and by outside was Derek Taylor, the press officer, this wonderful, mad person who would sit in his wing-back basket chair in this enormous room filled with all these freaks. If a freak arrived we would send him to Derek's office where they would be given a joint and a bottle of vodka. The overheads on his office were £600 a month, just on entertainment. But underneath all that there was Ron Kass who was running our record company very successfully. There was a successful publishing company and there was Peter Asher. I was running the general administration. The company was running relatively smoothly considering the crazy operation. There was no question that a lot of money was being lost, but at the same time there was also a lot of money coming in. It was never quite as chaotic as people sometimes believed. It was simply our way of dealing with it.'

There was one freak, however, who couldn't be sent up to Taylor's office and placated with a joint and a drink, one freak even McCartney couldn't order around or dismiss. John Lennon. While Paul was playing businessman (he would even check to see if there was enough loo paper in the lavatories), Lennon was hidden in a drug-lined black plastic bag with Yoko Ono. He seemed destined to stay there. He continued to consume prodigious quantities of LSD – and now he had added heroin to his menu. But somewhere inside his drug-addled brain a vestige of the old abrasive John Lennon was still ticking – like a time-bomb. And when Lennon decided to come back to claim his estate it exploded.

On 18 November 1968, Lennon and Ono were arrested at the flat in London's Montagu Square they had borrowed from Ringo and charged with possession of 219 grains of cannabis resin. The days when Beatle misdemeanours would be ignored were over for good.

The following month Lennon and Ono released *Unfinished Music No 1 – Two Virgins* on the Apple label. The cover featured a photograph of Lennon and his consort stark naked. They did not make a pleasing picture. When EMI's Sir Joseph Lockwood asked them what they were thinking of, Ono said that it was art. 'In which case, why not show Paul in the nude – he's much prettier!' Lockwood said. EMI refused to distribute the album and it was eventually issued on The Who's Track label in a brown-paper wrapper. The reaction it generated was predictable. In Britain people laughed; in the United States it was confiscated by the New Jersey police as pornography.

McCartney was outraged. *Two Virgins* offended his sense of

propriety. He was also astute enough to recognise the damage it would do to the Beatles whose own *White Album* had just been released. There was no diverting Lennon, however. In his own befuddled way, he was back on course – and he was gunning for McCartney. Where before he had been content to let his partner get on with it, he now started taking, if not quite an active, then certainly a destructive interest in the workings of Apple. Encouraged by Yoko Ono, he began turning up at the offices in Savile Row, firing orders, countermanding McCartney's instructions.

He would say, 'I don't like this, I don't want that.' McCartney would reply, 'Wait a minute, this is how we do it, this is Apple and this is how it's done. This is how we operate, this is how it's structured.' John would say, 'I don't care. I want it done differently.'

Says Brown: 'John wanted it to be a more erratic organisation. He wanted it to be more "artistic". Paul runs things in a very straight way. John was very different.'

McCartney could be capricious when the mood took him. The day after Jane Asher had walked out on him following her discovery of Francine Schwartz in the pre-marital home in Cavendish Avenue, McCartney had stormed into the Apple office intending to fire her brother Peter in retribution. The intervention of Kass saved Asher his job.

It was a rare eruption, however. On matters pertaining to business he was usually more level-headed, and McCartney's initial reaction was to ignore Lennon on the not unreasonable assumption that his enthusiasm was only an interlude between drug binges, that his interest in Apple wouldn't last long. When Lennon started sounding off about Apple's finances, however, McCartney was forced to take note.

'If Apple goes on losing money at this rate, we'll all be broke in six months,' Lennon told *Disc* magazine.

The fact that Lennon, through his sponsorship of 'Magic' Alex and his self-indulgent insistence on pushing ahead with the release of *Two Virgins*, was as responsible as anyone for the financial outpouring was an irrelevancy. It was Lennon's way of hitting out at

Paul and the organisation he had constructed in his own 'bourgeois' image. Apple, Lennon loudly declared, was losing around £20,000 a week and that he was down to his last £50,000.

That something was amiss was not in question. On the day *Two Virgins* was released, Harold Minsker, the Bryce-Hamner accountant who now supervised Apple's affairs, resigned in protest. Stephen Maltz, a junior partner in the accounting firm, took over. A few weeks later he too resigned, sending a warning to each of the four Beatles which read: 'You were never concerned where the money came from or how it was spent, and were living under the idea that you had millions at your disposal . . . your personal finances are in a mess. Apple is in a mess.'

The figures made depressing reading. The million-pound start-up fund had been spent, plus half of the £800,000 the Beatles had received for selling themselves into Apple. All of the Beatles were overdrawn on the Apple account; McCartney and Lennon by some £60,000 each, Harrison and Ringo by £35,850 and £32,080 respectively.

By McCartney's reckoning, however, it was not nearly as bad as Lennon was choosing to make out. The record division, after all, was a spectacular success and was generating millions of pounds. All that was needed, he said, was a springclean to clear the organisation of its more unprofitable ventures, and he set off looking for a suitable broom.

Lord Beeching, who had reorganised the British railway system by the draconian expedient of axing most of the branch lines, was offered the job but turned it down. Lord Poole, the chairman of Lazard's bank and financial adviser to the Queen, was also consulted and he did express interest. What McCartney was really looking for, though, was not a businessman but a father figure to guide him through the hazards. His own father, whatever other qualities Jim may have possessed, was certainly not qualified to deal with these kind of problems. His future father-in-law, however, most assuredly was.

Lee Eastman was an immensely successful lawyer who had

earned himself a considerable fortune looking after various showbusiness interests in New York. His expertise went beyond the law. As
McCartney explained: 'Lawyers in America aren't just like lawyers
here. They don't just do law, they often do business. So he was in
the music publishing business.'

McCartney had met the Eastmans at their sumptuous Manhattan
home a few months earlier and had been inordinately impressed by
their style, the way they played Mozart in their drawing room,
their confidence and acumen. 'He knew Irving Berlin and Hoagy
Carmichael,' McCartney proudly announced. Who better then,
than Lee Eastman, to take charge of Apple, he thought, and invited
him to London.

In a bad tactical mistake it wasn't Lee who flew to London to
meet the other Beatles, but his son, John, an elegant 28-year-old
Ivy Leaguer whose preppy style personified everything they professed
to detest. His advice was solid enough. The first thing they should
do, he said, was buy NEMS, now renamed Nemperor Holdings,
which provided no service but still, under Epstein's old contracts,
continued to take 25 percent of all the Beatles' earnings. Epstein's
brother, Clive, was anxious to sell in order to meet the death duties
of Brian's estate and the Beatles, Eastman counselled, would be
wise to acquire it for themselves. The £1,250,000 purchase price,
young Eastman explained, could be financed by an advance from
EMI against future royalties.

Lennon was singularly unimpressed. He eschewed interest in all
matters commercial almost as an act of artistic faith. 'I had always
felt guilty that I made a lot of money,' he said, 'so I had to give it
away or lose it.' More pertinently, he took an immediate dislike to
the carefully groomed Eastman and his attempt to engage him in a
conversation about Kafka.

This was the moment that Allen Klein had been waiting for. He
had been trying to get through to one or other of the Beatles ever
since the death of Epstein but had always been fended off by Brown,
the Apple 'gatekeeper'. Klein had then started leaning on one of the
Rolling Stones' entourage who leaned on Derek Taylor who in turn

went to Brown to complain that he was being blamed for keeping Klein at bay. He asked Brown, 'as a personal favour', to pass on Klein's message. Brown recalls: 'I, in my stupid fairness, felt that I wasn't there to be a gatekeeper, that I shouldn't turn people away just because I don't like them. I said to Derek, "OK, I'll arrange for Klein to see them." It was one of the biggest decisions I ever made.'

Klein met Lennon and Yoko at his suite at the Dorchester hotel. He promised them the world – millions of dollars, artistic control, freedom from responsibility. He thoughtfully served them macrobiotic rice. He flattered John with his knowledge of Lennon songs. He won Yoko round by talking admiringly of her art and music. He impressed them with his rough, tough street manner developed in the Bronx and so different to the smooth Fifth Avenue elegance of Eastman. He regarded Eastman's view with contempt. There was, he said, no need to pay £1,250,000 for NEMS. He would get it for them for free.

In three fast-talking hours he had Lennon and Yoko utterly convinced. Then and there Lennon wrote a note to Lockwood that said: 'From now on Allen Klein handles all my stuff.' He confirmed it the next day with another note to Lockwood which stated: 'I don't give a bugger who anyone else wants, but I'm having Allen Klein for me.'

McCartney was not too worried at first. His attitude was that this was just another of John's little whims he was going to have to deal with. Mick Jagger could have told him better – and tried to do just that. The Rolling Stones, after their initial enthusiasm for Klein and the money he had generated for them, had become disillusioned by his methods. He had taken them over and, try as they would, there seemed to be no way out of his grasp. When Jagger learned what Lennon was planning to do he telephoned Brown and warned him: 'You can't let this happen – doesn't John realise how awful Klein is?' Brown replied that he had tried, that Lennon wouldn't listen to him, that Jagger would have to tell him himself.

A special meeting was convened around the large octagonal rosewood table in Brown's office on the second floor of the Apple building in Savile Row. Ringo, Harrison and McCartney were waiting with Jagger when Lennon walked in – with Klein. Jagger took one look at Klein, mumbled a few words – and walked out. He had come along as a favour to warn them about what they were letting themselves in for. He had no intention of getting involved in a screaming match with Klein. If Lennon wanted to play the 'wandering minstrel', with a street fighter for a business minder, then so be it and on his own head.

Brown made one last attempt to talk Lennon out of appointing Klein. Lennon refused to be dissuaded. He told Brown: 'I've got my own dog to go after McCartney's dogs. You need a dog in this life to go after the dogs.' The dogs he was referring to were the Eastmans. It was a chilling indication of the savage in-fighting that lay ahead.

McCartney would later hold Yoko Ono primarily responsible for starting the war between him and Lennon. 'We were pretty good mates . . . until Yoko came into it,' he said. 'The thing is, in truth, I never really got on well with Yoko anyway. It was John who got on well with her – that was the whole point.' In McCartney's view, Yoko had assumed control over the drug-wrecked Lennon – and Klein had recognised that and was manipulating it to his own advantage. 'Klein, so I heard, had said to John – the first time anyone had said it – "What does *Yoko* want?" So, since Yoko liked Klein because he was giving Yoko anything she wanted, he was the man for John.'

That theory is fine, but only as far as it goes. For Klein would never have been allowed in if Harrison and Ringo had not sided with Lennon – and that is exactly what they did. Ringo and especially Harrison were becoming increasingly disenchanted with the way McCartney had taken over the Beatles, with them consigned to the role of backing group. Klein promised to go through their books and make them rich again. With dazzling hyperbole, he also promised to get McCartney off their backs. They liked what they heard and now there were three Beatles stacked up against McCartney.

Harrison's rebellion was recorded in music. During the making of the *White Album* he had got 'pissed off at Lennon and McCartney for the grief I was catching. I said I wasn't guilty of getting in the way of their careers. I said I wasn't guilty of leading them astray in our going to Rishikesh to see the Maharishi.' He put his thoughts into 'Not Guilty', which appeared on the *George Harrison* album.

Now the Beatles were working on *Let It Be* and the 'grief', as Harrison put it, was even worse, except this time it was all emanating from McCartney. The film was Paul's attempt to recapture the spirit of their early days, to 'Get Back' to the time when they enjoyed themselves. It is a record of disharmony. The others weren't interested in getting back; they wanted to get out. Lennon was too wrapped up with Yoko to pay more than passing attention to the proceedings, while Harrison was ever more irritated by what he saw as McCartney's dictatorial attitude. At one point he walked out.

'I just got so fed up with the bad vibes, and that arguments with Paul were being put on film,' he said. 'I didn't care if it was the Beatles, I was getting out. Getting home in that pissed-off mood I wrote that song, "Wah Wah".' The song, a snide attack on McCartney, would later appear on Harrison's *All Things Must Pass* album. '"Wah Wah" was saying,' he explained, 'You're giving me a bloody headache.'

Matters financial contributed to Harrison's dissatisfaction. Beatles records were either Lennon or McCartney compositions and there was intense competition between the two to produce the A side of their releases. But only because of ego – financially, because of their joint publishing, it made no difference. It did to Harrison. Every song (he was allowed only one per album and only three on the four-side, 29-track *White Album*) was an important source of income to him. He wanted to earn more and resented the fact that he wasn't being allowed to.

Ringo recalled that McCartney even started telling Harrison how to play his guitar solos, to Harrison's intense annoyance. 'He was writing more. He wanted things to go his way where, when we first started, they basically went John and Paul's way,' Ringo said. 'George was finding his independence and wouldn't be dominated as much by Paul.' And he certainly didn't want his business affairs ordered by Paul's impending in-laws.

McCartney could not see what the objection was. 'I was very upset when they said I was just trying to bring in Lee Eastman because he's my in-law. They'd known me twenty years, yet they thought that.' So intent had McCartney become on pursuing his own ends, and yet at the same time maintaining the appearance of Beatledom, that he had lost sight of the problems welling up behind him. The name of the film, of their life together, Harrison said, should have been 'Let it Rot'.

Yet however disgruntled Harrison might have been, it was still Lennon who posed the greatest and, as it would quickly prove, the insurmountable problem. In time McCartney and Harrison and therefore Ringo would most probably have straightened out their differences. Lennon was a different matter. It is easy to dismiss him as a drug-crazed victim of his own insecurity who had fallen under the spell of an oriental dominatrix. But of one thing John was certain: no matter how energetic and busy Paul had been on a day-to-day basis, he still felt 'It's my band, my group and my show.' It wasn't. The Beatles had become *McCartney's* group. Lennon refused to accept that and McCartney was almost certainly right when he observed: 'He became so jealous in the end.'

Lennon had found it difficult enough accepting McCartney as an equal ('It made him insecure,' Paul said). He found it impossible to consider a future under McCartney's artistic control. He would rather destroy the band than let McCartney take it away from him. And in Allen Klein he had found his Terminator. The battle lines were drawn, the battlefields were the Apple offices and the courts, and the fighting, when it came, was dirty and destructive. And it came soon enough.

It was at this juncture that John Eastman made another tactical mistake. He wrote to Clive Epstein on 14 February 1969. In his letter he questioned the 'propriety' of the nine-year agreement signed between EMI, the Beatles and NEMS when Brian renegotiated their recording contract. Clive and his mother Queenie were outraged by the implication and three days later sold out to Leonard Richenberg's Triumph Trust. When Klein and the younger Eastman met the air was fouled by insults. Eastman returned from the lavatory where he had found a glass jar of suppositories and said to Klein: 'I always knew you were an asshole.' Klein responded by calling Eastman a 'shithead'.

Lee Eastman flew over to try to work out some acceptable compromise. He flew straight into the most destructive row of them all. It took place at the Apple offices. Eastman, patrician, self-assured, coated with aristocratic gloss, knew all about Klein, about his more questionable dealings and the lawsuits involving him and his companies, and he treated him with barely concealed contempt. But Klein had been doing some research of his own. He had discovered that, far from being a high-born WASP of carefully polished appearances, Lee Eastman was a Jew whose original family name, by ironic coincidence, was Epstein. To compound the exposure, the change of faith was a recent one – childhood friends of Linda recall that, before the death of her mother and her father's remarriage to a woman she did not get on with, the Eastman family, while never Orthodox, had always observed the Jewish sabbath.

The Jew from the Bronx went straight for the jugular of the Jew from Manhattan. He called him 'Jew boy'. He persisted on referring to him as 'Mr Epstein' throughout the meeting. Lennon joined in the baiting. Whatever his other faults, Lennon was never anti-Semitic. What he despised was pretence. He thought it 'ludicrous' that Eastman should 'pretend to be something he wasn't'.

The meeting is remembered as a 'nightmare'. People were screaming at each other, racial and religious insults were being hurled. Klein kept interrupting Eastman with a stream of obscenities. Eastman and McCartney stormed out. There was no way back from this one. Klein had finally got the Beatles. But only its rotting body.

12

THE Beatles were in their death throes but frantic efforts were still being made to keep them alive. For McCartney this was a matter of emotional necessity. He *liked* being a Beatle. He liked the fame and the prestige. Most of all he liked the artistic sounding-board the group provided him with. 'When the four of us were together we were definitely better than the four of us individually,' he admits.

For Allen Klein it was a matter of money. Acting on the authority of Lennon, Harrison and Ringo and with the collusion of McCartney, he was indelicately renegotiating the Beatles' recording contract with EMI and Capitol. He was after a fortune and argued that any announcement of the group's imminent demise would fatally stymie his hand. McCartney agreed with him – partly because he was never averse to making money but also, and more honourably, because he still believed that the band had a future.

It didn't. The cracks had appeared and were widening. Harrison was frustrated. 'There were just too many limitations based on our being together for so long – everybody was sort of pigeonholed,' he said. Lennon just wanted out and he told McCartney so.

In September 1969 McCartney, desperately looking for a way to get back to the chummy comradeship of yesteryear, suggested the Beatles go back on the road again. He told the others: 'Look, something's wrong and we've got to sort it out.' He went on: 'What I think we ought to do is get back as a band – get back as the little unit we always were. I think we ought to hit small clubs and do a little tour.'

Explaining his thinking McCartney says: 'I just wanted to *learn* to be a band together again, because we'd become a business group. We'd become *businessmen*.'

Without giving the proposal the courtesy of consideration, Lennon replied: 'I think you're *daft*. In fact, I wasn't going to tell you – but I'm leaving the group. I've had enough. I want a divorce, like my divorce from Cynthia.' The businessmen they had become were on notice that their partnership was about to be dissolved.

That fateful meeting took place in the Apple offices in Savile Row. It was one of the rare occasions that McCartney had ventured in there in recent weeks. It was to be almost the last. For, following the brutal confrontation between Eastman and Klein, McCartney had been all but ousted from the running of the company he had been instrumental in setting up.

That was Klein's doing. He then embarked on a savage firing spree. As well as closing the door on all the hopeful visitors and dispensing with the services of such extraneous personnel as 'Magic' Alex, he also closed down the record division. Ron Kass was dismissed (and, on Brown's authority, collected as severance pay the Apple-owned Mayfair mews house he would later share with Joan Collins). So was Peter Asher, who took James Taylor with him. The one part of Apple Corp that was making real money had been cut out. The only people to survive the purge were Neil Aspinall and Peter Brown.

McCartney, Brown says, 'was horrified'. But he was powerless to prevent it. McCartney would have appealed to Lennon but his way was blocked. John had found a new partner, Yoko Ono, and she had her own priorities. They most certainly did not include Paul McCartney or 'the group'. Paul had initially dismissed the strange Japanese lady as just another of John's peculiar indulgences. He hadn't even protested unduly when, in violation of a cardinal Beatles rule, Lennon had brought her into the Abbey Road recording studio during the making of the *White Album*. But Yoko hadn't gone away. She had moved in for the duration.

In November 1968, Lennon had been unceremoniously divorced from Cynthia on the grounds of his adultery with Ono (but only after first shabbily trying to divorce Cynthia, accusing her of sleeping with 'Magic' Alex the night she found Ono in her marital home, wearing her dressing gown) and he had written her out of his life with a £100,000 pay-off. Four months later he married Yoko, with Peter Brown as best man.

By then McCartney had also taken a wife. Eight days before Lennon's nuptials in Gibraltar, he had married Linda Eastman, née Epstein, at Marylebone Register Office with Peter Brown as a witness. The civil ceremony was followed by a blessing at Paul's local Anglican church in St John's Wood. Linda was pregnant: Mary, named after Paul's mother, was born on December 28. McCartney had done the decent northern thing and made an honest woman of his expectant girlfriend. And like a typical northern man of his class, he expected his wife to stay at home and raise his family while he went out to work.

Lennon's union with Yoko was based on a very different premise. From now on, he said, they were inseparable. In symbolic recognition of their oneness he changed his name by deed poll to John Ono Lennon. In another symbolic act, the name-changing ceremony took place on the roof of the Apple building where, just a few short weeks before, on January 30, the Beatles had given their last ever public performance and had sung 'Get Back', McCartney's appeal to the past. But there was no going back.

Was there more than just coincidence in Lennon and McCartney getting married almost within a week of each other? Could it have been another example of the blatant rivalry that now marked everything they did, though, on this occasion, the competition was all McCartney's. Lennon had been trying to find a suitable place to marry Yoko ever since her Virgin Island divorce from Cox had come through in February. McCartney knew of Lennon's plans, and made his own arrangements which anticipated the Lennon wedding.

It was not surprising, given the building acrimony, but rather sad none the less, remembering their years of friendship, that no other Beatles attended either of the two ceremonies (Harrison couldn't have, even if he had wanted to – on the day McCartney got married and in confirmation that it was now open season on the Beatles, he was busted by the police and charged with possessing cannabis resin). By now, however, Lennon and McCartney's paths were diverging, both in their personal and their professional lives.

Lennon, proving as good as his promise to be inseparable from Yoko, set up peace camp with her in various hotel beds. McCartney, more prosaically, went back to work on the *Abbey Road* album. It was not a happy experience. The co-operation between Lennon and McCartney that had been such an essential feature of the Beatles was now all but at an end. 'By the time we made *Abbey Road* John and I were openly critical of each other's music, and I felt John wasn't much interested in performing anything he hadn't written himself,' Paul said. John countered by accusing Paul of 'subconsciously trying to destroy' his great songs, like 'Strawberry Fields' and 'Across the Universe', by over-experimenting with the arrangements and the electronic effects.

McCartney also had rows with Ringo and Harrison who, after years of quiet subservience, were starting to challenge his studio authority. Harrison had had enough of the 'superior attitude which for years Paul had shown towards me musically'. 'I was beginning to be too definite,' McCartney conceded. 'George and Ringo turned around and said, "Look, piss off! We're grown-ups and we can do it without you fine." For people like me who don't realise when they're being very overbearing, it comes as a great surprise to be told. So I completely clammed up and backed off – "Right, OK, they're right, I'm a turd."' He became, he said, 'paranoid'.

Dick James was someone else who was feeling uncomfortable. The good fortune that had brought Brian Epstein into his office and handed him Lennon and McCartney's publishing had made him a millionaire. Northern Songs had been floated as a public company in 1965, with James retaining almost a third of the shares. It should have been a lifetime's investment but James was sorely worried by Lennon's increasingly eccentric behaviour. He also distrusted Allen Klein who, he had just been informed, was now handling all of Lennon's business affairs. He wanted out and in Lew Grade, his own agent in his music-hall days, he found a willing buyer. In March of 1969 Dick James sold out his shareholding to Lew Grade's ATV for just over a million pounds. ATV then offered another £9.5 million for the rest of the company.

Grade had waited a long time to get his hands on the Beatles. Now he had them, though not without a fight. Lennon and McCartney between them still owned 30 percent of the shares and on this issue, if nothing else, they were united. They were appalled at what they saw as James's underhand disloyalty. And the last person they wanted to own their songs was Lew Grade. With the backing of merchant bankers Henry Ansbacher they mounted a counter bid for a controlling interest in Northern Songs and threatened that, if they lost, they would stop writing songs.

Grade dismissed that last point for the arrant nonsense it was. As he pointed out, apart from any creative considerations, 'songwriting plays an important part in the boys' income'. The threat, however, had been enough to swing a consortium of City investment houses, which controlled a crucial 14 percent of the votes, behind Lennon and McCartney and ATV was all but resigned to defeat when Lennon lost his temper. 'I'm not going to be fucked around by men in suits sitting on their fat arses in the City,' he stormed. The consortium promptly switched sides and sold to ATV. Grade had won. The majority of royalties from everything that Lennon and McCartney had written, including 'Yesterday', and everything they would write together, if they did, until 1973, would now go to Grade, the epitome of the cigar-chomping man in a suit. Lennon's self-defeating tantrum had in part been provoked by his discovery of just who owned what in Northern Songs. At a meeting at Ansbacher's offices on April 20 when all the stock was tallied it had been revealed that, while Lennon owned 644,000 stocks, McCartney had been quietly buying up more and now owned 751,000.

Lennon was livid. According to Brown he screamed, 'You bastard, you've been buying up stock behind our backs.'

'Oops, sorry,' McCartney replied. Better to invest in his own talents than supermarkets, he explained.

Lennon was having none of it. 'This is fucking low,' he shouted. 'This is the first time any of us have gone behind each other's backs.'

'I felt like I had some beanies and I wanted some more,' McCartney said.

It was, says Brown, the 'final wedge between John and Paul'. After that Lennon and McCartney could hardly bring themselves to exchange a civil word. And with Ringo and Harrison backing Lennon, and Klein off the leash, McCartney found himself all but ostracised. Brown became his only dependable link with Apple.

'The only way Paul would communicate to the office was through my private line,' Brown says. 'He wouldn't even go through the switchboard.'

McCartney retreated to his farm in Scotland and started work on a solo album, something he would never have contemplated doing only a few short months before. He was completely cut off from the outside world, with only his wife, his daughter, step-daughter and sheepdog for company. The only telephone was in one of the out-houses and he often didn't hear it, even when it rang for as long as 45 minutes, which is how long Brown tried to get through to him one day. He might as well have been dead – which was the rumour sweeping America and why Brown was trying to get hold of him.

On October 12 the previous year a disc jockey named Russ Gibb working for WKNR-FM in Detroit announced that he had received an anonymous telephone call informing him that McCartney was dead. The story caught on like Beatlemania had five years before. Beatles songs were searched for clues. It was Paul, not Tara Browne, who 'blew his mind out in a car'. If the final groove of 'Strawberry Fields' was played, John was said to be heard chanting, 'I buried

Paul.' The walrus, a symbol of death, was Paul (and so it was, but only because he was the one who fitted into the walrus costume in the taping of a sequence for *Magical Mystery Tour*). The photograph on the cover of *Abbey Road* of the four Beatles walking across the pedestrian crossing outside the recording studio is supposed to be a funeral procession with Harrison the gravedigger, Ringo the undertaker, Lennon the priest and a lookalike for the 'dead' McCartney.

Those executives left at Apple tried to deny the rumour but without success. McCartney, in seclusion and feeling persecuted, wasn't helping. When Brown at last got through to him, he was told: 'Why are you phoning me about this stupid thing. Deal with it – you deal with it. I don't want to know about it. What can I do that you can't do?' Brown replied: 'You can come out and show that you're not dead.' McCartney answered: 'That's stupid; you deal with it,' and hung up.

It was left to *Life* magazine to breathe life back into McCartney. The magazine sent a photographer and a reporter up to Scotland. McCartney told them to get off his land and threw a bucket of water over the photographer. When the photographer took a picture of that, McCartney's cultivated cuteness reasserted itself. He chased after the journalists and, in return for the roll of film showing him in bucket-waving temper, gave an exclusive interview and photographs of himself with his newborn daughter – taken, of course, by Linda. Even in depression, McCartney was too conscious of his public image to let it slip. If McCartney was still very much alive – 'If I'm dead, I'm sure I'd be the last to know,' he told *Life* – the Beatles weren't. Like a painted corpse, the group was only being kept on show for the money Klein was negotiating for.

After an unpleasant confrontation with Richenberg, involving court action and smear campaigns, Klein had managed to extricate the Beatles from Triumph in exchange for £800,000 cash and a quarter of the £1.3 million in royalties EMI had frozen because of the legal wrangles. Triumph in its turn bought the Beatles' 10 percent holding in NEMS for a little under half a million pounds' worth of its own valuable stock.

It was success of a sort and it was certainly more than John Eastman had managed to achieve with that letter to the Epsteins which had caused such offence. Klein fared even better with Capitol. By verbal muscle, reinforced by the not insubstantial fact that he was selling the world's most successful recording act, Klein cajoled Capitol's head Bob Gortikov into agreeing to increase the royalty rate on old material to 50 cents an album until 1972 and 72 cents thereafter. Better still, he agreed to 58 cents on two new albums a year until 1972, rising to 72 cents through until 1976 when the contract would again be renegotiated. It was the most lucrative deal in recording history and even Paul appeared impressed. According to Klein, 'Paul congratulated me on the agreement. He said, "If you are screwing us, I can't see how."'

The only flaw was that there were going to be no new Beatles albums except the two that had already been recorded: *Let It Be* and the lyrical *Abbey Road*, which, despite the terrible bitterness, showed what the Beatles were still capable of producing and, in 'Something', revealed the extent of Harrison's long-suppressed songwriting talent. By keeping quiet about their imminent disintegration, the Beatles had been offered a fortune they would never collect. But it had been a tawdry exercise in deception, as McCartney was by now well aware.

He refused to sign anything Klein put before him, to make any legal commitment to the future, and even the entreaties of Ringo, the most understanding of the other three, could not persuade him to change his mind. One evening at Cavendish Avenue Ringo said to Paul that perhaps Klein wasn't as bad as he was painted. Every time he mentioned Klein's name, Linda started crying. 'In a few minutes I'd be saying the same – "Well, maybe he isn't *so* bad" – and Linda would start crying again. "Oh, they've got you too," she kept saying.'

Linda, for her part, was horrified at the venom of the battle she found herself being drawn into. 'I was just some chick from New York when I walked into all that,' she recalled, adding, 'I thought the Beatles were above all that. I never thought there were any problems that could happen to these people, these Beatles.'

McCartney, as would be proved, was right to reject Klein, but at that moment that was an irrelevance. The Beatles, so recently the epitome of youthful optimism, had become a tangle of artistic differences and mutual distrust pulled taut by the personal animosity between Lennon and McCartney. Paul, who had never been able to deal with John head on, had resorted to his customary tactic of diplomatic evasion. But Lennon wasn't buying that any more. If he couldn't take charge of the musical direction and reclaim his position as leader of the gang, then, abetted by Yoko Ono, he was quite prepared to wreck the group.

'McCartney was placed in an impossible position,' says Brown. 'John wanted to go in another direction and McCartney couldn't follow him because there was Yoko in the middle and Yoko didn't want them to continue. Yoko wanted John for herself. And she was very single-minded.'

McCartney had imperiously assumed that he could deal with the problem, as he had always been able to deal with John's eccentricities. He was not going to allow anyone to disrupt what he himself had come to regard as one of the greatest songwriting partnerships of the twentieth century.

He was wrong. Lennon, adrift on a sea of a fame he despised and a drug excess he could not control, had found his anchor. Now it was McCartney who was cut loose and drifting. He had lost all control of the group he had helped found. He was *persona non grata* at Apple. He had even lost control of his own songs and projects.

The idea behind *Let It Be* had been to dispense with the overdubbing that had become the mark of Beatles records ever since *Revolver*. *Let It Be* – the title song was inspired by his dead mother who had appeared to Paul in a dream which 'gave me some strength' when he was feeling 'quite paranoid' – was supposed to return to a cleaner style of rock and roll and, so Paul hoped, restore the group's sense of unity. It did nothing of the sort.

The film exposes the Beatles in all their back-biting estrangement.

The music suffered as a consequence of the feuding and walk-outs and when the project finally collapsed under its own dead weight, no one could be bothered to sort through the hours of tapes to put together an album. For want of any better idea, and because he had done such a good job on the *Instant Karma* single for Lennon and Yoko, Harrison and Lennon handed the tapes over to Phil Spector, whose 'wall of sound' style of production had proved so successful on records like the Righteous Brothers' 'You've Lost That Loving Feeling'. The Spector sound was hardly what McCartney had in mind.

Spector remixed and re-arranged the tracks, adding strings and putting on the overdubs McCartney had specifically wanted left off. It was Spector's treatment of 'The Long and Winding Road' that particularly upset McCartney. He had recorded it as an unadorned ballad with just an acoustic guitar. Spector added an orchestra and overdubs. McCartney was furious and demanded that his original version be used on the album. Klein refused, and it was Spector's orchestrated version that was released as a single in the United States on 11 May 1970. It went to number one but by then it didn't matter anymore. Paul McCartney had quit the Beatles.

13

T HE break-up of the Beatles, says Linda, 'shattered' Paul
McCartney. He suffered what was possibly a nervous break-
down. 'I felt my life was over,' he said. 'I thought, I'm not worth
anything any more.' He became a virtual hermit on his Scottish
estate. The shiny hair which he used to wash every day became
tangled and matted. He didn't shave.

'I was fairly wiped out. For the first time in my life I was on the
scrap heap, in my own eyes. It was just the feeling, the terrible
disappointment of not being any use to anyone any more. It was a
barrelling, empty feeling that just rolled across my soul.'

In a state of what he described as 'catatonic' despair, he lost his
sense of self-preservation – and started sniffing heroin. The drug
initially induces nausea, then cuts out reality. The user ends up in
a self-contained stupor. With no one to order around, McCartney
became disordered, uncommunicative, 'impossible' to live with,
alternately angry and depressed.

McCartney's life was a mess. Even his beloved Rupert the Bear,
that innocent symbol of his childhood, had been turned into a
rampaging sex fiend by the underground newspaper, *Oz*, and was
about to become the subject of the longest obscenity trial in British
legal history.

'I couldn't cope,' he recalled. 'I remember days when I woke up
at three in the afternoon and thought, There's no point in getting

up, it'll soon be bedtime.' If he did get up, he 'wanted to go back to bed pretty soon after'. And what was the point of shaving or bathing or bothering about what to wear, 'because where was I going?' 'It was frightening beyond belief,' Linda said.

'Until then,' McCartney recalled, 'I really was a kind of cocky sod. It was the first time I'd had a major blow to my confidence. When my mother died I don't think my confidence suffered. It had been a terrible blow, but I didn't feel it was my fault.' This was proving at least as painful as the loss of his mother had been – and this time McCartney did hold himself responsible. If only he had been more understanding of George Harrison's maturing ambitions, less dismissive of Ringo, more receptive of Yoko Ono ('I often do feel not too clever about not taking to her,' he would say).

It was his feelings towards Lennon that caused him the most distress. They were ambivalent and contradictory. He could not come to terms with them. In the effort to emerge from Lennon's shadow, McCartney had lost himself in the penumbra. He would say, 'I realise now we never got to the bottom of each other's souls. We didn't know the truth. Some fathers turn out to hate their sons.' He would then counterbalance that by declaring: 'The bottom line is we loved each other.'

Either way, he found the prospect of life without Lennon all but impossible to contemplate. It was not just the loss of a friend that so upset him. It was also the loss of a dream. 'It was like a Rodgers and Hammerstein trip,' he said. 'That romantic image of collaboration . . . that always appealed to me, that image. Lennon and McCartney were to become the Rodgers and Hammerstein of the sixties.' Now the dream had died in legal confrontation and personal antagonism.

The end, when it came, was suitably unpleasant. McCartney had returned from his Scottish hibernation in the March of 1970. He brought with him the solo album he had been working on. It was entitled simply *McCartney*. It had been recorded at High Farm on a basic 4-track machine he had borrowed from EMI, and he wrote all the songs and played all the instruments. The most memorable track is 'Maybe I'm Amazed', written for 'me and Linda with the Beatles breaking up, that was my feeling. Maybe I'm amazed at what's going on, maybe I'm not, but *maybe* I am! "Maybe I'm amazed at the way you pulled me out of time, hung me on the line." There were things happening at the time and these phrases were my symbols for them. It was a very free album for me to do. I'd get up and think about breakfast and then wander into the living room to do a track. It had a certain kind of rawness.' The sound of 'kids screaming and the door opening' can be heard in the background.

McCartney wanted it released at the beginning of April. That, Klein informed him, was impossible. April was the release date for the now-completed *Let It Be*. Ringo's first solo album, *Sentimental Journey*, was also scheduled for around that time. McCartney flew into a rage. He telephoned Sir Joseph Lockwood and told him that the others were trying to 'sabotage' him. When Ringo went on a peace mission to Cavendish Avenue to explain why April was such a difficult date, McCartney 'went completely out of control, prodding his fingers towards my face, saying, "I'll finish you all now", and "You'll pay!"' He then threw Ringo out.

Ringo, convinced by that display of temperament of the importance McCartney attached to the record, went back and persuaded Klein and the others to juggle the release dates. *McCartney* was issued on April 17. On McCartney's instruction a note was inserted in the sleeve announcing the end of the Beatles. It came in the form of an interview. 'What,' the question asked, 'is your relationship with Klein?'

'It isn't,' McCartney replied. 'I am not in contact with him and he does not represent me in any way.'

'Are you planning a new album or single with the Beatles?'

'No.'

'Is your break with the Beatles temporary or permanent, due to personal differences or musical ones?'

'Personal differences, business differences, musical differences, but most of all because I have a better time with my family. Temporary or permanent? I don't know.'

'Do you foresee a time when Lennon–McCartney become an active songwriting partnership again?'

'No.'

Now it was Lennon's turn to be outraged. He accused McCartney of using the announcement to generate publicity for his solo album. 'I suppose, in a way, I was,' McCartney conceded. But so what? After all, it was Lennon who had first declared that he was leaving the Beatles, a decision that had only been kept secret so that Klein could renegotiate the recording contracts. 'Personally, I don't think it was such a bad thing to announce to the world after *four months* that we'd broken up,' McCartney said. 'It had to come out sometime. It was a conscience thing with me . . . I didn't like to keep lying to people.'

The other Beatles, and Lennon most of all, did not see it that way. The announcement of the end of the Beatles, they furiously pointed out, should have been a joint one. That would have been the honourable way to have gone about it. It should certainly not have been contained in a note surreptitiously slipped into a solo album. It was yet another hammer blow to their relationships.

Fifteen years later, with the full benefit of hindsight, McCartney said: 'I think maybe the manner of doing it I regret now. I wish I had been a little kinder, or with the others' approval.' He did not, he said, want to hurt Lennon, who none the less took McCartney's note as a personal insult (not least for the reason that if anyone was going to make a unilateral declaration, it should have been him – because, in his own mind at least, the Beatles were *his* group). 'But I didn't realise it would hurt him so much or that it mattered who was first,' McCartney said.

At the time, though, McCartney didn't really care. He was strung out in the Scottish Highlands, locked in his own desolation. Marijuana, the drug he has always resorted to in moments of stress to help settle him down, was not powerful enough to cut out this sense of despondency. He was using heroin instead.

'I had a friend who told me heroin was OK as long as you could afford it,' he recalled. '"You're all right," he said. "You wrote 'Yesterday'. You'll always be able to pay for your heroin."' He became, he said, 'a zombie'.

This was one drop-out with a self-righting mechanism, however. While Lennon was always prepared, as McCartney had pointed out, to throw himself off the cliff, McCartney always held back and his flirtation with heroin was short-lived. McCartney's self-image was too clearly established for him ever to allow himself to move on from snorting the drug to being a needle addict. However else McCartney may have seen himself, it was not as someone crawling around on the floor being sick and thinking it was wonderful.

'Something in my brain went, ping! A little light went on,' he said, adding, 'I didn't want to be a junkie. I didn't even enjoy taking the drug. I was just doing it to escape, to be numb.' He was ashamed by this display of weakness. Whenever he was asked if he had ever followed Lennon's example and taken heroin, he would always answer with a categoric 'No'. It was not until 1991 that he at last confirmed what had long been whispered; that he had indeed opted, if only briefly, for the ultimate and potentially fatal means of artificial release from life's pressures. 'It was Linda who made me realise what a complete fool I was,' he said.

Linda, the groupie from New York who had set out to hook a Beatle, had had a profound effect on McCartney. They were physically compatible – as they had wasted no time in discovering. Their relationship was quickly settled on to more durable ground, however. Whereas Jane Asher had always been intent on pursuing ambitions of her own, Linda made McCartney her career. McCartney, usually so casual with his women – and so dismissive of them – found himself able, anxious even, to unburden himself to her. He wanted to talk to her, to tell her about himself and his hopes and goals, and she was just as anxious to listen. In a cathartic exercise they told each other about the affairs they had each had before they met.

'You prove how much you love someone by confessing all that

old stuff,' McCartney explained. 'Both Linda and I were ravers back then. But that's one of the reasons our marriage has worked. We had both sown our wild oats and gotten it out of our system. We got it all out before we were married.'

By revealing the infidelities and deceptions from his past, McCartney was limiting his options for the future. But that, with his professional world in a shambles, was what he wanted to do. He had just been through what he called a divorce. It had been particularly painful. He had lost one partner. Now he looked to Linda for the support which before he had always sought from Lennon. In a very real sense, Linda was Lennon's replacement. And just in case anyone missed the point, he insisted on making Linda a member of his band when he pulled himself together and went back to work.

The other Beatles were not impressed by the prospective change of personnel. Lennon was gone but Harrison and Ringo were still on the sidelines. 'I think George and Ringo *did* want to save things,' McCartney said. There was tentative talk of doing something together in the future. Nothing came of it; as Ringo explained to his friends out on London's nightclub circuit, working with Linda was not a possibility to be considered.

Linda didn't want it either. She wanted McCartney for herself, just as Yoko wanted Lennon, though for homely reasons: while Yoko was intent on leading John in her own artistic direction, Linda wanted to rein Paul into domesticity. The Beatles had been a self-absorbed, all-male unit closed to outsiders, wives and girlfriends included – and as such represented a threat to the life she was determined to build for herself. Linda's 'hanging-out' days were over. Having claimed one of the greatest prizes in pop, she now wanted to be a wife and mother. McCartney was happy to go along with that. Linda promised the stability which McCartney declared himself so desperately in need of. She is, he says, 'loving, emotional, practical – and sexy'. More than that, she also seemed rejuvenatingly devoid of what he now regarded as the hollow pretensions that had driven him for so many years.

'I consider myself a peasant,' Linda said. 'I guess I rebelled against the privilege I was born into.' She was determined to get back to simpler and what she insisted were sounder values and McCartney was determined to join her.

In doing so he was implicitly rejecting the values of his dead mother – the mother who had always wanted her son to better himself, to get a better education, to live in a better house. He had adhered to those precepts. He had become a millionaire. He had immersed himself in intellectual culture. He had acquired the mansion in St John's Wood. And where had it got him? Smacked out on heroin. 'Then along came Linda and sense kicked in,' he said.

He set about remaking himself. Out went the exotic cars, the flashy, titled friends, the avant-garde art galleries, the limousines and the chauffeurs, the tins of caviar he used to eat round at comedian Peter Cook's house. Never the tidiest of men and married to a woman who, as Hunter Davies noted, 'was never the most houseproud of mothers', he retreated into a messy domesticity from which he has not emerged.

Instead of continuing to educate himself he went the opposite way. 'I just want to stay unlearned, that really is my intention,' he said. The artist who had grappled with the complexities of Stockhausen and Bergman now wanted to look at the world 'through child's eyes'.

He converted to vegetarianism. He had tried it once before. Author and broadcaster Ned Sherrin recalls McCartney turning up for a lunch with Jane Asher and telling his host when the lamb was served: 'Oh dear! Didn't you know? We became vegetarians this morning.' This time he stuck it out. 'It was soon after our marriage when Paul and I were in Scotland that we decided to become vegetarians,' Linda recalled. 'There we were, tucking into our plates of roast lamb, when Paul pointed through the window to our herd of sheep and said, "Look! You realise we are eating *those!*" We were both disgusted and we took the decision then and there to stop.'

Henceforth, McCartney ruled, no animal in his charge would

be killed, not even the toothless old sheep, who instead would be hand-fed on a mixture of oats and alfalfa chopped up in the kitchen blender, until nature claimed them. The McCartney dogs could not be persuaded to follow their master's example, however, and Wings guitarist Denny Laine tells how they kept killing the chickens, much to the distress of Linda 'who can't bear to see anything killed'. 'You can't change the course of nature to my mind,' Laine remarked. But Paul and Linda are still trying, campaigning for animal rights, giving money to the League Against Cruel Sports, buying land in the West Country to provide sanctuary from the stag hunts for red deer, insisting, much to the chagrin of the road crew, that everyone on tour with them has to follow a vegetarian diet.

Even his father, the most supportive of parents, was taken aback. In 1964 the elder McCartney had remarried and his young wife, Angela, a widow twenty-eight years his junior, would complain that when they visited the farm in Scotland they had to sleep on dirty mattresses thrown on a cold concrete floor. She did not approve. Nor, she said, did Jim. There is no question, though, that despite the strains which Angela said appeared in their relationship after Linda came on the scene, Paul remained close to his father right to the end and, in a gesture of filial affection, included 'Walking in the Park with Eloise', a tune Jim had composed, on the *Venus and Mars* album released the year before his death.

Old friends were less tolerant. They were astonished, and blamed Linda for the change which, though less extravagant in its manifestation, was almost as profound as the transformation Yoko wrought on Lennon. Winona Williams says: 'It was a shock to me. Paul was constantly seeking social status, in the same way that Mick Jagger was, although Mick was much better read. That's what he pursued when he was with Jane. Then all of a sudden this woman turns around, and now she's the grand Earth Mother who grows her own cows and changes Paul from this social-seeking demon into a born-again countryman. And not even a country gentleman. Just a countryman, which was never him.'

It was now. The city boy whose country holidays had provided him with some of his happiest childhood memories, was searching for old and homely values. Where he was going professionally was another matter. 'I only had two alternatives,' he said. 'Give up, or carry on.'

It was always going to be more complicated than that. The Beatles had ceased to exist as a musical entity, but they were preserved in memory and on record, a perpetual reminder of glories past, setting the standard with which McCartney would always be compared and against which he would always have to compete.

His initial efforts as a solo artist did not stand up well in the comparison. The response to *McCartney* was luke-warm. Lennon dismissed it as 'rubbish'. His second attempt fared no better. Stung by the critical reaction to *McCartney*, he had tried to produce a tighter, more coherent record. He called it *Ram*, because it 'seemed like a good word because it not only meant ram forward, press on, be positive and those kinds of things, but I was also letting a lot of people know . . . we're into sheep'.

If that explanation wasn't banal enough to invite derision, his decision to involve Linda in its production certainly was. They sang harmonies together. 'She hadn't done an awful lot, so it was a little bit out of tune,' he acknowledged. 'I gave her a hard time, but we were pleased with the results. It paid off for us. It was very much us against the world at that point.'

The album was a million-seller, and went to number one in the United States. The music critics, however, dismissed it. But then music was not getting his full attention. He had other preoccupations. On 31 December 1970, on the advice of the Eastmans, Ringo, Lennon and Harrison were served with writs. Paul McCartney was taking his former partners and friends to court. It was a move that would forever cast him as the villain in the break-up of the Beatles. 'I didn't want to,' he said. 'I went up to Scotland and agonised for three months, cut myself off, before I decided it was the only way. It was a terrible decision. I wanted to sue Klein but the only recourse was to sue my former mates.'

The case came before the High Court on January 10. McCartney demanded that the Beatles' formal union be dissolved because they no longer worked together; because Allen Klein had been appointed against his wishes; and because he had not been given any audited accounts since their partnership was formed in April 1967. The other three countered by producing evidence to show that, under Klein's direction, the Beatles' earnings had been increased by £9 million over the previous nineteen months.

On March 10 the High Court appointed a receiver to take charge of the Beatles' assets. That night, according to one unchallenged account, Lennon, with Harrison and Ringo in attendance, drove round to McCartney's Cavendish Avenue home and threw a brick through the window.

The feud continued on record. The inside cover of *Ram* was a photograph of one beetle screwing another, which was what McCartney felt Lennon was doing to him. The album also contained two songs directed at Lennon – 'Dear Boy' with its line, 'I hope you never know how much you missed', and, more pointedly, 'Too Many People'. 'Certain little lines, I'd be thinking, "Well, this will get him,"' McCartney said. 'Christ, you can't avoid it. "Too Many People", I wrote a little bit in that: "Too many people preaching practices" . . . He'd been doing a lot of preaching and it got up my nose a bit. That was a little dig at John and Yoko.'

Challenging Lennon to a direct confrontation had always been perilous, as McCartney well knew, which was why he had always avoided doing so. However spaced out on drugs he might be, there was still enough of the Liverpool tough left in Lennon to make him a dangerous adversary. McCartney didn't have long to wait for the counterattack.

In September Lennon released *Imagine*. As well as the title song, a dreamy, idealistic plea for peace, the album included a track brutally entitled 'Crippled Inside' and another called 'How Do You Sleep'. With Harrison playing accompanying guitar, Lennon sang: 'Those freaks was right when they said you was dead . . . The only thing you've done was yesterday . . . a pretty face may last a year

Linda with Denny Laine in Wings.
(Pictorial Press)

Mr and Mrs McCartney, 1975. 'We have our barnies, like every married couple,' Linda says. *(Harry Benson)*

The key to success? With daughter Stella, 1975. *(Harry Benson)*

or two / but pretty soon we'll see what you can do / The sound you make is Muzak to my ears . . . Oh, how do you sleep.'

McCartney, ever the PR man, tried to excuse Lennon. 'I think it was some kind of jealousy,' he said. 'I had to try and forgive John because I sort of knew where he was coming from. I knew that he was trying to get rid of the Beatles in order to say to Yoko, "Look, I've even given that up for you. I'm ready to devote myself to you and to the avant-garde."'

Lennon could not be placated. Like a Teddy Boy outside the Litherland Town Hall, he continued to put the boot in at every opportunity. He compared McCartney to Englebert Humperdinck, a doubly wounding remark because it had been Humperdinck's 'Release Me' that had kept McCartney's 'Penny Lane' off the top of the British hit parade in 1967. He got hold of a picture of Paul and Linda's wedding, crossed out the word 'wedding' and substituted 'funeral'. He accused McCartney of being 'all pizza and fairy tales'. He criticised McCartney's solo albums. He went out of his way to create an impression that McCartney's noteworthy work, with the exception of 'Yesterday', had been achieved either with his help or on his prompting. And because Lennon – tough, hard, iconoclastic, *honest* John Lennon – enjoyed the 'street cred' and McCartney – sentimental, smiling, thumb in the air – didn't, people believed him.

Englebert Humperdinck went so far as to blame McCartney for the slur. 'I said, It wasn't me, it was John slagging me off, saying I sounded like you,' McCartney recalled. 'And he said, "John Lennon would never have said that."'

McCartney could not compete in this street fight. His upbringing, with its emphasis on politeness and decency, would not allow it. 'I'm always sensible,' he said. 'That's me. I would never say the things he said.'

What really hurt was that Lennon had a point – and McCartney knew it. His first two albums, interesting though they might be in parts, were not of the quality expected of a major rock artist. The point was emphasised by Lennon's own work with the Plastic Ono

Band and, even more gallingly, by the individual success of George Harrison whom McCartney had so contemptuously kept in the background. While McCartney was squandering his gifts turning out throwaway ditties like 'Ram On' and 'Singalong Junk', Harrison had spent six fastidious months producing *All Things Must Pass*, the beautifully crafted three-record set that is one of the most widely acclaimed albums of the rock era. *Rolling Stone* magazine dismissed *Ram* as 'the nadir in the decomposition of sixties rock this far'. England's *Melody Maker* magazine hailed *All Things Must Pass* with the headline, 'Garbo talk! George Harrison is free!' McCartney was too competitive to miss the comparison. It was time to dispense with the ennui and get back to business.

14

I N the first eleven years of their marriage, Linda McCartney told me, she did not spend a single night apart from her husband. It was not John and Yoko who were joined at the hip. It was Paul and Linda. Lennon would soon be heading for the Hollywood Hills without Yoko but with May Pang, his former office assistant, on a 'lost weekend' which lasted for over a year.

McCartney, on the other hand, never strayed far from his wife's side. And when McCartney, never one to take criticism lightly and stung by the scorn his two solo albums had attracted, decided the way back was to get another band together, his first recruit was his wife. The answer to losing your job, he explained, which was how he regarded the end of the Beatles, was 'let's try and find another job'. It was not, he admitted, the most satisfactory solution to the problem of confidence crippling him. 'You can't top the Beatles,' he said. The Beatles had been together for over a decade. They had been forged by the experience. 'It made us very tight, like family almost,' he explained. To attempt to recreate that cohesion would be an impossible task. 'Even existing, without topping it, is really tough to do.'

The alternative to trying was worse, however. 'I thought, Well, if I don't sing for a year, I'm going to get croaky. And if I don't sing for two years, I'm going to think I'm not a singer any more. So I had to try and get a band together, just to give me something to do.'

The Beatles were over 'and there we were, left with the wreckage. I just thought, That's the end of me as a singer, songwriter, composer, because I hadn't got anyone to do it with – unless I work out another way to do it.'

It was now, in the interest of togetherness, that he decided to turn Linda, who couldn't play a note or sing one, into a rock star. 'I just basically wanted Linda with me instead of her staying at home while I was out on tour somewhere. I showed her middle C, told her I'd teach her a few chords, and have a few laughs. It was very much in that vein.'

Linda, it must be said, had her reservations. The glamour of the profession which, McCartney admitted, 'we talked about', appealed to her – she had been around too many rock stars for too many years not to be attracted by the prospect of acquiring some stardust of her own. But she harboured justified doubts as to her musical ability. As she said, 'How do you go out with Beethoven and say, "Sure, I'll sing harmony with you," when you've never sung a note? Or, "Sure, I'll play piano with you" when you've never played?'

McCartney, however, is never less than persistent. He had to get out there again, 'just so I don't forget how to do it, like an athlete keeping in some form, some kind of condition'. And he wanted Linda out there with him, as his personal security blanket. Enthralled by the idea of returning to the out-of-the-back-of-the-old-Austin-van simplicity of the early Beatles, he overruled his wife's objections. It was, he later admitted, a 'naïve' decision on his part. There was no turning back the clock of rock and roll history. McCartney, no matter how hard he willed it, could never again be a pop minstrel, taking work where he could find it. That didn't prevent him making a valiant attempt to do just that, though.

On 13 September 1971, ten days after Lennon left England for what would prove to be the last time, Linda gave birth to another daughter at King's College Hospital, London. She was named Stella. It was a difficult birth performed by Caesarean operation. 'Our baby was in intensive care, so rather than just sitting around twiddling my thumbs, I was thinking of hopeful names for a new group, and somehow this uplifting idea of Wings came to me at exactly that time,' he recalled. 'It just sounded right.'

A band was formed to complement the name. The line-up consisted of Paul and Linda, Denny Seiwell who had been recruited to play drums on the *Ram* album, and Denny Laine, the former singer in the Moody Blues whose hits included 'Go Now'. A major 1960s pop star in his own right and a songwriter of some talent – he composed the Moodies' hit, 'Say You Don't Mind' – Laine had known the Beatles well. He had drunk and nightclubbed with them, and at one point Epstein had expressed an interest in managing him. Indeed, Epstein had made a business appointment with Laine on the night he killed himself, and Laine was outside knocking vainly on the door of his Belgravia house while Epstein was inside dying.

Of Laine, McCartney remarked, 'I'd always liked his voice and stuff, so I thought he might be a good person to work with. Our voices kind of complemented each other.' Linda also approved; she told Laine that 'Go Now' was one of her favourite records.

Laine's collaboration with McCartney lasted for ten years, for almost as long as Lennon's had. They toured the world, playing to sell-out audiences, and together they co-wrote 'Mull of Kintyre', the first record to out-sell Lennon and McCartney's 'She Loves You' in Britain. But they were never partners in the way McCartney and Lennon had been. Laine, as talented a songwriter as he was, never rose much above the position of hired hand and his parting from McCartney, when it came, was nearly as acrimonious as Lennon's had been, with the former Moody Blue levelling the familiar charges of egocentricity and meanness at the former Beatle. He had been happy enough to respond to the call, however, when McCartney telephoned him one morning and said, 'I'm forming a new band to go on the road – are you interested?'

'Too right I am,' he answered, and flew up to Scotland that night to join the McCartneys at High Farm. The Moody Blues, in their Laine-led incarnation, had slipped out of the charts and into memory, the money had stopped rolling in, his taste for the high life had consumed what he had earned before, and he was reduced to sleeping on a mattress in the back room of his then-manager Tony Secunda's office. The chance of working with McCartney was an opportunity not to be missed, not if you were as desperate as Laine was. And Laine had to be desperate to accept the wage McCartney was offering – a mere £70 a week, according to Laine, an even more derisory £35 a week according to his ex-wife, Jo Jo. The accommodation which came with the job matched his salary – an outbuilding on the McCartneys' Scottish estate which Laine said 'wasn't really habitable'. He had exchanged one mattress for another.

The first album Wings made was equally threadbare. McCartney, in his determination to keep everything as simple as possible, had taken inspiration from Bob Dylan who, he heard, was now recording 'everything in one take'. He would have done better to have followed Dylan's sophisticated lyrical example rather than his proto-recording methods. *Wild Life* was produced in two weeks and died almost as quickly. Even McCartney, despite his inability to separate the wheat from the chaff in his own works, admitted, 'It wasn't that brilliant as a recording.'

Linda inevitably attracted most of the flak. A four-piece band carrying one musically illiterate member might be 'family', but it was never going to be tight. As Laine observed: 'Not that I minded Linda being around, but as a musician I wasn't too keen on the idea . . . I always resented it because I thought we could have been a better band a lot quicker if we'd had a proper keyboard player.'

It was more than just a problem of performance, however. In his keenness to produce something 'honest', by which he meant fast, McCartney had put together a collection of songs that would never have survived Lennon's critical appraisal. 'Dear Friend' was written for John. 'It was like a letter,' he explained. 'I wrote "Dear Friend" as a peace gesture.' Lennon wasn't interested. Nor was the record-buying public; it was an act of artistic arrogance to expect it to spend its money financing a personal feud. 'Mary Had a Little Lamb' was written for his daughter. 'I thought I'd record a song for her,'

McCartney said. 'I had an idea in my head that it would be interesting for everyone to find out what the words were to the original nursery rhyme. I thought it was all very deep and all very nice, and would make a nice little children's song, like "Yellow Submarine". I see now it wasn't much of a record.' There wasn't even an attempt at an excuse for 'Bip Bop'. 'I still cringe every time I hear it,' McCartney confessed. McCartney would try to argue that an artist should be judged by his lows as well as his highs, that there was more to Picasso than his blue period, that the lesser works help 'make up the final picture'. But he was forced to concede, 'You have to like me to like the record.'

Not many other people, by his own top-ten standards, liked Wings' first single, either. Entitled 'Give Ireland Back to the Irish', it was released in Britain on February 25, three and a half weeks after Bloody Sunday when British paratroopers opened fire on rioters in Londonderry's predominantly Catholic area of Bogside, killing thirteen and wounding a further seventeen. McCartney had 'always vowed that I'll be the one who doesn't do political songs. I always used to think, God, John's crackers doing all those political songs.' The tragic developments in Northern Ireland provoked him into changing his mind. British troops had been sent to Ulster in August 1969, a month after Mick Jagger (dressed in a little girl's party frock) and the Rolling Stones had given a free concert for 250,000 in London's Hyde Park and released clouds of white butterflies in memory of guitarist Brian Jones who had died three days before. The butterflies had quickly expired, as did the cheers with which Northern Ireland's Catholic minority had initially greeted the soldiers. Committed to a peace-keeping role, the troops soon found themselves inexorably caught in the crossfire of Ulster's sectarian violence and shot back in a savage confrontation that bloody Sunday in January.

'I'd grown up with this thing that the Irish were our brothers,' McCartney said. 'So when the English paratroopers, *my* army who I'm paying rates for, go into Ireland and shoot down some innocent bystanders, for the first time in my life I go, Hey, wait a minute, we're the goodies, aren't we? And I'm moved to make some kind of protest . . . I thought, Wait a minute, this is not clever, and I wish to protest on behalf of us people. So I tried.'

'Give Ireland Back to the Irish', which was banned by the BBC, would be McCartney's only Lennon-style song for two decades, until 'All My Trials', his song to the homeless with its attack on the government of Margaret Thatcher. 'All My Trials' was not a big-seller, nor was the Irish record. The record-buying public on the British mainland bought the record only into the number-13 spot on the charts. It fared even worse in the United States, where it made it only up to number 21.

'Paul was quite innocently trying to solve a problem which obviously can't be solved with a song,' Denny Laine said. Political protest was not McCartney's natural forte. He did not share his former songwriting partner's ability to turn issues into music, as Lennon had done on 'Imagine' and 'Give Peace a Chance'. He was better when he stuck to what he called the 'general issues for humanity', like love, for instance, or the nostalgia of 'Yesterday'. And yesterday was where he wanted to be which is why, on February 9, he loaded up his band, now extended to include guitarist Henry McCullough, into the back of a bus and set off on an impromptu tour of Britain.

'For me this was like going back to the Cavern, a whole new life starting again,' he explained. 'We decided, let's do whatever we want, it's allowed in this world, and what we wanted was to get in a van and take off up the motorway with a few musicians and play for student unions,' he said. 'Someone would go and say, "We've got Paul McCartney in the van, do you want him to come in and play?"' The band's first gig was at Nottingham University and for the next few weeks they popped up at universities around the country – in Wales, in Yorkshire, eventually at Oxford – charging 50 pence admission for the shows they played and splitting the proceeds up in the bus afterwards.

'With the Beatles you used to get paid massively but you never saw it, because it went straight into the company. You had to draw on it,' he explained. 'So for me one of the big buzzes of that first tour was actually getting a bag of coins at the end of the gig. It wasn't just a materialistic thing; it was the feeling of getting physically paid again. It was like going back to square one. I wanted to take it back to square one. I wanted to take it back to where the Beatles started, which was in the halls. We played poker with the money afterwards, and I'd actually pay the band physically. You know, "Fifty pence for you . . . and fifty pence for you." It brought back the thrill of actually working for a living.'

It was an artificial situation and one that did not endear itself to the non-McCartney members of the band who were keener on the sex and drugs aspect of rock and roll than they were on eating fish and chips bought at the local take-away and staying in second-class boarding houses. The idea certainly hadn't attracted John Lennon. When McCartney had suggested just such a tour for the Beatles, Lennon had replied, 'You're daft.' And though McCartney had at last got his own way, albeit without the Beatles, the financial reality of what he had become continued to intrude on his fantasy.

The *Ram* album had given Linda McCartney joint songwriting credits which effectively deprived Northern Songs of 50 percent of the royalties. Lew Grade's ATV instigated legal action on the grounds that Linda was clearly not musically competent to compose songs like 'Another Day'. McCartney steadfastly defended his wife and his right to write with anyone he chose. 'As I wasn't writing with John any more, I looked for someone else to collaborate with. If my wife is actually saying, "Change that" or "I like that better than that", then I'm using her as a collaborator. I mean, John never had any input on "The Long and Winding Road" and Yoko still collects royalties on it.'

The case went to court where Linda took the stand to testify to her musical talents. The court ruled that she could keep her share (and just as well, McCartney said, because thanks to the legal battles still raging over the Beatles' money, 'Linda was the only one getting paid in our household'). As part of the settlement, however, McCartney agreed to appear in a Lew Grade produced television special entitled 'James Paul McCartney', which was shown on 10 May 1973. It featured McCartney doing a top-hat-and-tails routine originally devised for Twiggy. There was nothing in that of the foot-stomping urgency of the early Beatles he had been so keen to recapture.

In one sense, though, the 'tour' around the universities had been a success; it had given the group the opportunity to play together before going on the commercial stage. 'With Wings I didn't think it was a good idea after the Beatles to come out with a little group that wasn't rehearsed, so we had to find some way of getting to know each other, playing the songs to the audience,' McCartney explained. The universities helped restore some of his confidence, as did the ensuing tour of Europe. And when Wings embarked on their first proper British tour in 1973, McCartney had regained his composure – and all of his confidence.

'For the first few months I thought, Oh Christ, it'll never work, they'll criticise us every time we open our mouths because we're not the Beatles,' he said. 'But it's worked out. We're growing. I'm satisfied with how we are now. I think I'm good. I like me. I *am* good. I can dig me.'

At the start of the tour a reporter asked, 'You don't expect Wings to be as big as the Beatles – obviously not?' McCartney retorted, 'Crap to that "obviously not". The Beatles were guys coming down from Liverpool who wanted the lot. Now I've got the lot.' His records, too, were showing an improvement in quality. The *Red Rose Speedway* album which includes 'My Love', was well received, as was his 'Live and Let Die' single written for the James Bond film.

'I see music as a craft,' he said. 'I like the idea that I could turn my hand to a Chippendale-style table or a rude country peasant table. I see that as part of the craft. From the very early days I was interested in doing film music. That's why I did the Bond theme.' It was a new discipline for him. 'I don't normally write to titles,' he said. By wisely enlisting the help of George Martin for both *Red Rose Speedway* and 'Live and Let Die' in what was their first collaboration since *Abbey Road* – 'I always needed someone like George

Martin to help me because technically it's quite a hard game to get together', he said of the Bond theme – McCartney had gone some way to regaining his old zest.

He turned out 'Helen Wheels', a catchy single which attempted to do for England what Chuck Berry had done for America. 'That song was my attempt to put England on the map,' he explained. 'All the Chuck Berry songs you ever heard always had things like, "Birmingham, Alabama!" These American places like "Talahassee!"', which had been a hit for Freddie Cannon in the late 1950s. The attempt hardly challenged Berry, who had never been that enamoured of the Beatles, despite the royalties Beatles' cover versions of his songs had earned him, and had once remarked, 'I don't think the Beatles were as good as the Everlys.' As McCartney admitted, 'Scunthorpe', or 'Warrington' were never going to sound 'as funky' as Oklahoma City or Memphis, Tennessee. But the fun had been in the attempt and the record made the American Top Ten.

There was much better to come. While Lennon was wrestling with his *Mind Games*, McCartney was embarking on what would prove to be the artistic high point of his Wings career. In August 1973, Linda, Paul and Denny Laine flew off to Lagos in Nigeria to start work on a new album. 'I thought it would be good to get out of the country to record, just for a change,' McCartney said. 'Sometimes you get bored and think, I'm going to the same studio every day, and you think it will make your album boring.'

Lagos, a hot and damp, overcrowded city built on an island, was an ill-starred choice. It was the rainy season when they got there. The EMI studio wasn't ready. Fela Ransome-Kuti, a militant African, accused McCartney of attempting to steal the continent's musical soul and warned him to leave the country. Paul and Linda were mugged when, ignoring the warnings they had received, they went on a night stroll and were accosted by five men wielding knives. McCartney, sensibly, handed over his money and cameras while Linda screamed, 'Please don't kill us! We're musicians – and he's Beatle Paul!' Soon afterwards McCartney collapsed in the unfinished studio and passed out suffering from what the doctor diagnosed as acute bronchial spasm.

It was chaotic and dangerous. But it had its artistic reward. 'Out of adversity,' McCartney remarked, 'came one of our better albums. The friction helped a bit on that one. It gave us something to really fight against. We were going uphill all the way.' The album he came back with was *Band on the Run*. 'I love the album,' McCartney would later say. 'I must say, it's great,' adding: 'It sort of relates to me escaping.' One track was entitled 'Picasso's Last Words'. It was written in a show of virtuosity for Dustin Hoffman when the singer and the actor met up in Jamaica where Hoffman was filming *Papillon*.

'Dustin was saying he thought it was an incredible gift to be able to write a song about something,' Paul recalled. McCartney said he could write a song on demand. Hoffman produced a newspaper clipping which said that Picasso's last words were, 'Drink to me, drink to my health, you know I can't drink any more.' He asked McCartney to write a song around them. 'I happened to have my guitar with me,' McCartney recalled. 'I'd brought it around and I said, Yeah, sure. I strummed a couple of chords I knew couldn't go wrong and started singing, "Drink to me, drink to my health", and he leaps out of his chair and says, "Annie, Annie!" – that's his wife – "The most incredible thing! He's doing it! He's writing it! It's coming out!" He's leaping up and down, just like in the films. And I'm knocked out because he's so appreciative.'

Band on the Run received the plaudits McCartney desperately wanted and which he had been denied since the break-up of the Beatles. Even Lennon liked it. And due to the judicious inter-vention of a West Coast promotions man who persuaded McCartney to release 'Jet' as a single, it was also an outstanding commercial success, topping the American charts on four separate occasions, something even the Beatles hadn't managed.

His next album, *Venus and Mars*, while not in the same league, also did well. So did the one after that, *Wings at the Speed of Sound*, which contained such memorable or, depending on musical taste, forgettable tracks as 'Let 'Em In' and 'Silly Love Songs'. There were some ruffled feathers in the Wings set-up, however.

McCullough had quit the band shortly before the Lagos trip. Like Laine, he had reservations about working with Linda. It was McCartney's dictatorial attitude to his playing that caused the final rift, however. It might have been McCartney's band, but when Paul ordered him to play a solo in a certain way, as he had once done to Harrison, he exercised his artistic freedom and stormed out.

Seiwell resigned an hour before they were due on the aeroplane for Nigeria. 'Apparently someone had been to his house and made him very nervous about Africa,' McCartney said. The perennial problem of being without a drummer no longer worried McCartney, though, 'Because it meant I could play drums,' said the bass guitarist cheerfully. Seiwell was replaced by Geoff Britton, but he soon ran foul of McCartney and was in turn replaced by the bearded American, Joe English.

'It's all right if a band has come up together and they're all millionaires – they can talk to each other as equals,' Britton later remarked. 'But with Wings there were these incredible imbalances . . . for instance, we were offered to play a gig with Stevie Wonder for half an hour. The money being offered was a fortune. My cut alone of that would have bought me a house . . . But Paul didn't want to do it.'

In McCullough's stead McCartney hired the brilliant but emotionally erratic Jimmy McCulloch, who had followed such luminaries as Eric Clapton, Jeff Beck and Mick Taylor as lead guitarist with John Mayall's Blues Breakers. But as talented as he undoubtedly was, McCulloch was not temperamentally suited to the pressures of rock stardom. He disappeared into a twilight zone of drugs and drink. After wrecking the outhouse on the McCartney farm – not that there was much to wreck but McCulloch still managed it – which led to a furious row with the hysterical Linda, he too left the band. He died two years later in 1979 in mysterious circumstances, with the coroner recording an open verdict.

The roadies weren't very happy in Scotland, either. One night, in bored desperation, they drew a television set on the wall of the outhouse. When they got tired of watching that they invaded the McCartney residence, only to discover that, apart from the fact that there the television set was real, conditions were no more salubrious.

It wasn't just the hired hands who found the going tough. So did Linda. McCartney's insistence on including her in the group had subjected her to a torrent of invective which made Yoko appear almost loved by comparison. McCartney would later admit, 'It was mad, really.' Linda's inclusion, he said, 'was like saying, "Would you like to play tennis with Bjorn Borg?" We can see that now. We couldn't see it then. It might have been wise to insist that Linda take a lot of lessons, for both of us to go on a big TV talk show to explain ourselves.'

Instead she was wheeled into the spotlight with only a middle C and an off-key voice for protection, which proved no protection at all. She wanted to quit. Denny Laine recalls her crying on his shoulder in distress. 'She told me over and over again that she did not want to be in Wings,' he said. 'She wanted to pack it in and just be a mother.' A son was born on 2 September 1977, and was named James, after Paul's father. Linda said she wanted to stay at home and look after her children. 'But Paul wanted her there . . . he wanted her around him,' Laine said. 'He wouldn't allow her to leave.'

He needed her on stage, McCartney admitted, 'for my confidence. That was really the major point.' His wife's discomfort, it seemed, wasn't. For all McCartney's new-man image, he remains true to his northern roots and if he wanted his wife up there on stage with him, then it was her duty to oblige. 'The thing is, it caused a lot of trouble between us,' he admitted. But whatever rows they had in private – the McCartneys are too reserved, too image-conscious ever to give full vent to their feelings in public – Linda was always out on stage the next night, bashing away at her tambourine, beating away on the synthesizer, gamely smiling her way through the catcalls. If Paul criticised her playing, which he sometimes did, 'Linda would turn away . . . she's a very passive person,' Laine observed. 'She won't be involved in arguments – she isn't good at it.'

She didn't need to be. She was living in an artificial world where the ordinary dictates of talent and legality did not apply. By marrying Paul she had become 'a personality, I guess', and had retreated into the cocoon McCartney had constructed for himself and his family. It was his show and he had the wealth and the fame to do virtually what he wanted, or so it must have seemed, for none of his hired helpers was going to go out of his way to persuade him otherwise. In this court anything was possible. If McCartney ordained that Linda would be a successful musician, then so be it: the emperor had spoken.

In 1976 Wings toured the United States. They were received enthusiastically. McCartney chose to share the praise that was rightly his with his wife. 'It doesn't matter who hated her on the way – we did it,' he said. 'On the 1976 tour there she was, by God, doing it all.' The plain fact that no one would have crossed the street to see Linda McCartney perform was an irrelevance to be ignored. Having vacated the palace of Beatledom, McCartney had enthroned himself in another one. Not all the courtiers were happy, however. There had been that rapid changeover of personnel in the band. And now Denny Laine was becoming irritated with life inside the spartan Scottish farmhouse, McCartney's personal version of the ivory tower.

On the tour of Europe which followed the bus ride around the universities, Laine had met his wife, American model Jo Jo Patrie. Linda didn't take to this new member of the entourage. She regarded Jo Jo as a groupie – an attitude Laine regarded as the height of hypocrisy – who had her sights set on her husband. When Wings went cruising in the West Indies to record the *London Town* album aboard the yacht, *Fair Carol*, Jo Jo was not allowed to join them. Laine was weak enough to go along with the prohibition. That put a strain on the Laines' marriage – and his relationship with the McCartneys.

It was money, however, that caused the real grief between the two old friends. Laine, counting up the record sales and seeing the millions roll in, became justifiably displeased with the pitiful seventy or so pounds a week he claims was all McCartney paid him in the first five years. When he threatened to leave Wings, McCartney 'gave me £30,000. After that I averaged about £70,000 a year.' It was a colossal leap. But it still wasn't enough to placate Laine.

With McCartney he co-wrote 'Mull of Kintyre'. 'Paul had written the chorus, we wrote the rest of it together and most of the lyrics are mine.' The record, notable for its haunting bagpipe refrain, sold over two million copies in the United Kingdom alone, making it the biggest-selling single of all time. It earned McCartney another fortune. 'But I got very little of it,' Laine insisted. 'I was on a wage when we wrote the song. When I asked Paul for a special deal on the song, his answer was virtually: 'I'm Paul McCartney and anyone who writes with me is privileged.'

Even so, the royalties from 'Mull of Kintyre' and the other songs he wrote for Wings should have guaranteed him a lifetime's income. And they would have, had Laine not fallen foul of his own disorganisation. His divorce from Jo Jo, plus the demands of the inland revenue, left him in urgent need of cash. He was looking for a loan. McCartney, determined to rake in every penny as though to make up for the millions given away by Epstein, took a more businesslike approach to Laine's problem. According to Laine, he parted with all his Wings song rights, including 'Mull of Kintyre', and received £90,000 from McCartney.

McCartney viewed it as a straightforward business transaction. He calculates that in the ten years Laine was with Wings he earned in the region of one million pounds, 'and that was worth more than a million is worth now'.

Those financial statistics did not assuage the bitterness Laine felt about having to sell his catalogue. In 1986, nine years after 'Mull of Kintyre' topped the charts for nine weeks, he was declared bankrupt with debts of £76,035. 'Mull of Kintyre' and the other Wings songs continue to earn at least that every year. All of it goes to McCartney. 'Most people in the music business are a bit dim with money and I'm dimmer than most,' Laine poignantly observed, before he shambled off into obscurity.

These disagreements, coupled with the changes in line-up, seemed to sap the band of its artistic inspiration. Wings holds the distinction of being the most successful pop act of the 1970s, notching up twenty-seven US Top 40 hits, compared with Elton John's twenty-six. But, try as he did, McCartney was not able to recapture the form he had shown on *Band on the Run*. There were some interesting moments. Harrison thought 'I'm Carrying', from *London Town*, was 'sensational . . . I've always preferred Paul's good melodies to his screaming rock-and-roll tunes.' His attempt at New Wave on *Back to the Egg*, released in 1979, was singularly lacking in new ideas, however. The memorable track was 'Rockestra Theme' and that only because of its all-star line-up featuring Led Zeppelin's John Paul Jones and John Bonham, the Who's Pete Townsend, Pink Floyd's Dave Gilmour, and one Hank B Marvin, the previously much maligned guitarist from the Shadows.

'I don't really feel the need for everything to be incredible and great,' McCartney opined defensively when the album took a critical pasting. No one believed him. McCartney is, by his own admission, one of the most competitive people working in popular music. He is not one to accept failure, however relative (the album reached number eight in America and number six in Britain). Laine, still on the McCartney payroll, suggested a solution. Wings, he argued, should get back on the road. McCartney agreed. It was time, he said, to get back to basics and, in a slightly refined repeat of that jaunt around the universities, Wings did an eighteen-date tour of small British cinemas and theatres in the autumn of 1979. It was intended as a warm-up to what McCartney believed would be the most spectacular tour of his career. It almost ended it.

15

O N a bad day it can take up to three hours to get from Narita International Airport into the centre of Tokyo by car. There was nothing good about 16 January 1980 for Paul McCartney but he made it into the city in half that time, with sirens flashing and an armed escort of police outriders. The problem was that he made it in handcuffs. Paul McCartney, family man and father, had just been busted for trying to import 219 grams, more than half a pound, of high-grade marijuana into Japan. He was guilty of an act of the grossest folly which, in the most anti-drug nation in the industrialised world, could be punished by a prison sentence of up to eight years.

It was, in fact, always unlikely that the world's richest entertainer would spend the rest of the new decade behind bars. With a lingering and not always disguised distaste for foreigners, the Japanese see little reason in detaining alien miscreants at their taxpayers' expense and the authorities, from the day after his arrest, were quietly letting it be known, in off-the-record briefings, that deportation was the likeliest legal action. But McCartney didn't know that. Neither did his wife and children who had flown into Narita with him. And the authorities were not inclined to tell him. For McCartney in his stupidity had not only broken the law, he had also insulted them and, in their view, quite deliberately so.

They hadn't wanted to allow him in at all and had refused to grant him a visa when he had applied to tour there with Wings in 1975. With every justification, Japan, still firmly authoritarian underneath its US-imposed democracy, is resolutely determined to keep itself drug-free. McCartney, just as resolutely, continued to exercise what he perceived as his individual right to smoke as much dope as he wanted and he had already paid the legal penalty for his stance. In 1972, on the Wings tour of Sweden, he, Linda and drummer Denny Seiwell had been arrested and later fined £800 after half a pound of grass which had been mailed ahead from London for them was intercepted by the police. Later that same year marijuana plants were discovered by a policeman growing in the greenhouse on McCartney's Scottish farm. He was fined £100 for cultivation after disingenuously explaining that the seeds had been sent to him by an American fan and he had innocently planted them to see what they were.

In 1975 it was Linda's turn to fall foul of the law when she and Paul were stopped while driving in Los Angeles and 17 grams were discovered in her purse. Linda insisted that the reefers were hers. The courts accepted that, which was just as well for Paul who was now having visa trouble with US immigration because of the other two busts. Linda was bailed for $500 which Paul, who still never carried cash, had to borrow from Peter Brown, who was staying at the same Beverly Hills hotel that Winona Williams had gone to in the futile attempt to borrow money off Paul to extricate a girlfriend from the same jail Linda was now in. McCartney's daughters, Mary and Stella, and his step-daughter, Heather, were in the car when they were stopped by the police and Linda was fortunate to escape being indicted on the much more serious charge of contributing to the delinquency of minors.

'The only real unfortunate thing is that it starts to get you a reputation as a kind of druggie,' McCartney complained. He did nothing to dispel the image. After the Swedish bust he had got round to singing what Dylan thought he had sung on 'I Want to Hold Your Hand': 'Hi, Hi, Hi' went the way of the Irish record and was banned by the BBC. And *Band on the Run*, while not a 'concept' album, did have a drugs thread running through it. 'Most bands on tour are bands on the run,' McCartney explained. 'There were a lot of musicians at the time who'd come out of ordinary suburbs in the sixties and seventies and were getting busted. Bands like the Byrds and the Eagles. The mood amongst them was one of desperados. We were being outlawed for pot.'

After the Swedish bust he said, 'At the end of the day most people go home and have a whisky. We play a gig and we're exhausted and Linda and I prefer to put our kids to bed, sit down and smoke a joint.' After his British court appearance he said, 'I think the law should be changed, make it like homosexuality with consenting adults in privacy.' These were not sentiments likely to endear him to the Japanese authorities and they rejected all his visa applications. McCartney would have been happy to leave it at that. His promoter, Harvey Goldsmith, had other ideas. Wings were on tour and, as Goldsmith says, 'Japan is very important in the marketplace and when we put the tour together Japan was an integral part of it. He said, "I can't get into Japan." I said, "That's my bit." He was intrigued but reticent.'

The British embassy in Tokyo became involved, giving its assurance that Paul McCartney, MBE, was indeed an upstanding, law-abiding citizen. Pressure also came from the Japanese end, with *Yomiuri*, the Tokyo newspaper, offering to sponsor a series of concerts. Japanese promoters were lined up. 'I did my bit,' Goldsmith said.

In their desire to be seen to be fair-handed, the Japanese authorities finally relented. And what thanks did they receive? Half a pound of marijuana staring them in the face. McCartney hadn't even bothered to conceal it. It was lying on the top of the suitcase. Japanese officialdom was outraged. McCartney had caused them 'loss of face', that strong Eastern concept of honour. Despite what the senior officials were saying, there was a body of opinion inside the narcotics squad and the customs agencies saying punish him with a long-term prison sentence. And until a final decision was made, they were certainly going to make him sweat.

He was given the number 22 and confined to an eight-by-four-foot concrete cell in the grey prison building in the centre of Tokyo. He slept on a thin roll-up mattress with only one thin blanket for warmth. The guards woke him at 6 a.m. when he had to sit crossed-legged for morning inspection. He recalled: 'It was like *Bridge over the River Kwai*. They shouted out "Twenty-two" in Japanese and I had to shout back, "Hi",' as in the Japanese for 'yes', rather than 'Hi, Hi, Hi'. 'I did it – I wasn't going to go against the system.'

He breakfasted on seaweed and onion soup – 'Not the greatest thing in the morning if you're used to cornflakes,' he told me – followed by twenty minutes of exercise. After a lunch of bread and jam he was taken to the narcotics headquarters, 'handcuffed with a rope tied around my neck like a dog. They wanted to know everything about me – my age, where I was born, my father's name, my income.' He was returned to his cell at 5 p.m. for a supper of rice and soup before lights out at 8 p.m. The prince was well and truly out of his palace. 'At first I thought it was barbaric,' he said. 'The first thing I expected was rape, so I slept with my back to the wall.'

Prisoners in Japanese jails are only allowed one bath a week and because he was arrested the day after bath night he had to wait six days before being allowed to share a hot tub with three other inmates. In the meantime he had to wash in the water from the cistern of the flush toilet in his cell. 'It is perfectly hygienic,' his jailer, Yasuji Ariga told me. 'The water running into the toilet is fresh water.' The vegetarian Paul wasn't allowed bananas because, as Ariga explained with steely-eyed seriousness, the guards might slip on the skins. His request to be allowed a guitar and a tape-recorder was refused. Nor was he permitted pencil and paper.

Linda, installed with her children in the £500-a-night luxury of a suite at the Okura hotel, was distraught. 'I take things in my stride but this has been hard,' she said. 'I haven't been able to sleep. I'm exhausted and I do get very low.' It was the first time in over a decade that she had slept apart from her husband. She was not allowed to see him for six days. When she did, Paul, ever the dutiful family man, was more concerned about their welfare than his own. 'He told me, "Keep your chin up – for me and the kids",' Linda said.

By then McCartney had settled into the routine of prison life with fatalistic resignation. 'I really thought I was going to be inside for years,' he said. He turned down the morning bread and coffee offered to Westerners because, he said, if he was going to be there for a long time, he might as well get used to Japanese food. He started to get on with the guards – 'Underneath their inscrutable exterior they were quite warm,' he said. He became as friendly as the language barrier would allow with two other inmates, one a murderer, the other, like McCartney, a putative drug user. 'We joked and had singsongs, singing songs like "Baby Face" and "Red Red Robin",' he said. 'And, yes, I also got a few requests for "Yesterday". I would sing and they would clap. It was a bit of a laugh.'

The laugh was not shared by his advisers on the outside who were working frantically to get him released. Expensive lawyers were hired and representations made to the Japanese government. They refused to involve themselves directly and the matter went back down to the investigating officers. By then, however, the authorities in Tokyo were tiring of the international scrutiny of their legal system McCartney's arrest had provoked and the police enquiries were starting to wind down. The jet freighter that had flown in Wings' eleven tons of hired equipment, protected in another eleven tons of packing cases, had been impounded when McCartney was arrested. The head of the customs services considered searching the cases to see if any other drugs were hidden away. After due deliberation, he decided not to. The case, he explained, was against McCartney and they already had all the evidence they needed to bring a successful prosecution.

The Japanese were clearly trying to avoid backing themselves into a corner. Had a search been instigated and any other incriminating evidence found, there would have been little alternative but to bring McCartney before the courts where he would certainly have been convicted. Better to get rid of the problem by expelling him. All that was required now, therefore, was for McCartney to show contrition, an important element in Japanese justice. This McCartney, trimming his sails to necessity, duly did. He apologised for the inconvenience he had caused. And he paid the Japanese promoters $200,000 to cover their losses on the now-cancelled tour. That bag of pot had proved very expensive indeed. But at least the way was clear for his release and on January 25 he was put on a plane bound for Amsterdam, where he was reunited with his family who had been given an hour's notice of his impending deportation.

As he was being bundled into the first-class cabin, his 8-year-old daughter, Stella, hugged him by the crumpled trouserleg of his dark green suit and said, 'Daddy, please don't go away again.' 'I promise I never will,' McCartney tearfully replied. The prince was on his way home to his palace.

Why he had been permitted to escape from it in the first place has become the subject of a minor industry of conspiracy theories, with Yoko Ono cast in the role of villainess. On their way to Tokyo the McCartneys had passed through New York where Linda had bought what Paul called 'some dynamite grass'. He telephoned the Lennons at their home in the Dakota building on the other side of Central Park from the Stanhope hotel where he was staying and suggested he came round so they could smoke it together in a hippy version of a peace pipe. Yoko, who took the call, rejected the suggestion out of hand. Paul is then said to have boasted that he was going to be staying in the presidential suite at the Okura hotel. This sent Lennon and Ono into a frenzy of agitation. The suite was their official residence when they were in Tokyo and having the 'McEastmans', as John called them, staying there would destroy the hotel's 'karma'. 'Mother', as he called Yoko, promised to take action.

According to Frederic Seaman, Lennon's personal assistant for the last two years of his life, Ono employed the services of John Green, her tarot-card reader who was also a 'voodoo priest', to cast a spell on McCartney to ensure that he never made it to the Okura.

According to Albert Goldman in his book, *The Lives of John Lennon*, Yoko went further than that. Quoting Sam Green, an art-dealing intimate of Yoko's, Goldman recorded, 'She has a cousin over there who runs customs. One call from Yoko and Paul was finished.'

I must discount Goldman's theory as highly improbable. The man who ran Tokyo customs was not a relation of Yoko's. Nor did he place any store in tarot cards or spells. Foreigners' suitcases are opened as a matter of routine, he told me, which is true. McCartney's was opened, he said, for what would have been no more than a cursory search because he was a prominent visitor and Japanese officials like to be seen to be doing their duty. The customs officer, he added, was surprised and embarrassed when he found the marijuana lying there on the top. It was as simple as that, he insisted.

But why did McCartney not even bother to attempt to hide his illicit contraband? Denny Laine, who flew in with McCartney and left Japan and Wings five days later, said he did it for kicks. The McCartneys, he said, had once smuggled £200-worth of marijuana past British customs hidden in the hood of their baby son James's coat. 'I think that he and Linda thought that if they managed to smuggle grass through the Japanese customs it would be one up to them – "Everyone thinks you can't do it so we'll show them we can,"' Laine said. 'Paul and Linda are the couple who have everything. That can get boring. What they crave is excitement. They did it for the thrill.'

McCartney gave me his own explanation. He said: 'I'd just come from America and I still had the American attitude that marijuana isn't that bad. I didn't realise how strict the Japanese attitude is. I know it sounds daft but that's the truth. I didn't try to hide it. I'd got some good grass in America and I was silly enough to think I could get it past. It was a fair cop – nick, nick.' Is this the end of your pot-smoking? I asked him on the flight out of Tokyo. He lit an unfiltered Senior Service cigarette, gave what was tantamount to a wink, and replied, 'From now on all I'm going to smoke is these.'

Four years later, while on holiday in Barbados, Paul and Linda were arrested and fined $200 each for possession of cannabis. Linda was searched by customs on her return to England. A small quantity of cannabis was discovered. She was charged and fined. The McCartneys' resolutions on marijuana have a habit of going up in smoke. These habitual offenders always managed to get away with it, however. It was only in Japan that McCartney's wealth and celebrity failed to provide him with the protection he had come to take for granted and he had spent ten days in jail as a consequence. It was a rotten start to the year. It would finish on a far, far lower note.

16

J OHN LENNON was gunned down outside his home in the Dakota
  building at seven minutes past eleven on the evening of 8
  December 1980, and became a myth and a martyr.

Paul McCartney's first reaction to his death was one of shocked
bewilderment. Irritation came later. For in dying so violently, so
senselessly, Lennon had forever claimed the glorious immortality
in which McCartney dearly wanted to share. He was at home in
the small house in Sussex that the McCartney family made their
English base when his office telephoned him with the news of
Lennon's murder. It was early in the morning, British time, and
Linda was out taking the children to school.

'It was all blurred,' he recalled. 'You couldn't take it in.' He
responded by sticking to the banality of his ordinary routine and
went to the recording studio in London where he was working.
'Nobody could stay home with that news,' he explained. 'We just
had to keep going. So I went in and did a day's work in a kind of
shock.'

That evening, as he was leaving, a reporter asked him how he
felt. He replied, 'It's a drag.' It was a trite answer that has dogged
him ever since, and cast him irretrievably as glib and insensitive.
Words had failed the songwriter in speech, as they sometimes did
in song.

'I meant drag in the heaviest sense of the word – you know, It's a *drag*,' he explained later, though conceding that, in hard type, it did look too 'matter of fact'. It had been the same when his mother died and he asked, insensitively, 'What are we going to do without her money?' That was another remark he regrets. 'I've never forgiven myself for that,' he says. 'Really, deep down, you know, I never have quite forgiven myself for that. But that's all I could say then.' And when Lennon died, all he could say was, 'It's a drag.'

He sat at home that night, watching the news on television, holding hands with his wife and children and crying. 'We just couldn't handle it, really,' he said.

And what hurt most of all, in those desperate days after Lennon's death when the enormity of the loss was still sinking in, was, McCartney said, that 'we never actually sat down and straightened our differences out'. A decade and a host of debilitating lawsuits later, Lennon and McCartney were still at war over the spoils of the Beatles' fortune. It was a feud that had carried through till death finally parted them. It would continue beyond the grave.

In 1973 Lennon, at last coming round to McCartney's way of thinking, and detesting his former partner all the more because he had been right all along, joined Ringo and Harrison in bringing a lawsuit against Allen Klein alleging that he took excessive commission and practised fraud. Klein promptly countersued for $63,461,372 and 87 cents. In a separate suit, he accused McCartney of conspiring against him in business and demanded $34 million in damages. Klein was nothing if not pugnacious in litigation and it eventually cost the Beatles $5 million dollars to get rid of him. That infuriated McCartney, who had to contribute to Klein's pay-off. 'And he never wanted that man as a manager in the first place,' Linda stormed. Klein's going did not resolve the dispute between the four ex-Beatles, however, which had now acquired a dynamism of its own.

'There was incredible bitterness,' McCartney remembered. When he suggested that the four of them should simply split the

Beatles' money up four ways, Lennon, concerned about the potential tax liabilities, refused. 'Everyone thinks I'm the aggressor but I'm not, you know – I just want out,' McCartney remarked. To which Lennon riposted: 'If you're not the aggressor, as you claim, who the hell took us to court and shat all over us in public? As I've said before – have you ever thought that you might possibly be wrong about something?'

The answer to that, of course, is rarely. But even when McCartney tried to compromise, he ran into hostility. At one point, 'to get some peace in the camp', as he put it, he offered to give Lennon the indemnity he was seeking for a certain clause in one of the myriad Apple contracts. Passing through New York, he telephoned Lennon to break the news to him.

'But there was so much suspicion, even though I came bearing the olive branch,' McCartney said. When McCartney said he wanted a meeting, Lennon replied, 'What for? What do you *really* want?'

Lennon brought one meeting to a premature conclusion by asking for a million-dollar loan. He didn't show up at all for what had been billed as the 'big dissolution meeting' at the Plaza hotel. Harrison, Ringo and McCartney had flown in from London. Lennon only had to walk the five hundred yards along Central Park South. He didn't even make the effort. John Green had read his tarot cards and the portents weren't right. Harrison lost his temper. He telephoned Lennon and shouted, 'Take those fucking shades off and come over here, you!' Lennon sent a balloon instead with the message, 'Listen to the Balloon.'

When McCartney went to see Lennon's son, Sean, who was born on John's own birthday of 9 October 1975, and two days after Lennon finally won his protracted legal battle against deportation from the United States, Yoko shouted at him, 'Don't touch the baby – he doesn't know you!' When he went round to the Dakota, guitar in hand just as he had done when they were teenagers, in yet another of his increasingly pathetic attempts to regain the friendship of the partner he had lost, Lennon refused him entrance. 'You can't just drop in on people in New York like you did in Liverpool,' Lennon told him. 'The old days are over.'

It wasn't all one-way traffic on this long and vitriolic road. 'We all accused one another of various business things,' McCartney admitted. To add to the ferment of hostility, McCartney again found himself accused of going behind the backs of the others.

In early 1985 Ringo, Harrison and Yoko Ono, representing the Lennon estate, filed suit against McCartney in the New York State Supreme Court. No explanatory papers accompanied the summons and when the matter was wrapped up in a larger settlement five years later, the terms were sealed. What can be ascertained is this – that Paul McCartney was earning a higher royalty rate on Beatles records than George Harrison, Ringo Starr or even John Lennon. Capitol Records confirmed that. With Klein gone and Apple Records no longer extant, McCartney had gone shopping for a record deal for Wings. Like a homing pigeon he returned to the people he knew, and from 1975 onwards until he moved across to Columbia Records in early '79, Wings records were released by Capitol, the Beatles' original American label. He was an artist every important record company was anxious to have and Capitol were delighted; of all the ex-Beatles, McCartney was the one sure fire winner.

Lennon had disappeared into an experimental phase and then stopped recording altogether. Harrison's musical inspiration had dried up, and in 1980 he suffered the indignity of having an album turned down by his own record company. Ringo had scored a couple of hits with songs like 'Back off Boogaloo' and 'It Don't Come Easy' and then faded out of the charts. That left McCartney as the only guaranteed commercially productive member of the old Fab Four; and with Wings scoring million sellers with virtually every record, he was in a position to demand a hefty financial recompense for his artistic output. Still smarting over the parsimonious way the Beatles had been treated, McCartney demanded a lot. As his later deal with Columbia would prove, he was in a position to get it.

That contract would earn him an astonishing twenty percent royalty rate. It was a poor deal from Columbia's point of view. Such an up-front rate could only be sustained by massive sales of a kind McCartney no longer generated; in effect he became the company's loss leader. Capitol, however, had that catalogue of Beatles records which continued to earn millions. It was a large cake and McCartney, the others complained, was being treated to an extra helping. His former partners took legal umbrage and instigated a series of lawsuits against McCartney, his father and brother-in-law, his company, and MPL, alleging 'breach of fiduciary duty, breach of contract and other wrongs'. They demanded 'at least $8 million'.

The matter was finally resolved in 1989. It was included in the settlement the Beatles reached with Capitol Records after a separate ten-year legal battle over royalties they claimed had not been paid. Leonard Marks, the New York attorney who represented the surviving members of the group in the drawn out case, says: 'The claim was that Capitol allegedly sold records they had claimed they had scrapped. There were numerous other charges, including false accounting.' The settlement, the largest of its kind, included an $80-million cash payment. Also included was the agreement that McCartney would not be taken to court by Harrison, Ringo, and the Lennon estate. McCartney vigorously defended himself against the charge that he had had his hand in the till of Beatles' royalties. 'That was a bum law suit,' he said when the settlement was announced. 'I half wish they would bring that lawsuit against me. I wanted to fight the case.'

There is no doubt, however, that Lennon, who found out about the arrangement when he went looking for a deal for *Double Fantasy*, his comeback and, as it would tragically turn out, last album, was very embittered. It was even worse, he said, than learning that McCartney had been buying up shares in Northern Songs all these years before. Harrison, too, was angered. 'I don't think George will ever really forgive Paul for that', says one long-time Beatles' confidante.

On matters of money, however, McCartney is very much his own master. By sticking to what he does best, music, he has made himself into one of the richest men in the world. It is not just his own songs that generate him an income estimated at £20 million a year. He also owns the publishing rights to such standards as 'Stormy Weather', 'Hello Dolly', and 'Till There Was You', the song from *The Music Man* which McCartney had sung on the *With the Beatles* album.

It was Linda's father, Lee Eastman, who suggested he get into publishing. McCartney recalled: 'He said originally, "If you are going to invest, do it in something you know. If you invest in building computers or something, you could lose a fortune. Wouldn't you rather be in music? Stay in music." I said yeah, I'd much rather do that. So he asked me what kind of music I liked and the first name I said was Buddy Holly. Lee got on to the man who owned Buddy Holly's stuff and bought that for me.'

The next Eastman-led move was to acquire control of the Edwin H Morris publishing house in New York. That cost him, McCartney said, 'all my savings, plus, so it was a big move.' It quickly paid off. As McCartney recalled: 'When we were shaping up to get it, slightly nervously, because I was putting it all on the line to do it, somebody from the company rang up and said, "Seeing as you're going to become the new owner, we've got a little show in here, which is in Boston and off-Broadway and doing the rounds. Will you continue to fund it, or do you want us to lay them all off?" I said, "No way am I going to lay them all off, you're kidding; an artist comes in and lays everyone off, that's not my kind of game. Of course we'll continue to fund it." That turned out to be *Annie*.'

Since then *A Chorus Line*, *La Cage aux Folles*, *High Society*, and *Grease* have been added to the collection, along with the rights to *Happy Birthday*, the most sung song of all time. McCartney takes an almost innocent delight in their ownership. The money, he insists, is of secondary importance; when his annual income was first computed at over £20 million, he said, 'It doesn't mean anything – they're just a string of zeros.'

The set of publishing rights he doesn't own are his own. In 1981 he tried to buy ATV Music which had absorbed Northern Songs. Unwilling to lay out himself the $20 million it would have cost, he

Under arrest and facing up to eight years in Japanese prison after half a pound of marijuana was found in his luggage at Tokyo Airport in 1980. *(Syndication International)*

Celebrating after the London première of *Give My Regards to Broad Street* with a few friends – Olivia Harrison, Barbara Bach and Ringo. *(Pictorial Press)*

The McCartney family striding out in the States, 1991. *(Pictorial Press)*

First-night triumph: Dame Kiri Te Kanawa, Jerry Hadley, Paul, Carl Davis, Sally Burgess and Willard White at the première of *Paul McCartney's Liverpool Oratorio.* *(David Modell/Katz)*

tried to enlist the financial assistance of Lennon's widow, but Yoko declined to become involved and the deal fell through. The company was then bought by the Australian entrepreneur, Robert Holmes a'Court, 'an Australian asset stripper, mate', as McCartney scathingly referred to him.

In 1984 ATV Music again came up for sale and once again McCartney expressed an interest in acquiring it. He was beaten to it by Michael Jackson who paid what was then considered an astounding $47.5 million for it. Once again the rights to his own work had been snatched away from him, though this time he had only himself to blame.

'I was quite friendly with Michael at the time,' McCartney recalled, 'and he used to keep coming up to me and asking me for a lot of advice. I gave him three pieces of advice.' The first was to get a business manager in whom he had confidence. 'So he immediately went and fired his manager.' He did more than that. By the summer of 1983, eight months after the release of their duet, 'The Girl is Mine', Jackson had disposed of not one, but three managers; Ron Weisner, Freddy DeMann, and, most controversially (though, as it turned out, not finally), his own father, Joe, who had handled the business affairs of Michael and his siblings, known collectively as the Jackson Five, since the 1960s when they had been hailed as Motown's black answer to the Beatles.

'I didn't quite mean *that* but he took me at my word there,' the unwitting Svengali observed. He told Jackson to 'get into videos because you'll own them and they'll be amazing assets in a number of years'. Jackson had only done *Beat It* at that time. Acting on McCartney's advice he went and made *Thriller*. 'So again he took me at my word.'

It was the third nugget of wisdom that proved so detrimental to McCartney's own interests. 'I said, "The other thing, think about music publishing for an investment." I said, "I love it, it's a hobby, it's something you and I can do, Michael, you'll be very good at it." He looked at me coyly and said, "I'm going to buy your songs." I thought, Good joke. I just laughed it off. The next time I saw him he again looked at me coyly and said, "I'm going to buy your songs." I thought, Still a good joke.'

It was a joke that turned very sour when Jackson, cash rich from *Thriller*, the biggest-selling album of all time, telephoned to tell him that he had done exactly what he said he was going to do – and bought the rights to 251 Lennon and McCartney compositions, including 'Yesterday'. It still rankles.

'I wrote and sang "Yesterday",' he complains. 'I pick up about fifteen percent of the money earned on that song and I don't think it's good enough. I deserve a little more than fifteen percent. It would be very noble of Michael to ring up and say, "I think it's time to renew your deal."' Denny Laine, who was last heard of camping out in a car park in Windsor, might say exactly the same thing, but then McCartney has always held decidedly subjective views on matters pertaining to business.

But if his reaction to Jackson's move on what he still regards as his own property was predictable, his decision not to buy ATV Music for himself still engenders surprise within the music industry. He could certainly afford it; given his earnings, he could have had it for little more than a year's income. Peter Brown offered an explanation during a television interview in the United States. Asked why McCartney hadn't bought back his own works, Brown replied, 'Because he's too cheap.'

This reluctance to risk a single one of the noughts he claims to be indifferent to is a disconcerting and less than attractive characteristic in McCartney's make-up. When Neil Aspinall married in 1968, for instance, McCartney was of the opinion that a modest gift would suffice. It was the other three Beatles who insisted on buying their longest-serving employee, who had made such a contribution to their success but had never been particularly well remunerated for his loyalty, a Knightsbridge flat as a wedding present.

It was Yoko Ono, however, who had the greatest cause to feel aggrieved by McCartney's penny-pinching ways. In his last telephone conversation with Lennon, McCartney had managed to exchange a few civil words, 'about his family, my family', as he recalled later. His relations with Yoko, however, were always fraught. 'Being her business partner is a real problem,' Linda said in 1984. And vice versa, Yoko would say.

Shortly after Lennon died the three surviving Beatles flew to New York for a meeting at the Plaza with Yoko who moved into a suite in the hotel in readiness. The object was to devise a strategy to deal with the financial difficulties posed by John's death. Yoko claimed that she was not consulted, that she was kept waiting outside the conference room while Ringo, Harrison and McCartney worked out what to do, which was in effect to do nothing; on Ringo's suggestion and with McCartney's acquiescence, Yoko later told her staff, all monies were to be frozen 'while things were sorted out'. That, Yoko bitterly complained, effectively cut off her cash flow. According to one employee, 'Yoko was left virtually penniless for months afterwards.'

Yoko could possibly have been exaggerating the case in order to highlight what she liked to call the 'heartlessness' of her late husband's partners. There is no doubt, though, that she felt that she had been ruthlessly squeezed – and that money was only a part of it. But then, it was a difficult time for everyone connected with the Beatles – and most especially for McCartney.

He had always been closest to John (as Lennon had pointed out, they *were* the Beatles because they wrote the songs) and he was disorientated by his death. He was also frightened. Always the most open and relaxed of pop stars, he had made a point of travelling by bus and train, happy to sign an autograph or give a wink and a cheery thumbs-up sign to passing fans. He now felt compelled to hire professional bodyguards and to turn his home in Sussex into a fortress protected by the latest surveillance equipment. He decided to give up touring.

At the same time, he was going through one of the creative troughs that afflict him every decade, a crisis exacerbated by Lennon's death. After the Japanese bust, Wings had disbanded. By then McCartney had signed up for Columbia for an estimated $20 million plus the requisite 'sweetener', in this case Frank Music, the publishing catalogue of Frank Loesser of *Guys and Dolls* fame. Money had proved no inspiration, however, and the quality of McCartney records went into further decline. Yoko, never one to use a rolling pin when a steamroller will do just as well, took great delight in telling her staff how she had told McCartney: 'You're the person who wrote "Hey Jude" – and now you write all this crap. How come you don't write great songs any more?'

In the effort to rekindle his creative embers, McCartney went into musical partnership again, first with Stevie Wonder on 'Ebony and Ivory', and then with Jackson on 'The Girl is Mine' and 'Say Say Say'. They were successful, in the commercial sense, and McCartney would steadfastly defend 'Ebony and Ivory' as an honourable statement on the need for racial tolerance. They were not songs likely to earn Yoko's applause, however.

Lennon, shortly before his death, remarked: 'Paul is quite a capable lyricist who doesn't think he is. So he doesn't go for it. Rather than face the problem, he would avoid it.' McCartney himself was honest enough to acknowledge that his music lacked the bite it once had. Songwriting, he observed, 'is like the thumb in the mouth. The more crises you have, the more material you have to work on.'

The problems now besetting McCartney were unfortunately not the kind that could be readily transmuted into song. He was as rich as he could ever wish to be. 'The greed has gone,' he said. He was a married man, he explained, whose primary interest was his family, who stayed in at night and watched television. 'If you get a bit content,' he said, 'then you might not write savage lyrics and stuff.'

To kick-start himself he decided to make a film. He must have wished he had stayed at home and watched some more TV rather than venture back into the world of cinema to make *Give My Regards to Broadstreet*. McCartney, exercising what he called the 'ultimate luxury, professionally' of being able to change into another medium, wrote and starred in the $9-million film. The story, he said, 'is about me and what happens to me'. No one cared. *Give*

My Regards to Broadstreet was an unmitigated disaster which makes *Magical Mystery Tour* look almost coherent.

Professional help was available. McCartney, convinced of his own ability, chose to ignore it. 'I think if it's someone else's idea, it's not as easy as if it's your own,' he said. The Liverpool playwright, Willy Russell, who wrote the successful play, *John, Paul, George, Ringo and Bert*, produced a draft script. 'It wasn't quite in my line of thinking,' McCartney said, and wrote his own script based on an idea – about a musician losing some tapes – which occurred to him in a traffic jam.

On the recommendation of *Chariots of Fire* producer David Puttnam, Peter Webb was hired to direct. Webb was a commercial film-maker of some repute. He was hardly allowed a look-in. McCartney wanted everything done his way. It was another manifestation of the old problem, of McCartney's insistence on having the final say, which had caused such dissension on the set of *Let It Be*.

'It was one of the most embarrassing experiences for everyone involved, including CBS records and 20th Century Fox, who just couldn't bring themselves to tell the emperor that he had no clothes on,' says one person connected with the ill-fated project. Webb's view of McCartney is still scarred by the experience. 'A little difficult?' the director says. 'It was one of the most horrible experiences of my life.'

The film opened simultaneously in 311 American cinemas in the autumn of 1984 – and was pulled within days. It was a stunning failure. He had made another home movie – and this time it had cost $9 million. The tailspin in McCartney's career was turning into a free fall. McCartney was shaken. He dislikes criticism and his self-confidence, so complete when he is secure in an environment he can control, so fragile when his talents come under unfavourable scrutiny, was unravelling again.

In 1985 he appeared on stage for the first time in six years in the Bob Geldof-organised Live Aid concert. He appeared nervous and unsure of himself. He attempted a collaboration with Eric Stewart of 10CC on *Press to Play*. Stewart was no John Lennon, however, and it was not a success. The album, with its front cover of Linda pressing her face in adoring sublimation into her husband's, was a poor seller, getting no higher than number 30 in the US charts. He was called 'mawkish, insipid, silly, vacuous – and worse', by one reviewer. McCartney, the prodigy of the 1960s, the best-selling artist of the 1970s, appeared to be a spent force.

Even his place in musical history was being called into question. For in death Lennon had regained the leadership of the Beatles that had eluded him for the last years of the group's existence. It was, said McCartney, 'eulogy time'. It had happened to James Dean, to Jim Morrison of the Doors, and to Buddy Holly. Now it was happening to Lennon. McCartney found himself relegated to the role of glorified sessionman in the burgeoning mythology growing up around the Beatles. 'There are times,' he complained, 'when you read about how the Beatles was John and these other three guys just sort of stood around.'

McCartney was one guy who certainly hadn't. He had been the driving force behind *Sgt Pepper*. He had provided the majority of their hits in the later years, and had written the group's biggest-selling single, 'Hey Jude'. As much as anyone in a four-man band could be, Paul McCartney *was* the Beatles for half of their eight recording years together.

'A lot of the artistic and creative things that John got the credit for were in fact done by Paul,' Linda said. 'But you can't prove that to people and I think it still hurts him that people think John was the genius while he was only the cute, melodic one. I keep saying it doesn't matter what people think, he knows what he is and what he's done. But he still resents it.'

He is rich enough for it not to matter but that is not McCartney's way. He has a firm view of his position in rock's pecking order. 'I'd put me at the top,' he says forcefully. 'Just because I'm a competitor . . . You don't find Mike Tyson saying, "Sure, there's a lot of guys who could beat me."'

Lennon had not been able to dominate McCartney in life. He

was not going to be allowed to do so in death. And as he proved after the death of the Beatles, he has a remarkable ability to rise, Phoenix-like, from catastrophes of his own making. It was time to get back to the slog, 'because you've got to slog, man', of proving himself yet again – to a public in danger of being allowed to forget how good he could be, and to himself.

He went back into the recording studio, this time with New-Waver Elvis Costello as his sidekick and co-composer. 'I really wanted to show that I can still do it and not just rely on the old hits,' he explained. The album was *Flowers in the Dirt*, his best offering of the decade. His collaboration with Costello worked well. Always at his best when working with someone else, he described Costello as 'a very good foil for me'. On the track entitled 'You Want Her Too' McCartney even managed to catch a distant echo of the Lennon days. 'I'm saying, "I've loved her so long", and he's saying, "I know you did, you stupid git!"' he recalled in the sleeve notes. 'I said, "My God, that's me and John's whole style, I'd write some romantic line and John does some sort of acid acerbic put down."'

Yet for all McCartney's fine words, there is very little of Elvis Costello to be heard in *Flowers in the Dirt*. Because of his apparent need to control everything he is involved in, the input of his post-Lennon partners tends to be washed out. When his talent was in its youthful bloom this did not matter. It does now. The well of his inspiration is running shallow and all too often his melodies are little better than the pastiches he insists he is anxious to avoid. In 'My Brave Face' on *Flowers in the Dirt*, he sings, 'I've had this sentimental inclination not to change a single thing.' That, sadly, includes too many of his songs, which continue to play the same old three- or four-chord trick in ways too derivative of work he has done before to stimulate the critical interest he still craves. The edge of modernity is missing. His albums, including the comparatively well-regarded *Flowers in the Dirt*, have an old-fashioned feel to them.

Roy Orbison, another 'dinosaur' singer-songwriter of the rock age who had seen his career stumble on the hurdle of changing taste, came back, just before his death, with the Travelling Wilberries, then with the delightful *Mystery Girl* album. It was still unmistakably Orbison, but with a new freshness to it. He achieved his artistic renaissance by putting his songs in the charge of others, including Bono of U2, Tom Petty of the Heartbreakers, and, most notably, Jeff Lynne, one-time member of the Move, founder of the Electric Light Orchestra and now a major record producer.

McCartney shows no such willingness to surrender himself to outside direction. He believes in his own musical genius and is reluctant to accept advice. But without Lennon's cynicism on hand to define the parameters, his songs all too often drift off into slushy sentimentality. There is little quality control – or if there is, it is difficult to discern. Flashes of the old, sharper McCartney still manage to struggle through, however, and *Flowers in the Dirt*, while certainly no *Sgt Pepper* or *Band on the Run*, did top the British charts for one week in the summer of 1989 and restore some credibility to his flagging reputation. And to confirm to himself that he really could still cut it, he embarked on a worldwide tour, his first in over a decade.

There were no apologies this time, no attempt to hide the glories of his past behind the mundanity of his present. Fifteen of the songs he sang at each performance, a full half of the set, were Beatles songs.

'I'd shied away from the Beatles stuff with Wings – it was a bit too near the break-up of the Beatles and it was a painful break-up,' he said. 'Now I thought, I don't have to deny the Beatles songs – *or* the McCartney songs because some of them were recorded by the Beatles but *I* wrote them.'

In the tour's free programme which cost $1 million to print and distribute, McCartney wrote: 'The thing I find myself doing – which is a pity really, but it's just because of the unfortunate circumstances – is trying to justify myself against John and I hate to do that. There are certain people who are starting to think he was the Beatles.'

McCartney was out there proving that Lennon wasn't. The songs he sang, as he emphasised, were all *McCartney* songs, including

'The Fool on the Hill', 'Can't Buy Me Love', 'Hey Jude', 'Back in the USSR', 'Sgt Pepper', 'Good Day Sunshine', and, of course, 'Yesterday'.

'One reason I decided to tour,' he said, 'is that I realised I'd never performed a lot of my own songs. When I was touring with Wings, it wasn't right yet. Too soon after the divorce. So "Pepper" has only been performed once, the day we did it in the studio. Same with "Hey Jude".' Now he was performing them in front of millions – in April 1990, at the Maracana stadium in Rio de Janeiro, he played to a world record paying audience of 184,368.

'I'm not trying to claim the history and achievements of the Beatles for myself,' he insisted. 'I'm just trying to reclaim my part of it.' The Beatles, McCartney said, would never have got back together again because Lennon's life had moved on and he didn't want to go back. That didn't matter so much any more. McCartney had discovered he could do it himself. 'It was the great unblocking,' he said. In his determination to lay the ghost of Lennon, he also set out to prove that he is capable of going forward.

17

THE two thousand people who congregated in Liverpool's cavernous Anglican Cathedral on a fresh summer's evening in 1991 were treated to decidedly more yet, conversely, confusingly, distinctly less than they had expected.

What they witnessed was the partial renaissance of a talent so often stalled in a rut of complaisant, unchallenging mediocrity. What they heard was *Paul McCartney's Liverpool Oratorio*, a grand, sweeping work far distant, both in time and intent, from the rudimentary four-bar tunes he had belted out three decades before in the dingy Cavern only a few hundred yards away.

It was an immense project for a composer whose best works had never run for longer than three minutes, who cannot read or write music and who admits that, when he started on it, didn't know what an oratorio was. It had been two years in the preparation and it had stretched McCartney's ability to its limit and, in some respects, beyond it. Yet whatever its flaws – and they are the same ones that have dogged everything else he had done in the previous decade – the Liverpool Oratorio stands up as a substantial piece of work.

The reaction that Friday night, however, was muted and confused. It was not until McCartney walked up to the front to bow and embrace Carl Davis, the conductor and his fellow composer, did the applause acquire real life – and that was in appreciation more of the man than his music.

Dame Kiri Te Kanawa, the distinguished New Zealand soprano whose voice had helped give authority to the Oratorio, said afterwards, 'I find it quite marvellous to be at the front end of something like this. It is a great honour. The orchestra was superb, and the singers were wonderful.'

Others were less sure. They had gone to the Cathedral in the expectation of hearing a collection of 'McCartney tunes'. That was exactly what they hadn't heard. For that was what McCartney had specifically decided he was *not* going to turn in.

No matter what he does or how hard he tries, Paul McCartney is forever destined to be Beatle Paul in the minds of a public still clinging to its illusion of perpetual adolescence made incarnate. But the Beatles no longer exist, except in memory, and with Lennon dead they can never exist again. McCartney may talk wistfully of getting together with George Harrison and Ringo Starr but that is more wishful thinking than probability; when Paul said he would like to write with Harrison, George snapped back, 'It's not for me. We had our chance to write together – 25 years ago.'

So it is to others that McCartney must now turn for stimulus for his work – and his compulsion to work remains as strong as ever. However proud he may be of his Beatling past, there are times when it becomes oppressive. That was why he had teamed up with Carl Davis, the American-born, London-based conductor – as a way of breaking out of what he called 'this pigeon hole – "Ex-Beatle, ballad writer, rocks occasionally."' And whenever Davis said, 'What we need now is a McCartney-ish ballad,' he refused, 'because this was to be my first outing with a straight orchestra and I didn't want it to be a pastiche of what I'd already written.'

It had been Davis's idea, when asked for ideas for the 150th anniversary of the Royal Liverpool Philharmonic Orchestra, to involve Liverpool's famous son. A meeting was duly arranged through Linda's fellow animal rights campaigner, Carla Lane, who wrote the television series *Bread* which starred Davis's actress wife, Jean Boht. Initially, however, McCartney, wasn't keen.

'In the first hour we got on rather falteringly,' Davis recalled. 'He likes to be led to things quite gradually. He's very cautious.' It was only through the good offices of Linda, he added, that their relationship 'started to build'.

As well as his caution, McCartney had inherited his father's distaste for classical music.

'The problem was those fruity classical voices; he couldn't stand them,' McCartney says. Nor could the son.

Davis persevered, however, and when he started making notes for movements based on the stories McCartney was telling about his childhood, Paul became interested. A rough outline for a work of eight movements set to a semi-autobiographical story was developed. Then, over the next two years, Davis and McCartney set about composing the music, with Davis providing the orchestration and the filler passages, McCartney the melodies and the words which, says Davis, 'he conceives together'.

McCartney, who refuses to learn how to write music – 'It's almost a superstition,' he says – and rejected Davis's offer to loan him a recording of Benjamin Britten's *Young Person's Guide to the Orchestra* ('too late for that, love'), would picture the music in his mind, rather like a film, and then describe it to Davis, just as he had done with George Martin back in the wonderfully creative 'Penny Lane' days with the Beatles.

'He talked about his collaboration with George Martin and this sort of dictating, discussion, indicating, and trying, was all part of the process on all the arrangements he did with George Martin, so he wasn't unfamiliar with orchestral sounds and colours,' said Davis.

McCartney knew what he wanted – and what he didn't. The ninety-minute oratorio which, he learnt from a magazine article he read aboard a plane, is a 'religious work sung by solo voices with a chorus and orchestra but without costume or drama', was going to be a 'serious, grown-up entertainment'.

It was also the fulfilment of a musical development long in the gestation. 'I remember around that time, I must have been in my mid-twenties, looking at thirty as being a very dangerous age, and

I thought, "God, what am I going to be then?" And I imagined myself in a tweed jacket writing "serious" music. "Eleanor Rigby" and those things were the start of it.' The Oratorio was the culmination.

There were moments, though, when he felt embarrassed about being involved in a project so divergent from anything he had attempted before.

'The fruit barrier was the problem,' he said, 'and while I was writing the piece I was apologising to friends like Elvis Costello and Chrissie Hynde (of the Pretenders). But in fact they love classical music and this got me over the hurdle.'

Those early misgivings did not prevent him from insisting on taking the major credit for the piece. McCartney has never been too bashful lay claim to a work he felt was rightfully his and, to Davis's surprise, he insisted on it being entitled *Paul McCartney's Liverpool Oratorio.*

Davis had assumed that the work would be called *The Liverpool Oratorio* with *By Paul McCartney and Carl Davis* as the main rather than the sub-title. With some good reason. If McCartney contributed the tunes and the lyrics, it was Davis who provided the orchestration, and the harmonic structure, taking, for instance, a McCartney-suggested D Major and turning it into a D Major with an added sixth, so giving colour and character to an otherwise bland chord – and, by extension, giving the work its distinctive texture and flavour.

McCartney's need to dominate, however, is urgent and profound. 'He's used to being the boss,' Davis says. On the *Flowers in the Dirt* album he goes to the extent of crediting himself in the sleeve notes with providing the handclapping. On the *Oratorio*, he explained, 'I had to lead the dance. I was getting paranoid that on the day of the performance he would be up on the podium working away like Stravinsky on heat and I'd be sitting in the audience like a soft Mick and that I'd be coming over as the scruff from Speke who couldn't read music and who'd just done one or two little tunes and people would think it was Carl who had written it all.'

Given McCartney's personality, there were other, inevitable, moments of tension. McCartney, Davis said, could be 'shockingly brusque sometimes. I'm not used to that but we got over it . . . If you're going to do something with Paul McCartney, you know what you're biting off. He's not going to remain inconspicuous.'

The *Oratorio*, however, was new musical territory for McCartney. He had to rely on Davis, who had the musical advantage of knowing exactly how every written note would sound. 'Look, you know what this is going to sound like and I don't,' he explained to Davis when he ordered a full rehearsal. When the orchestra struck up 'I think Paul was terrified,' Davis said. 'He had a look of terror, of the unknown, on his face. I felt very warm about that moment, because I knew it was going to be wonderful.'

McCartney thought so too. Not everyone in the Cathedral that first night shared his opinion. The consensus amongst the bemused first audience was that it worked better when 'classical' music came to McCartney, as on 'Eleanor Rigby', than when McCartney went to 'classical' music, as he did in the Oratorio. The local Liverpool *Daily Post* heard 'memorable passages . . . interspersed with periods of near tedium', while *The Times*, so fulsome in its praise of Lennon's 'Not a Second Time' twenty-seven years earlier, complained that the 'churchy choral passages and laboured orchestral interludes make Brahms's *Requiem* seem like a hotbed of syncopation.'

The real problem was the lyrics, as it so often is with the later McCartney. His touch was surer in his youth. 'Eleanor Rigby' stands out as clearly in the memory as a black and white photograph, its story sharp and poignant, its lyrics good enough to stand by themselves. The *Liverpool Oratorio*, by comparison, is soft centred and sentimental. As good as it is musically – and in parts it is very good indeed – the lyrics lack the verve and resonance for the *Oratorio* to be considered a truly major work of art. As Paul Fisher of the *Guardian* noted, 'McCartney's literary self is more uncertain than his musical self and the sugary libretto needed an editor with even a fraction of Lennon's cynicism. It is true there is a sturdy classical tradition of flaky librettos, but the suggestive snap of, say, "She's just seventeen, if you know what I mean," will remain clearer in the memory than any of the Oratorio's words.'

Back in the sixties, when everyone knew exactly what McCartney meant, his interests were what he sang about – having a good time playing hard, driving, foot-stomping rock and roll and maybe getting lucky afterwards with the mini-skirted dolly bird screaming in the front row. He still plays rock and roll. But now he touches his fans only with his eyes. He is a family man whose notion of a good time is an evening spent at home with his children, which is the message of the *Oratorio*, whose final movement contains the line: 'What people want is a family . . . moat around the castle, pull up the drawbridge.'

That is exactly what the McCartneys have done, keeping themselves to themselves, only inviting the closest of acquaintances to their 200-acre farm in Sussex (like his parents, McCartney has few friends outside his family), devoting themselves to being as ordinary as possible, looking after their animals and practising their philosophy of letting everything live naturally – which means refusing to trim their horses' hooves or put down their aged sheep.

'Being ordinary is very important to me,' he explained. 'It's really quite rational, my ordinariness. It's not contrived at all. It's actually my answer to the question: What is the best way to be? I think ordinary.'

It is a philosophy he has tried to pass on to his children, all of whom were educated at the local state school. 'Linda and I aren't strict but we do have values we impress on our kids,' he says. 'You see, if my kids are going to inherit money – and they will – then they should have their feet on the ground' – and preferably back in the Liverpool suburb where their father spent his own childhood.

'I considered sending James to Eton but I couldn't bear the thought of him coming home, talking all posh and saying, "Hello, pater".'

His efforts to live by that code sometimes smack of affectation.

When they are invited to dinner by neighbours the McCartneys have been known to annoyingly insist that they will only come if they eat in the kitchen – and then only if the food is vegetarian. He also insists, as a matter of domestic policy, on Linda doing her own housework. Yet as absurd as this can seem to outsiders, it is vital to McCartney. Trapped in the shadow of his own fame, cocooned by his wealth, he is hanging on to reality the only way he knows how.

'Linda really doesn't like housework,' he once explained, 'because when she grew up her family had maids and she wasn't taught to do anything. But it's something I've tried to tell Linda about because in the kind of family I'm from, housework is considered a pleasure. The smell of ironing and the laundry . . . Where I'm from, once a week, the women would sort of get the laundry out and smell the washing and feel it and see it and iron it all, and they'd be chatting or listening to the radio. It was a very peasant thing. It was an event, like treading the grapes.'

Linda might object that, with a fortune estimated at over £500 million, McCartney is rich enough to afford her an army of house-keepers, chauffeurs, nannies. She doesn't. The girl from the Upper Eastside of Manhattan is happy in her role as Mother Earth, living in messy comfort, campaigning for animal rights, writing her best-selling vegetarian cook books, cooking for her family, worrying about the future of the planet, catering to her man, happy with her husband.

'We have our barnies, like every married couple,' she says. Paul, she says, can 'definitely be quite horrible' because he is a perfectionist who 'knows how he wants things and gets angry when they are not done properly'. After two decades together, however, they are still in love. 'I am very proud of Linda,' Paul says. Linda, for her part, has said: 'Kindness is the thing I find most attractive in a man. That's what I find so attractive about Paul – even after all these years he still stops off after meetings to bring me flowers home.' He also makes her tea in the morning.

People with a casual acquaintanceship with the couple insist that

275

Linda is the dominant partner in the marriage. She denies it. 'I was never a mother substitute, if that's what you're thinking,' she has remarked. 'Paul's always had the upper hand. Still does. He's the boss.' She doesn't even know how much money her husband earns.

'My dad never told my mum how much he earned,' McCartney explained. Jim McCartney had died on 13 March 1976, in the home in Heswall Paul had bought for him, with the last words: 'I'll be with Mary soon.' Paul, always reluctant to expose his emotions, did not attend his father's funeral and, as he did when Lennon died, covered his grief by spending the day at work. But although there were no public ululations, he paid Jim the greater respect of re-creating him in his own home life.

It is a strange emotional resting place for a pop icon whose talents took him from the suburbs of Liverpool and made him one of the richest people in the world; whose music has thrilled millions; whose thumbs-up gesture and cheery smile is one of the most famous images of the twentieth century; who is as determined at his half-century as he was when he was a mop-topped teenager to keep proving himself; who plans to keep on recording and touring; who still wants everyone to like him. Yet by living 'a normal life' mod-elled on his own upbringing he has managed to hang on to his sanity. And that, amongst the burnt-out carcasses that litter the foot-stomping, mind-blowing world of rock and roll, is its own remarkable achievement.

While Rock's cemetery continues to fill, he is happily shopping for the groceries, angrily campaigning to keep his local hospital open, making donations to charities like Amnesty International (he isn't as stingy as reputation would have it), taking the train to the office every morning, bringing flowers home for his wife at night, enthusiastically looking forward to becoming a grandfather, sub-scribing to many of the values, albeit with a cushion of half a billion pounds under him, as his father and mother had before him.

There is danger in this domestic contentment. As the critic Cyril Connolly observed: 'There is no more sombre enemy of good art than the pram in the hall', and McCartney's Muse has trouble making itself heard above his household clamour. In his teens McCartney was writing songs like 'When I'm 64'. His twenties had produced such lyrical classics as 'Yesterday', rockers like 'I Saw Her Standing There', and the quintessential Beatles anthem, 'Hey Jude'. The break-up of the Beatles provided him with the inspiration for 'Maybe I'm Amazed' with its brilliant use of chromatic scales. With that springboard to work from he might now, at his half-century, be expected to be producing work of rounded maturity. Instead he continues to turn out silly love songs. While there is nothing inherently reprehensible in that, a public which can still remember, if only just, how incisive his music used to be has a right to wonder into which vegetable pie the inspiration went.

But if the critics' judgement over the past few years has often been severe, creating music still gives him pleasure and satisfaction, despite the lapses and the frustrations and the periods of apparent complacency that have punctuated the glories. Paul McCartney has produced some of the most memorable popular music of all time and we owe him that. By extending himself, as he did with the *Oratorio*, he has shown he can still produce work of at least intermittent quality. He plans to keep on trying. And given the store of talent at his disposal, it would be foolish indeed to write him off just yet. Linda certainly hasn't.

'She always wants Paul to keep developing,' Carl Davis observes. 'She's a very positive force in his life.' The challenge now, as it is with all artists sooner or later, is with himself and McCartney seems determined to try and rise to it.

'I can't see myself giving up,' he says. 'Even if no one wanted to record any album by me ever again, I'd still write songs.'

Until he's 64. And beyond.

Bibliography

Among the books I have consulted, the following are the most important:

Brown, Peter, and Gaines, Steven, *The Love You Make* (Macmillan, London, 1983)

Clayson, Alan, *The Quiet One; A life of George Harrison* (Sidgwick & Jackson, London, 1990)

Davies, Hunter, *The Beatles* (Heinemann, London, 1968); Second Revised Edition (McGraw-Hill Book Company, 1985)

Dowlding, J., *Beatlesongs* (Fireside, Simon & Schuster, NY, 1989)

Epstein, Brian, *A Cellar Full of Noise* (New English Library, London, 1981)

Flippo, Chet, *McCartney, the Biography* (Sidgwick and Jackson Ltd, London, 1988)

Gambaccini, Paul, *Paul McCartney in His Own Words* (Omnibus Press, London, 1976)

Giuliano, Geoffrey, *Blackbird; the Unauthorised Biography of Paul McCartney* (Smith Gryphon Ltd, London, 1991)

Goldman, Albert, *The Lives of John Lennon* (William Morrow and Co, NY, 1988)

Gross, Edward, *Paul McCartney: 20 Years on his Own* (Pioneer Books Inc, Las Vegas, 1990)

Lennon, Cynthia, *A Twist of Lennon* (Star Books, London, 1978)

Lewisohn, Mark, *The Beatles Live!* (Pavilion Books in association with Michael Joseph Ltd, London, 1986)

Lewisohn, Mark, *The Beatles Day by Day* (Harmony Books, NY, 1990)

Martin, George, with Hornsby, Jeremy, *All You Need is Ears* (Macmillan, USA, 1979)

McCartney, Linda, and Cox, Peter, *Linda McCartney's Home Cooking* (Bloomsbury Publishing Ltd, London, 1989)

McCartney, Mike, *Thank U Very Much; Mike McCartney's Family Album* (Weidenfeld & Nicolson Ltd, London, 1981)

Norman, Philip, *Shout* (Fireside, Simon & Schuster, NY, 1981)

Schwartz, Francie, *Body Count* (Straight Arrow Books, San Francisco, 1972)

Seaman, Frederic, *John Lennon; Living on Borrowed Times* (Xanadu Publications, London, 1991)

Somach, Denny and Kathleen, *Ticket to Ride* (Macdonald and Company, London, 1989)

Taraborrelli, Randy J., *Michael Jackson* (Birch Lane Press, NY, 1991)

Taylor, Derek, *It Was Twenty Years Ago Today* (Fireside, Simon & Schuster, NY, 1987)

Williams, Allan, and Marshall, William, *The Man Who Gave The Beatles Away* (Coronet, London, 1975)

Wyman, Bill, *Stone Alone* (Viking, London, 1990)

The Rolling Stone Illustrated History of Rock and Roll (Picador, London, 1980)

Other invaluable sources include: *The Playboy Interview*, (December 1984, January 1989), *Record* (September 1984), *New York Newsday*, (10 December 1989), *Newsweek* (29 September 1980), *Vox* (July 1991). *USA Today* (19 May 1989), *Sunday Times Magazine* (9 June 1991), *Daily News Magazine* (10 December 1989), *Rolling Stone* (19 April 1979, 28 February 1985, 25 January 1990, 8 February 1990), *The People Magazine* (21–27 July 1991), *US* (30 November 1987), *Musician Magazine* (November 1987), *Viva* (February 1978), the *Economist*, *Playgirl*, the *Daily Telegraph*, the *Daily Express*, the *Mail on Sunday*, the *Sun*, the *Guardian*, the *Independent*, *Washington Post*, the *Daily Mirror*, and the BBC Radio 1 interviews. I would like to thank Mike McGovern, Christopher Wilson, Mike Cowton, and many others without whose help and guidance this book would not have been possible.

Index

Abbey Road album, 210, 213, 214, 236
Abbey Road studios, 76, 127, 144, 159, 161, 172, 209
Abrams, Steven, 168
'Across the Universe', 210
Ali, Mohammad, 117–18
'All My Loving', 109
'All My Trials', 234
All Things Must Pass, 204
'All You Need is Love', 165
'Another Day', 235
Apple Boutique, 196
Apple Corp, 194–206, 208, 212–13, 215, 255
Apple Records, 197, 208, 256
Arden, Don, 91–2
Ardmore and Beechwood, 75, 87
Ariga, Yasuji, 248
Arnez, Desi, Jr, 186
Asher, Jane:
    career, 95, 95–6, 126, 221
    Cavendish Avenue house, 129–30
    family, 85, 94–5, 124
    Maharishi, 169, 179
    Paul break-up, 190–1, 199
    relationship with Paul, 96, 115, 150, 171, 182–3, 188–91, 223, 224
Asher, Margaret, 94–5, 179, 191
Asher, Peter, 110, 197, 199, 208
Asher, Dr Richard, 94–5
Askew, John, 38
'Ask Me Why', 78
Aspinall, Neil:
    Apple, 208
    Best's sacking, 80
    marriage, 260
    orgies, 135–6
    road manager, 57, 58, 74
    Sgt Pepper, 157
    'She's Leaving Home', 151
Astaire, Fred, 17

ATV, 211, 235, 258, 259–60
Avalon, Frankie, 102, 105

'Back in the USSR', 114, 267
Back to the Egg, 243
Bambi-Filmkunsttheater cinema, 46, 55
Band on the Run, 238, 243, 246, 266
Barratt, Brian, 144
Barrow, Tony, 140
Bart, Lionel, 167
Basie, Count, 126
BBC, 28, 161, 234, 246
Beach Boys, 105, 142
Beatles:
    Apple *see* Apple
    audience reaction, 90, 98, 135
    boots, 63, 73, 86
    break-up, 207–16, 217–20, 222, 225–6, 255
    contracts, 75–7, 86, 111, 145, 164, 205, 207
    death threats, 138–9
    drugs, 51–2, 125–6, 159, 161
    haircut, 61–2, 63, 86
    Hamburg, 42–55, 61–3
    jackets, 62, 86
    Jesus popularity row, 138–9
    MBEs, 133–4
    merchandising, 86, 111–12, 113, 174
    name, 36, 45
    Royal Command Variety Performance, 98–9
    tours, 135–7
    US tours, 101–21, 137–40
Beck, Jeff, 239
Beeching, Lord, 200
Bee Gees, 194
'Being for the Benefit of Mr Kite', 153, 159–60
Bennett, Barbara, 189

Bennett, Cliff, 142
Benson, Harry:
  on Best's sacking, 80
  US tour memories, 101, 104, 106, 117–18,
    120, 139
Bergman, Ingmar, 148, 223
Bernstein, Sid, 102–3, 109
Berry, Chuck, 53, 56, 237
Best, Mona, 35, 57, 61–2, 72–3, 80
Best, Pete:
  background, 35–6
  Hamburg, 47–8, 50–2, 55, 61
  Lee Curtis and the All Stars, 91
  opinion of McCartney, 113
  position in group, 57, 60–1, 71–2, 80–2
'Big Bop', 233
'Birthday', 186
Black, Cilla, 110, 151, 171
Blackwells, The, 58, 110
Blake, Peter, 157–8
Bloomfield, Mike, 185
Blue Angel club, Liverpool, 37
Blue Flames, 184
Blues Breakers, 239
Boht, Jean, 270
Bonham, John, 243
Bono, 266
Bowery Boys, 158
Bowie, David, 186
Boyd, Patti see Harrison
Brando, Marlon, 40, 157
Britten, Benjamin, 271
Britton, Geoff, 239
Bron, Eleanor, 126
Brown, Peter:
  Apple, 16, 194–5, 196, 197, 201–2, 208
  Beatles involvement, 16, 91, 137, 209
  Epstein's death, 170–1
  Linda–Paul introduction, 16, 184–6
  Linda's bail money, 246
  McCartney death rumour, 213
  Maharishi, 170, 180
  NEMS, 16, 67
  on Epstein, 70–1, 75, 109, 112, 163, 169
  on Hamburg, 52
  on Lennon–McCartney relationship, 127,
    144, 178–9, 212, 215
  on Linda, 185, 191
  on McCartney, 7, 16, 23–4, 73, 87, 96,
    114, 139, 149, 195, 260
  on Ringo, 107
Browne, Tara, 124, 131–3, 153, 159, 212
Bruce, Lenny, 157
Bryce-Hamner, 86, 200
Burdon, Eric, 185
Butler, Rab, 120
Byrds, The, 247
Byrne, Nicky, 105, 111–12, 113, 119

Cage, John, 180
Cannon, Freddie, 237
'Can't Buy Me Love', 267

Capitol Records, 102–5, 145, 207, 214,
    256–7
Carson, Johnny, 195
Cas and the Casanovas, 36–7
Casbah club, Liverpool, 35, 57, 61, 72
Cash, Johnny, 56
Cavern club, Liverpool:
  Beatles at, 57–60, 69, 72, 93, 269
  Best's sacking, 80, 82
  Cilla Black, 110
  Epstein's visits, 65, 69–70
  Jim's attitude, 59
CBS, 109, 263
Chandler, Chas, 185
Charles, Ray, 128
Clapton, Eric, 239
Clay, Cassius, 117–18
Cochran, Eddie, 23, 27, 56
Cogan, Alma, 127
Collins, Joan, 197, 208
Collins, Lewis, 51
Columbia Records, 74, 256, 262
Connolly, Cyril, 277
Cook, Peter, 223
Costello, Elvis, 265, 272
Coward, Noël, 130–1
Cox, Kyoko, 180
Cox, Tony, 180–1, 209
Cronkite, Walter, 102
'Cry for a Shadow', 63
Curtis, Tony, 26

Daily Express, 118, 173
Daily Post, 273
Darin, Bobby, 164
Datebook magazine, 138
Davies, Hunter, 62, 191, 223
Davies, Meta, 150–1
Davis, Colin, 269, 270–3, 277
'Day in the Life, A', 153, 161
Dean, James, 264
'Dear Boy', 226
'Dear Friend', 232
Decca, 74
Delfont, Bernard, 97–8
DeMann, Freddy, 259
Derry and the Seniors, 43, 46, 47
De Stael, Stuart, 38
Deutsche Gramophon, 63
Dick James Music, 87
Dimbleby, David, 169
Disc magazine, 199
Donegan, Lonnie, 27, 32
Double Fantasy, 257
Dresner, Buddy, 116
Dunbar, John, 181
Dylan, Bob, 125–6, 145, 183, 232, 246

Eagles, The, 247
Eastman, John, 201–2, 205–6, 214, 225
Eastman, Lee, 200–1, 205–6, 208, 225, 258
Eastman, Linda see McCartney

'Ebony and Ivory', 262
Eckhorn, Peter, 54–5, 61
Edwin H. Morris, 258
'Eleanor Rigby', 21, 125–6, 272, 273
Electric Light Orchestra, 266
Ellington, Duke, 126
Ellis, Geoffrey, 170
EMI:
  Beatles contracts, 75–7, 86, 111, 145, 164,
    205, 207
  Capitol see Capitol Records
  George Martin, 75, 152
  Klein, 207, 213
  NEMS deal, 201
  Nigerian studio, 237
  profits, 86
  Sgt Pepper, 157–9
English, David, 118–19
English, Joe, 239
Epics, The, 116
Epstein, Brian:
  background, 65–8
  Beatles contracts, 75–7, 86, 111, 145, 164,
    205
  Beatles management, 52, 71–7, 83, 86–8,
    91, 97–8, 112–13, 145, 163–5, 174,
    193–4, 196
  Best's sacking, 80–2
  drugs, 125, 137, 143, 166–9
  homosexuality, 66, 68, 91–2, 119, 143
  house plans, 124
  Lennon relationship, 65, 70–1, 75, 92–3,
    168, 174
  meets Beatles, 8, 64, 65, 68–71
  Noël Coward, 130
  Philippines tour, 136–7
  Sgt Pepper, 157–8
  suicide, 163, 170–1, 231
  suicide attempt, 143–4
  US tours, 102–3, 109–13, 116, 119–21,
    138
Epstein, Clive, 91, 194, 201, 205
Epstein, Harry, 72
Epstein, Queenie, 66, 67, 205
Evans, Mal, 98, 116, 136, 142, 156, 159
Evening Standard, 138
Everly Brothers, 27, 34

Faith, Adam, 75
Faithfull, Marianne, 148, 154, 167, 170
Fame, Georgie, 184
Family Way, The, 142
Fascher, Horst, 54
Fenton, Shane, 58, 76
Fernald, John, 67
Fisher, Paul, 33–4, 273
'Fixing a Hole', 150–1
Flowers in the Dirt, 265, 266, 272
'Fool on the Hill, The', 173, 267
Fool, The, 154, 157, 160, 167, 196
Fourmost, The, 93
Francis, Connie, 164

Frank Music, 262
Fraser, Robert, 148, 157
Freed, Alan, 105
'From Me to You', 85
Fury, Billy, 37

Gandhi, 157, 158
Geldof, Bob, 263
Gentle, Johnny, 38–9
George Harrison album, 204
Gerry and the Pacemakers, 39, 43, 78, 110
'Get Back', 204
'Getting Better', 153, 160
Gibb, Russ, 212
Gibson, Brian, 159
Gilmour, Dave, 243
Ginsberg, Allen, 105–6, 148
'Girl is Mine, The', 262
'Give Ireland Back to the Irish', 233–4
Give My Regards to Broadstreet, 8, 35, 262–3
Goldman, Albert, 104, 251
Goldsmith, Harvey, 247
'Good Day Sunshine', 267
Goodman, Arnold, 193
'Good Morning, Good Morning', 153, 160
Gorcey, Leo, 158
Gormanston, Lord, 131–3
Gortikov, Bob, 214
'Got to Get You into My Life', 142
Grade, Leslie, 97
Grade, Lew, 97, 211, 235
Green, John, 250, 255
Green, Sam, 251
Greene, Graham, 169
Griffiths, Eric, 31
Gruenberg, Eric, 154
Guardian, 274

Haley, Bill, 26
Hard Day's Night, 123, 124, 128, 141
Harrison, Carl, 38
Harrison, George:
  All Things Must Pass album, 204, 228
  Apple, 200, 203–5
  background, 12, 31–3, 42
  Beatles break-up, 222, 225–6, 255
  Best's sacking, 80–1, 82
  clothes, 32, 61
  drugs, 141, 159, 210
  Epstein meeting, 71
  Epstein's party, 167
  finances, 87–8, 114, 193, 200
  George Harrison album, 204
  hairstyle, 62
  Hamburg, 42, 48, 51, 54, 61–3
  Klein appointment, 203–5
  Klein case, 254
  Lennon estate, 261
  Let It Be tapes, 216
  London move, 94
  McCartney relationship, 117, 203–5, 210,
    212, 218, 225–6, 256–7, 270

Harrison, George – *cont'd.*
  Maharishi, 169–70, 179–80, 204
  marriage, 124
  Martin meeting, 77
  Noël Coward, 130
  on tour, 135–6
  position in group, 33–6, 60–1, 141, 143,
    149, 177–8
  Sgt Pepper, 153, 157, 159, 162
  songwriting, 214, 256
  success, 228
  US tour, 107, 114–18
Harrison, Louise, 32
Harrison, Patti (Boyd), 124, 169
Haworth, Jill, 114–16
Haworth, Nancy, 115
Heartbreakers, The, 266
Heine, Heinrich, 42
'Helen Wheels', 237
'Help', 146
Help! (film), 126, 139, 141
'Helter Skelter', 60
Hendrix, Jimi, 185, 186
Henry Ansbacher, 211
Herald Tribune, 106
'Hey Jude', 197, 262, 264, 267, 277
'Hi, Hi, Hi', 246, 248
Hitler, Adolf, 47, 157, 158, 196
HMV, 74
Hoffman, Annie, 238
Hoffman, Dustin, 238
Holingshead, Michael, 131, 132
Holly, Buddy, 36, 56, 118, 258, 264
Holmes a'Court, Robert, 259
Hopkin, Mary, 197
How I Won the War, 141, 146, 150
Howe, Suzanne, 186
Hughes, Vic, 58, 110
Humperdinck, Englebert, 227
Hutchinson, Johnny, 37, 81
Huxley, Aldous, 157
Hynde, Chrissie, 272

Ichiyananagi, Toschi, 180
'I Feel Fine', 177
Ifield, Frank, 90
'I'll Follow the Sun', 53
Imagine, 226, 234
'I'm Carrying', 243
Indra club, Hamburg, 45–6, 51
International Times, 148
'I Saw Her Standing There', 109, 127–8, 277
'I Want to Hold Your Hand', 85, 103–6, 109,
    125, 246

Jacaranda club, Liverpool, 35, 42
Jackson, Joe, 259
Jackson, Michael, 259–60, 262
Jacobs, David, 111–12, 174
Jagger, Mick:
  accent, 125
  Beatles relationship, 164, 202–3

'Day in the Life', 154
Epstein's party, 167
Hyde Park concert, 233
Klein, 202–3
Linda, 187
Maharishi, 170
status seeker, 224
James, Dick, 87–8, 152, 210–11
'James Paul McCartney' television special,
    235–6
Jan and Dean, 128
'Jet', 238
Jim Mac's Band, 18
John, Elton, 30, 243
Johnny and the Moondogs, 31
Johnson, Olive, 19
Jones, Brian, 133, 185–6, 233
Jones, Casy, 36
Jones, John Paul, 243
Jones, Raymond, 68–9
Joyce, James, 128
Juke Box Jury, 94

Kaiserkeller club, Hamburg, 43, 46–9, 54
Kass, Ron, 186, 197, 199, 208
Kaufman, Murray 'the K', 108, 116
Kelly, Brian, 57
Kerouac, Jack, 49, 50, 105
Kesey, Ken, 171–2
Kirchherr, Astrid, 48–50, 61–2, 80
Klein, Allen:
  Apple takeover, 205–6, 208, 212
  background, 164
  Beatles approach, 164–5, 201–2
  Beatles contract negotiations, 207, 213–15
  Beatles lawsuit against, 254
  departure, 254, 256
  Eastman investigation, 185, 206
  Lennon agreement, 202–3, 211
  McCartney case, 225–6
  record release dates, 219
Koestler, Arthur, 49
Koger, Marijke, 154, 160
Kooper, Al, 185
Koschmider, Bruno, 43, 46, 54–5
Kramer, Billy J., 110
Krupa, Gene, 82

Laine, Denny, 224, 231–2, 234, 237,
    239–43, 251, 260
Laine, Jo Jo, 232, 241–2
Lane, Carla, 270
Leander, Mike, 151
Leary, Timothy, 131
Led Zeppelin, 243
Lee Curtis and the Allstars, 91
Leeger, Josje, 154
Lennon, Cynthia (Powell)::
  divorce, 209
  Epstein, 72, 167
  Hamburg, 47
  Lennon break-up, 182, 197, 209

Lennon relationship, 35–6, 38, 92–4, 117, 182
Liverpool Art College, 35–6, 38
Maharishi, 170
marriage, 83
memories of McCartney, 59–60, 95, 129
son, 92, 94, 197
Weybridge, 124
Lennon, Fred, 27
Lennon, John:
  Apple, 194, 198–206
  Beatles break-up, 215–16, 220, 225–6, 255
  Best's sacking, 80
  Cavern, 58
  childhood, 12, 27
  clothes, 61, 65, 73
  cruelty, 24, 75, 98, 168, 187
  death, 253–4
  divorce from Cynthia, 208, 209
  drugs, 51–2, 125, 141, 144, 150, 159, 160–1, 182, 198
  Epstein relationship, 65, 70–1, 75, 92–3, 168, 174
  Epstein's party, 167
  estate, 256, 257, 261
  finances, 87–8, 193, 200
  'Give Peace a Chance', 234
  groupies, 117
  hairstyle, 62, 63, 141
  Hamburg, 48, 50, 51–2, 55, 61–3
  Imagine, 226, 234
  In His Own Write, 128–9
  'Instant Karma', 216
  Jesus popularity row, 138–9
  Linda, 186, 187
  Liverpool Art College, 27, 29, 36, 38
  London move, 94
  McCartney relationship, 22–4, 27–31, 59–60, 117, 144, 174, 198–9, 205, 209–10, 212, 215–16, 218, 225–7, 232, 250, 254–5, 264–5
  McCartney songwriting partnership, 24, 78–9, 85–8, 125–9, 142, 153–4, 178–9, 210, 218, 261, 264–5
  Maharishi, 169–70, 179–80
  marriage to Cynthia, 117, 197
  marriage to Yoko, 209
  May Pang affair, 229
  MBE, 134
  Mind Games, 237
  Noël Coward, 130
  Northern Songs, 211–12, 257
  'Not a Second Time', 273
  opinion of George, 32
  opinion of McCartney, 7
  Quarry Men, 22–3, 31, 32, 35
  Rolls decoration, 132, 141
  self-examination, 140–1
  Sgt Pepper, 149–62
  Silver Beatles, 36–41
  stage act, 22, 47, 51
  'Strawberry Fields', 146, 210

  Two Virgins, 198–200
  US tour, 107–8, 115–17, 119–20
  Weybridge house, 124, 148, 160
  Yoko Ono, 180–2, 188, 203, 208–9, 215–16
Lennon, Julia, 28
Lennon, Julian, 92, 94, 160, 197
Lennon, Sean, 255
Lester, Richard, 141, 197
'Let 'Em In', 239
'Let It Be', 215
Let It Be, 204, 214, 215–16, 219
Lewis, Jerry Lee, 56, 106
Lewis, Vic, 137
Liberty Records, 197
Life magazine, 165, 167, 213
'Like Dreamers Do', 75
Liston, Sonny, 117–18
Litherland Town Hall, 56–7
Little Richard:
  chases McCartney, 83, 91–2
  musical influence on McCartney, 23, 27, 30, 50, 70, 91
  priesthood, 56, 91
  songs, 34, 53
Live Aid concert, 263
'Live and Let Die', 236
Liverpool Oratorio, 8, 269–74, 277
Lloyd, John, 29–30, 31
Lockwood, Sir Joseph, 157–8, 159, 198, 202, 219
Loesser, Frank, 262
London Town, 241, 243
'Long and Winding Road, The', 216, 235
'Lovely Rita', 151, 155
'Love Me Do', 31, 78, 79, 82–3, 87, 146
'Love of the Loved', 75
Lowe, Duff, 34
'Lucy in the Sky with Diamonds', 153, 159–60, 161, 188
Lynch, Kenny, 90
Lynne, Jeff, 266

McCallum, David, 154
McCartney album, 218–20, 225
McCartney, Angela (Jim's second wife), 224
McCartney, Florence (Paul's grandmother), 18
McCartney, James (Paul's son), 240, 251, 274
McCartney, Jim (Paul's father):
  background, 11–13
  bands, 17–18
  Beatles, 38, 44, 72
  Best, 80
  Cavern, 58–9
  death, 8, 276
  Jane Asher, 96
  jobs for Paul, 55–6
  music, 17–18, 67, 90, 224, 271
  relationship with Paul, 11–19, 25–6, 34, 200
  remarriage, 224
  retirement, 132

McCartney, Jim – *cont'd.*
  values, 12, 15, 17, 29, 33
  wife's death, 19, 25
McCartney, Joseph (Paul's grandfather), 18
McCartney, Linda (Eastman):
  appearance, 185, 187, 189
  background, 184–6
  Beatles break-up, 214–15, 217
  children, 185, 187, 188, 209, 212, 230, 240
  drugs, 188, 246, 247, 252
  fans' attitude, 191
  Japan, 248–9
  Klein case, 254
  lifestyle, 8, 274–7
  marriage, 209
  meets Paul, 175, 184, 186–8
  Northern Songs case, 235
  pregnancy, 187, 209
  relationship with Paul, 191, 195, 221–5,
    229, 240–1, 271
  religion, 15
  singing, 225, 230, 240
  Wings, 230–2, 235, 237–41
McCartney, Mary (Paul's daughter), 209, 232, 246
McCartney, Mary Patricia (Paul's mother),
    11–19, 94, 276
McCartney, Michael (Michael McGear –
    Paul's brother):
  childhood, 12, 14–17, 25–6, 44
  Jane Asher, 94, 96
  Maharishi, 169
  memories of Paul, 19, 29, 55, 59–60
  mother's death, 19, 25
  relationship with brother, 16, 26
McCartney, Paul:
  appearance, 7, 11, 21, 65, 217
  Apple, 194–206, 208, 212–13, 215
  Beatles' break-up, 207–16, 217–20, 225–6,
    255, 266, 267
  Cavendish Avenue house, 129–30, 151,
    190–1, 195, 226
  Cavern, 58
  childhood, 11–20
  children, 209, 212, 230, 240, 274
  clothes, 21, 26, 61, 73
  death rumours, 212–13
  Dorothy Rohne, 47, 95
  drugs, 51–2, 125, 129, 131–2, 159, 161–2,
    165–8, 170, 183–4, 217, 220–1
  drugs arrests, 245–52
  Epstein relationship, 71, 77, 92–3, 113,
    164–5, 167–8, 171–2
  finances, 12, 85–9, 113–14, 129–30, 193,
    200, 241–2, 257–60, 264
  George Martin relationship, 151–2, 236–7,
    271
  groupies, 117, 123
  hairstyle, 21, 26, 62, 63
  Hamburg, 44, 48–55, 61–3, 92
  Hamburg women, 52, 118
  Harrison relationship, 117, 203–5, 210,
    212, 218, 226, 256–7, 270

High Farm, 130, 212, 217–18, 231–2,
    239–40
Jane Asher, 94–6, 115, 129–30
Jane break-up, 189–91
Japanese tour, 136
Jill Haworth, 114–16
Lennon relationship, 22–4, 27–31, 59–60,
    117, 144, 174, 198–9, 205, 209–10, 212,
    215–16, 218, 226–7, 232, 250, 253–6,
    261, 264–5
Lennon songwriting partnership, 24, 78–9,
    85–8, 125–9, 142, 153–4, 178–9, 210,
    218, 261, 264–5
lifestyle, 8, 123–5, 129–33, 147–8, 175,
    184, 223–4, 274–5
Linda involvement, 175, 184, 186–8, 191,
    195
Linda relationship, 221–5, 229, 240–1,
    274–7
Liverpool Oratorio, 269–74
Maharishi, 169–70, 179–80
marriage, 209
MBE, 133–4
MD role, 82–3
mother's death, 19–20, 25–6, 28, 218
Northern Songs, 211–12, 235, 257, 258
on Beatles, 50
paternity suit, 118–19
PR role, 50, 59–60, 108, 130–1
publishing rights, 258–60
Quarry Men, 22–3, 31, 32, 35
relationship with father, 8, 15–17, 26, 38,
    59, 132–3, 224, 276
Ringo relationship, 106–7, 113–14, 210,
    212, 214, 218, 222, 226, 256–7
Sgt Pepper, 149–62, 165, 264
Silver Beatles, 37–42
Sussex farm, 274
US tours, 101, 104, 106–9, 113–20,
    139–40
vegetarianism, 223–4
Wings, 229–43, 261, 266–7
Yoko Ono relationship, 181, 203, 208–9,
    218, 250–1, 255, 259, 260–2
McCartney, Stella (Paul's daughter), 230, 246,
    250
McCulloch, Jimmy, 239
McCullough, Henry, 234, 239
McFall, Ray, 57
McGear, Michael *see* McCartney, Michael
Magical Mystery Tour, 8, 35, 172–4, 213, 263
Magritte, René, 148
Maharishi Mahesh Yogi, 169–70, 179–80
Makin, Rex, 68, 70, 71
Maltz, Stephen, 200
Mamas and Papas, 187
Mann, William, 89
Manson, Charles, 60
Marcos, Imelda, 136
Mardas, 'Magic' Alex, 196, 199, 208, 209
Markowitz, Beverly, 119
Marks, Leonard, 257

286

Martin, George:
  Beatles signing, 75–7
  Best's sacking, 80–1
  Epstein, 163
  Harrison, 177
  Lennon–McCartney song recordings, 78–9, 82–3
  Lennon tripping, 161
  'Live and Let Die', 236–7
  LSM student days, 94
  Northern Songs, 87–8, 152
  'Penny Lane', 148–9, 271
  Red Rose Speedway, 236–7
  Sgt Pepper, 151–5, 159
  'Strawberry Fields', 146
  'Yesterday', 128
Marvin, Hank, 63, 243
'Mary Had a Little Lamb', 232–3
Masked Melody Makers, 17
Mason, David, 149
Mason, Spencer, 51–4, 81, 93
Massey and Coggins, 55
Mayall, John, 239
'Maybe I'm Amazed', 219, 277
Melody Maker, 228
Merry Pranksters, 171
Mersey Beat, 69, 76
Mineo, Sal, 114
Minsker, Harold, 200
Moger, Wendy, 158
Mohin, Bill and Dill, 19
Mojos, 51
Montez, Chris, 96
Moody Blues, 231
Moore, Tommy, 37, 39, 40
Morris, Edwin H., 258
Morrison, Jim, 264
Move, The, 266
'Mull of Kintyre', 128, 231, 242
Murray, Mitch, 78
'My Brave Face', 265
'My Love', 236

Nemperor Holdings, 201
NEMS, 67, 69, 72
NEMS Enterprises:
  administration, 170
  Beatles contract, 205; *see also* EMI
  Byrne lawsuit, 113
  formation, 91, 110
  London move, 94
  Magical Mystery Tour, 173
  purchase advice, 201
  Stigwood negotiations, 194
  Triumph purchase, 213
Newfield, Joanne, 144
Newsweek, 150
Nichols, Jimmy, 153
Norman, Philip, 165
Northern Songs, 88, 152, 211–12, 235, 257, 258
'Not a Second Time', 89

O'Dell, Dennis, 197
'Oh Boy!' programme, 30, 37, 54, 56
Oldham, Andrew Loog, 164
Ono, Yoko:
  background, 180–1, 184
  Beatles break-up, 28, 202–3, 215–16
  drugs, 198
  Lennon relationship, 123, 144, 175, 181–2, 198–9, 209, 215–16, 229
  London Exhibition, 148, 181
  McCartney relationship, 208–9, 250–1, 256, 259, 260–2
  Two Virgins, 198
Oranmore, Oona, Lady, 131
Orbison, Roy, 99, 265–6
Orenstein, Bud, 111
Ormsby-Gore, Alice, 120
Ormsby-Gore, Sir David, 120
Ormsby-Gore, Jane, 120
Ormsby-Gore, Sylvia, Lady, 120
Owlsley (chemist), 166

Pang, May, 229
'Paperback Writer', 145–6
Parker, 'Colonel' Tom, 108, 110
Parlophone Records, 75–6, 87, 152
Parnes, Larry, 37–8, 39, 110
Patrie, Jo Jo, 232, 241–2
Paul McCartney's Liverpool Oratorio see Liverpool Oratorio
'Penny Lane', 145–7, 149, 227, 271
Perkins, Carl, 38, 53
Peter and Gordon, 110
Petty, Tom, 266
Philips, 74
Phillips, John, 187
Picasso, Pablo, 238
'Picasso's Last Words', 238
Pink Floyd, 243
Plastic Ono Band, 227–8
Playboy Club, 116, 182
Playboy magazine, 168
'Please Please Me', 82–3, 85
Please Please Me album, 85, 145
Polydor, 63, 69
Poole, Brian, 74
Poole, Lord, 200
Posthuma, Simon, 154, 160
Powell, Cynthia *see* Lennon
Precht, Bob, 103, 109
Preminger, Otto, 114
Presley, Elvis:
  army, 56
  death, 150
  films, 86, 141–2
  influence on Beatles, 27, 40, 70
  management, 108, 110
  Sullivan Show, 102
Press to Play, 264
Pritchard, John, 167
Procol Harum, 167
'PS I Love You', 78, 79

Puttnam, David, 263
Pye, 74

Quarry Men, 22–4, 31, 32, 35
Queen magazine, 165, 167
Quennell, Joan, 120

Rainbows, The, 31
Ram, 225, 226, 228, 231, 235
'Ram On', 228
Ramon, Paul, 38
Ransome-Kuti, Fela, 237
Rawls, Lou, 128
Red Rose Speedway, 236
Revolution, 190
Revolver, 142, 156, 215
Rich, Buddy, 82
Richard, Cliff, 30, 37, 56–7, 63, 78, 102, 141
Richenberg, Leonard, 206, 213
Rigby, Eleanor, 21
Righteous Brothers, 216
Robbins, Mike, 34
'Rockestra Theme', 243
Rodgers and Hammerstein, 218
Rodgers and Hart, 79
Roe, Tommy, 96
Rohne, Dorothy, 47, 95
Rolling Stone magazine, 228
Rolling Stones, 73, 133, 145, 164, 185, 201, 233
Ronettes, 116
Rosa (in Hamburg), 51, 54
Rowe, Dick, 74
Royal Caribbeans, 42, 43
Royal Command Variety Performance, 98–9
Russell, William, 263
Rydell, Bobby, 105

'Say Say Say', 262
Scaffold, The, 93
Schwartz, Francine, 189–91, 199
Seaman, Frederic, 250
Secunda, Tony, 232
See, Bob, 185
See, Heather, 185, 187, 188, 212, 246
Seiwell, Denny, 231, 239, 246
Seltaeb, 111
'Sgt Pepper', 149, 267
Sgt Pepper, 8, 95, 142, 143–5, 149–62, 165, 183, 186, 264, 266
Shadows, The, 37, 57, 63, 78, 243
Shapiro, Helen, 57, 90, 96
'She Loves You', 85, 109, 231
Shenson, Walter, 111, 130
Sheridan, Tony, 54, 63, 69
Sherrin, Ned, 223
'She's Leaving Home', 151–2
Shotton, Pete, 23, 31, 156
'Silly Love Songs', 8, 239
Silver Beatles, 37–41, 43, 45
Sinatra, Frank, 109, 128
'Singalong Junk', 228

Smith, Mimi, 27, 28, 32, 72
Society of Mental Awareness, 168
Somerville, Brian, 119
'Something', 214
Spector, Phil, 216
Spiritual Regeneration Movement, 169
Star Club, Hamburg, 61
Stardust, Alvin, 58, 95
Starkey, Maureen, 124, 169, 179
Starkey, Richard *see* Starr, Ringo
Starr, Ringo (Richard Starkey):
    Apple, 200, 203, 205
    background, 12, 40–1, 51
    Beatles break-up, 222, 225–6, 255
    drugs, 125
    finances, 87–8, 193, 200
    Hamburg, 48
    Hardy Day's Night, 124, 128
    joins Beatles, 80–2
    Klein appointment, 203, 205
    Klein case, 254
    Lennon estate, 261
    lifestyle, 141, 222
    London move, 94
    Maharishi, 169–70, 179–80
    marriage, 124
    position in group, 82, 106–7, 151
    Linda relationship, 222
    McCartney relationship, 106–7, 113–14, 210, 212, 214, 218, 222, 225–6, 256–7
    Sentimental Journey, 219
    Sgt Pepper, 151, 157, 162
    songwriting, 256
    US tour, 104, 106–7, 116, 119
Steele, Tommy, 37, 43, 141
Stevens, Margo, 191
Stewart, Eric, 263–4
Stigwood, Robert, 194
Stills, Stephen, 185
Stockhausen, Karlheinz, 148, 155, 223
Stone, Norman, 82
Storm, Rory, and the Hurricanes, 37, 43, 47, 51, 81, 95
Strach, Dr Walter, 86, 94
Stramsact, 111
'Strawberry Fields', 145–7, 149, 210, 212
Sullivan, Ed, 102–3, 108–9, 115
Sutcliffe, Stu:
    Astrid Kirchherr, 48–9, 61–2
    Cavern club, 69
    death, 41–2, 75, 83
    Hamburg, 48–9, 55, 61–2
    joins group, 35–6
    Lennon relationship, 36, 60
    McCartney relationship, 36, 48, 60, 62
Sutherland, Joan, 124, 130

Tamla Motown, 142, 259
'Taxman', 193
Taylor, Alistair, 195
Taylor, Derek, 150, 196, 197–8, 201–2
Taylor, James, 197, 208

Taylor, Mick, 239
Teddy Boys, 26, 28, 32, 40–1, 49
Te Kanawa, Dame Kiri, 270
Thatcher, Margaret, 18, 234
Thomas, Dylan, 148, 157
'Those Were the Days', 197
Tilletson, Johnny, 105
'Till There Was You', 109
Time magazine, 124
Times, 89, 168, 273
Times Literary Supplement, 128
'Too Many People', 226
Top Ten club, Hamburg, 54–5, 61
Town and Country, 185
Townsend, Pete, 243
Transcendental Meditation, 169
Travelling Wilberries, 266
Tremeloes, The, 74
Triumph Trust, 206, 213
20th Century Fox, 197, 263
Twiggy, 197, 236
'Twist and Shout', 85, 98
Two Is coffee bar, 43
Tynan, Kenneth, 156

United Artists, 111
U2, 266

Vaughan, Ivan, 21–2
Vee, Bobby, 105
Venus and Mars, 224, 238
Vincent, Gene, 23, 27, 47
Vivaldi, 148
Voorman, Klaus, 49

'Wah Wah', 204
Walden, Brian, 169
'Walking in the Park with Eloise', 224
Waller, Fats, 17
Wall Street Journal, 112
Warhol, Andy, 148

Webb, Peter, 263
Weisner, Ron, 259
Weiss, Nat, 118, 139, 158, 167
West, Mae, 158
'When I'm Sixty Four', 31, 149, 150, 277
White Album, 114, 156, 159, 199, 204, 209
White, Andy, 82
Whitman, Slim, 30
Who, The, 243
Wilde, Marty, 36
Wilde, Oscar, 157
Wild Life, 232
Williams, Allan:
    booking agent, 35, 39, 57, 62, 70
    Hamburg, 42–4, 45–6, 52–3
    Jacaranda club, 35, 42
    Parnes audition, 37
Williams, Larry, 53
Williams, William B., 106
Williams, Winona, 186–7, 189, 224, 246
Wilson, Brian, 142
Wilson, Harold, 18, 133–4, 193
Wings, 90, 229–43, 256, 261, 266–7
Wings at the Speed of Sound album, 238
WINS, 108
'With a Little Help from My Friends', 159–60
With the Beatles, 85, 89
'Within You Without You', 153, 162
WMCA, 105, 108
WNEW, 106
Wonder, Stevie, 239, 262
Woodbine, Lord, 43
Wooler, Bob, 57, 69, 71, 93
Wyman, Bill, 73

'Yellow Submarine', 233
'Yesterday', 8, 126–8, 211, 227, 234, 249,
    260, 267, 277
Yomiuri, 247
'You Want Her Too', 265
Young, Neil, 63

289